Advance Praise for
Your Drug May Be Your Problem

"In non-technical, easy to understand language, Peter Breggin and David Cohen bring an incredibly important and hardly ever recognized message to people who need to understand the dark side of psychiatric drugs and how to stop taking them. I heartily recommend it."

Candace Pert, Ph.D.
Research Professor of Physiology and Biophysics
Georgetown University Medical Center
Author of Molecules of the Mind
Washington, D.C.

"Confronting current psychiatric drug prescribing practice head-on is a daunting task—we owe Breggin and Cohen a vote of thanks for openly speaking the truth. Despite what the pharmaceutical companies would have us believe, we don't need 'a better life through chemistry.' This book will help debunk this myth and provide practical advice on how to avoid psychiatric drugs and get off them."

Loren Mosher, M.D.
Soteria Associates, Former Chief of the Center for
Studies of Schizophrenia, National Institute of Mental Health
San Diego, California

"This book is long overdue. Drs. Breggin and Cohen make possible the practice of psychiatry with a conscience."

Bertram P. Karon, Ph.D.
Professor of Clinical Psychology
Michigan State University
East Lansing, Michigan

"The modern medical approach to almost any human problem is to find a drug—a sort of magic bullet—to fix it. But many drugs do more harm than good, and some even cause the problems they are supposed to fix. And once on a drug, coming off may also be dangerous. In this clear and important book, Peter Breggin and David Cohen outline the problems and provide a step-by-step account of how to come off the drug which may be harming you."

Steven Rose, Ph.D.
Professor of Biology and Director, Brain and
Behaviour Research Group, Open Univer
Milton Keynes, England

"This is a courageous, compassionate book, and a much needed antidote to the pro-drug bias of modern psychiatry and psychology."

John Horgan
Author of The End of Science *and* The Undiscovered Mind
Garrison, New York

"Your Drug May Be Your Problem is a clear, accurate, and thorough look at the dangers of psychiatric drugs, and a prudent outline of what steps to take for those who want to stop taking them."

Thomas J. Moore
Author of Prescription for Disaster:
The Hidden Dangers in Your Medicine Cabinet
Washington, D.C.

"I wish I had this book when I was trying to come off psychiatric drugs. How wonderful that you have provided this guide."

Kate Millett
Author of Sexual Politics *and* The Loony Bin Trip
New York, New York

"Working as a consultant, I am constantly looking for ways to help clients achieve a more educated view regarding psychotropic medication. Breggin and Cohen have assembled a gold mine of information to assist in this process. I can think of no other book that has done such a superb job of making such information accessible at any point of decision regarding taking or discontinuing psychotropic medication."

Tony Stanton, M.D.
Psychiatric Consultant
Bremerton, Washington

"This book is one of the most important things that has happened to psychiatry and especially to so-called 'psychiatric patients' during this century. Having worked for more than 20 years with so-called schizophrenics—the main victims of the abuse by prescribed psychiatric drugs— I can say that Peter Breggin and David Cohen must be praised for the courage they have had to unmask many pseudo-scientific conclusions frequently present in supposedly scientific literature."

Alberto Fergusson, M.D.
Psychiatrist, Psychoanalyst, and Institute Director
Bogota, Colombia

"Your Drug May Be Your Problem provides much useful and very practical information, and it is much needed considering that there is such massive propaganda by the pharmaceutical and medical industries about such drugs. This propaganda must be combated, and this book contributes to that effort."

Wolf Wolfensberger, Ph.D.
Research Professor of Education
Syracuse University
Director, Training Institute for Human Service Planning,
Leadership and Change Agentry
Syracuse, New York

"Your Drug May Be Your Problem is an honest and straightforward attempt to present a clear picture of drug effects, why we turn to drugs, their role in society, and more. It fills a real need in our current drug culture and in our current complete trust in the drug dispenser himself. The book's main import will be to serve as a counter-balance to the myth of a 'miracle' drug cure. It's a must on everyone's bookshelf!"

Rhoda L. Fisher, Ph.D.
Clinical Psychologist
Syracuse, New York

"I recommend *Your Drug May Be Your Problem* as the number one self-help guide to coming off psychiatric drugs."

Steven Baldwin, Ph.D.
Senior Editor, Ethical Human Sciences and Services
Foundation Professor of Psychology
School of Social Sciences, University of Teesside, Teesside, UK

"Anyone considering saying 'yes' to psychiatric drugs, or wanting to 'just say no,' should first say 'YES' to buying and reading this essential, informative book. Breggin and Cohen's goal is empowerment of troubled people seeking help, not propaganda, pressure, or profit. This book questions, informs, warns, and leaves the reader far better able to choose wisely."

Thomas Greening, Ph.D.
Professor of Psychology, Saybrook Graduate School
Editor, Journal of Humanistic Psychology
Los Angeles, California

"I highly recommend this book to persons on psychiatric drugs, and to the physicians who prescribe them. These drugs are very powerful, either for good or for harm. Since the actions for almost all of them are still unknown, the people who use them are being experimented on, mostly without their knowledge. Drs. Breggin and Cohen are experts on the negative effects of drugs. Their views should be just as widely known as the misleadingly positive advocations of the drug companies."

Thomas J. Scheff, Ph.D.
Professor Emeritus of Sociology
University of California, Santa Barbara

"This groundbreaking book provides a comprehensive and honest source of information about adverse and withdrawal effects of commonly-used psychiatric drugs. It should be in the office of all medical and non-medical 'mental health' workers. It should also be read by anyone considering the use of psychiatric drugs and all those who want to stop."

David H. Jacobs, Ph.D.
Clinical Psychologist, Resident Faculty
California Institute of Human Science
San Diego, California

"Emotional maturity, self-confidence, and life competence come from struggling with stresses, fears, and adversities. When young people become addicted to drugs they remain emotionally immature until they quit and start learning to cope. Breggin and Cohen point out that the same is true of chronic users of psychiatric medications. It is not until they withdraw from the chemical dependency urged on them by psychiatry, that they can develop inner strengths for coping with life's difficulties."

Al Siebert, Ph.D.
Author of The Survivor Personality
Portland, Oregon

"Doctors Peter Breggin and David Cohen take the reader through the risky pathways of psychiatric medication with accurate information as a guide. Dr. Breggin was a voice in the night calling for responsibility with psychiatric medication. Now he leads an orchestra of protest."

Jay Haley
United States International University
Author of Leaving Home *and* Learning and Teaching Therapy
La Jolla, California

"Breggin has been a brave pioneer in not only pointing out but also meticulously documenting the ways that the 'Emperor' of traditional mental health treatment is naked. His relentless raising of questions and documentation of false advertising and cover-ups by drug companies and various forms of abuse of patients by a variety of therapists is invaluable and irreplaceable."

Paula J. Caplan, Ph.D.
Author of They Say You're Crazy *and* The Myths of Women's Masochism
Visiting Scholar, Pembroke Center
Brown University
Providence, Rhode Island

"Nowhere does the false medical thinking, that there is a drug cure for almost all common diseases, do more harm than in the modern psychiatric argument that mental illness is easily diagnosed and then cured by a side-effect-free drug. Nowhere is the correct psychiatric thinking more evident than in the books by Peter Breggin. In them he explains clearly that patients with mental illnesses are in almost all instances suffering from their inability to connect with important people in their lives and need help in making these vital connections. He supports safe, drug-free counseling as a more effective way to help people, and I enthusiastically agree with this premise."

William Glasser, M.D.
Psychiatrist, author of Reality Therapy *and*
the forthcoming Reality Therapy in Action
Chatsworth, California

Your Drug May Be Your Problem

Your Drug May Be Your Problem

How and Why to Stop
Taking Psychiatric Medications

Fully Revised and Updated Edition

Peter R. Breggin, M.D.
David Cohen, Ph.D.

Da Capo
LIFE
LONG

A Member of the Perseus Books Group

Copyright © 1999 by Peter R. Breggin, M.D., and David Cohen, Ph.D.

Text design by Heather Hutchinson
Set in 11 point Fairfield by the Perseus Books Group

Cataloging-in-Publication data for this book is available from the Library of Congress.

First Da Capo Press paperback edition 2000
Revised and updated Da Capo Press paperback edition 2007
ISBN-13: 978-0-7382-1098-8
ISBN-10: 0-7382-1098-6

Published by Da Capo Press
A Member of the Perseus Books Group
www.dacapopress.com

Note: The information in this book is true and complete to the best of our knowledge. This book is intended only as an informative guide for those wishing to know more about health issues. In no way is this book intended to replace, countermand, or conflict with the advice given to you by your own physician. The ultimate decision concerning care should be made between you and your doctor. We strongly recommend you follow his or her advice. Information in this book is general and is offered with no guarantees on the part of the authors or Da Capo Press. The authors and publisher disclaim all liability in connection with the use of this book. The names and identifying details of people associated with events described in this book have been changed. Any similarity to actual persons is coincidental.

Da Capo Press books are available at special discounts for bulk purchases in the U.S. by corporations, institutions, and other organizations. For more information, please contact the Special Markets Department at the Perseus Books Group, 2300 Chestnut Street, Philadelphia, PA 19103 or e-mail special.markets@perseusbooks.com.

10 9 8 7 6 5 4 3 2 1

To our wives
Ginger and Carole
Who inspire us
With their love, brilliance, and courage

Contents

A Warning Concerning the Use of Psychiatric Drugs

Psychiatric drugs are much more dangerous than many consumers and even physicians realize. All of these drugs produce numerous serious and potentially fatal adverse reactions, and most are capable of causing withdrawal problems that are emotionally and physically distressing. Some produce powerful physical dependence and can cause life-threatening withdrawal problems.

Although this is the first book to describe in detail why and how to stop taking psychiatric drugs, it is not intended as a substitute for professional help. Especially when psychiatric drugs have been taken in large doses for prolonged periods of time, experienced clinical supervision may be useful and even necessary during the withdrawal process.

This book is intended for anyone who is thinking about starting or stopping psychiatric drugs. It may also be useful to people who are taking psychiatric medications without any immediate intention of stopping. In addition, it is meant for anyone who has friends or loved ones who are taking these drugs.

Many professionals who are involved with the prescription or monitoring of medication may also find this book useful. The chapters that follow contain basic information about drug hazards and drug withdrawal of which many medical doctors may be unaware—including even those physicians who frequently prescribe psychiatric drugs.

Introductions to
the New Edition:
Scientific Confirmations
of the First Edition

When *Your Drug May Be Your Problem* was originally published in 1999 it was the first of its kind—the only book to examine the adverse effects of every class of psychiatric drug and how to safely withdraw from them. With this second edition, our book remains unique in its emphasis but in many ways it has become less controversial. In the past eight years, scientific research and the Food and Drug Administration (FDA) have further confirmed many of the concerns voiced in the first edition, including our emphasis on how antidepressants and stimulants cause harmful mental effects and dangerously abnormal behavior such as psychosis, violence, and suicide.

We have both been very active in scientific research in the intervening years since the first edition of *Your Drug May Be Your Problem*. I have published more than a dozen scientific articles and books that further develop and demonstrate many of the observations and concepts described in the first edition of this book.[1] In recent years, my testimony has been accepted in many additional criminal, malpractice and product liability cases involving the adverse effects of these medications

The FDA Finally Recognizes
Antidepressant-Induced Suicidality

The FDA has at long last confirmed the first edition's observations that antidepressants produce dangerous degrees of stimulation with aggressive behavior and that they also produce suicidality in children and adults.

At public hearings in 2004 the FDA presented re-evaluations of anti-depressant clinical trials for children and youth under age eighteen documenting that the suicide risk was doubled in children taking anti-depressants compared to similar individuals taking a sugar pill. The agency also reported that only one-fifth of controlled clinical trials demonstrated any usefulness for antidepressants in children and youth under age eighteen.[2] Antidepressants were not only proven ineffective in children and teenagers, they were proven to cause suicide.

The FDA applied its conclusions to all of the newer antidepressants including bupropion (Wellbutrin), citalopram (Celexa), fluoxetine (Prozac, Sarafem), fluvoxamine (Luvox), mirtazapine (Remeron), nefa-zodone (Serzone), paroxetine (Paxil), sertraline (Zoloft), escitalopram (Lexapro), and venlafaxine (Effexor). A more recent antidepressant, duloxetine (Cymbalta), shares similar risks.

In summarizing the hearings, panel chairman Wayne K. Goodman, M.D. confirmed an emerging "pattern" of "behavioral toxicity" and specifically referred to "activation" or over-stimulation as a root prob-lem. He suggested that symptoms or signs of over-stimulation "may represent a precursor to the symptom we most fear, that of suicide in-tent." Dr. Goodman reminded the hearing that only 20 percent of the clinical trials showed any effectiveness and warned, "So, in addition to adverse effects that were of concern, we had questions about the over-all benefit of this class of agents, raising then naturally questions about benefit/risk ratio."[3]

On March 22, 2004, the FDA issued a press release along with a pub-lic Health Advisory on "Cautions for the Use of Antidepressants in Adults and Children." The agency's press release stated that it is "known" that antidepressants are associated with "anxiety, agitation, panic attacks, insomnia, irritability, hostility, impulsivity, akathisia (severe restlessness), hypomania, and mania."[4] Without using the terms stimulation or activa-tion, the FDA for the first time confirmed that antidepressants cause a dangerous pattern of these effects along a continuum from anxiety and agitation through mania.

The FDA published a new required label for all antidepressants on Jan-uary 26, 2005 including a black box headlined "Suicidality in Children and Adolescents." The warning begins "Antidepressants increased the risk of suicidal thinking and behavior (suicidality) in short-term studies in children and adolescents with Major Depressive Disorder (MDD) and other psychiatric disorders."[5]

The FDA also added to the label a section entitled "WARNINGS—Clinical Worsening and Suicide Risk" for children *and adults*. In doing so, the federal agency confirmed my longstanding concern that antidepressants actually worsen the condition of many patients. Antidepressant labels must now warn that adults "should be observed similarly for clinical worsening and suicidality, especially during the initial few months of a course of drug therapy, or at times of dose changes, either increases or decreases."

Confirming Over-Stimulation

The media and the psychiatric profession have focused almost exclusively on the new suicide warnings in antidepressant labels, while the FDA's more far-reaching warnings about over-stimulation have been largely ignored. Every antidepressant label must now warn in detail about over-stimulation or activation. This critical new addition to all antidepressant labels applies to children and adults alike and is found in the section entitled, "WARNINGS—Clinical Worsening and Suicide Risk." Embellishing slightly on the initial FDA press release, the label states that antidepressants are associated with the production of "anxiety, agitation, panic attacks, insomnia, irritability, hostility, aggressiveness, impulsivity, akathisia (psychomotor restlessness), hypomania, and mania."

Another section of the new label informs doctors what information should be given to patients and their families. It points to "clinical worsening and suicide" and repeats the description of over-stimulating, adding "and other unusual changes in behavior, worsening of depression, and suicidal ideation."

The FDA also published a special booklet to be included in the labels and to be given to the parents of children placed on antidepressants.[6] In a heading entitled "What to Watch Out For in Children or Teens Taking Antidepressants," the booklet lists twelve psychiatric items with bullets. Almost all of them confirm antidepressant over-stimulation and several specifically mention manifestations of violence and suicidality. Here they are in their entirety:

- Thoughts about suicide or dying
- Attempts to commit suicide
- New or worse depression
- New or worse anxiety
- Feeling very agitated or restless

- Panic attacks
- Difficulty sleeping (insomnia)
- New or worse irritability
- Acting aggressive, being angry, or violent
- Acting on dangerous impulses
- An extreme increase in activity and talking
- Other unusual changes in behavior

Immediately after the list, the booklet additionally warns about withdrawal:

> Never let your child stop taking antidepressants without first talking to his or her healthcare provider. Stopping an antidepressant suddenly can cause other symptoms.

Antidepressant-Induced Suicidality in Adults

After establishing that antidepressants cause suicide in individuals under the age of eighteen, in 2005–2006 the FDA required the drug companies to re-evaluate their data on adult suicidality. As a result, in May 2006 GlaxoSmithKline sent a mass mailing to "Dear Healthcare Professional" warning that Paxil increases the risk of suicidal behavior for adults of all ages who suffer from Major Depressive Disorder as well as for younger adults who suffer from lesser depressive disorders and anxiety disorders.[7]

On December 13, 2006 the FDA's advisory committee[8] met to discuss the overall results of the re-evaluation of adult suicidality data. The FDA concluded that antidepressants cause increased rates of suicidality in people age eighteen to twenty-four taking antidepressants compared to those taking placebo.

The FDA seemingly would like to believe that at age twenty-five people change biologically or psychologically in some fashion so that the antidepressant suicidality warning need not apply to them; but common sense and clinical experience tell us that the risk is increased for all ages. Younger patients may be more likely to have these horrendous adverse drug reactions, but they occur as well in older people. Clinical trials are not meant to detect suicidality and due to their relative insensitivity to the problem, they only identified the greater vulnerability found in younger patients.

The FDA Resists the Facts

All of these "new" FDA observations and conclusions were already available in the first edition of *Your Drug May Be Your Problem*. The psychiatric community and the FDA have been slow to catch up with observations that I have been making for decades and that were summarized in the first edition of the book. In 1991 in *Toxic Psychiatry* I first described how Prozac can cause "murderous and suicidal behavior" by means of over-stimulation:

> Prozac often affects individuals as if they were taking stimulants, such as amphetamine, cocaine, or PCP. . . . Like amphetamine or cocaine, Prozac can produce the whole array of stimulant effects, such as sleeplessness, increased energy, jumpiness, anxiety, artificial highs, and mania. Some patients taking Prozac do indeed look "hyper" or "tense," and even aggressive, without even realizing it. . . . Indeed, the FDA's internal review of Prozac side effects by psychiatrist Richard Kapit twice mentions the drug's "stimulant" effects, but these important observations were not included in the final labeling requirements.[9]

In many books after 1991, I continued to warn about antidepressant overstimulation, violence, and suicide, drawing upon additional clinical and research studies in *Talking Back to Prozac* (1994), *Brain-Disabling Treatment in Psychiatry* (1997), and finally *The Antidepressant Fact Book* (2002). I also published scientific papers culminating in 2003 with the most detailed scientific review of the entire subject entitled "Suicidality, violence and mania caused by selective serotonin reuptake inhibitors (SSRIs)."

Meanwhile, in 1997 psychiatrist David Healy joined in with a critique of antidepressants, *The Antidepressant Era*, further describing the risk of suicidality; and in 2000 psychiatrist Joe Glenmullen wrote *Prozac Backlash*, extensively documenting the role of antidepressant-induced akathisia (psychomotor agitation) in causing violence and suicide.

The new language required by the FDA in antidepressant labels closely follows the thrust of my observations in my 2003 paper that was distributed to the FDA committee before it drew its conclusions. In that paper I described and documented how the antidepressants cause akathisia and a stimulant syndrome that begins with "insomnia, nervousness, anxiety, hyperactivity, and irritability and then progresses toward more severe agitation, aggression, and varying degrees of mania." Notice the similarity in the concept and language in the new FDA-approved label when it describes antidepressant-induced "anxiety, agitation, panic attacks, insomnia, irritability, hostility, aggressiveness, impulsivity, akathisia (psychomotor restlessness), hypomania, and mania."

It was of course gratifying to witness this outcome after years and years of work, often in the face of professional outrage, judicial hostility, and media disbelief; but for untold millions of patients and their families, the warnings came much too late.

How are we to account for such a long lag in the FDA's recognition of antidepressant-induced over-stimulation, as well as hostility, aggression, and suicidality? Most obviously, the drug companies and the FDA want to protect themselves from being criticized for denying problems that some of us have been warning about since the early 1990s. More insidiously, as I have recently documented on my Web site and in *Ethical Human Psychology and Psychiatry* concerning Paxil and GlaxoSmithKline, drug companies make extreme efforts to hide incriminating data about their drugs from the FDA, the health professions, and the public.[10]

Antidepressant Withdrawal Acknowledged

As we emphasized in the first edition of this book, all antidepressants can cause emotionally and physically distressing and dangerous withdrawal reactions. Because of a wide variety of symptoms from severe shock-like headaches to overwhelming depression, many patients feel they cannot stop taking them.[11]

Paxil produces some of the worst withdrawal reactions but GlaxoSmithKline, the manufacturer of the antidepressant, has fought recognizing the severity of these problems. A few years ago I was a consultant in a California suit to force the manufacturer of Paxil to increase its warnings concerning withdrawal. Attorney Don Farber of San Rafael reported to me that the company "resolved the case" satisfactorily, a pharmaceutical industry euphemism for settled without admitting guilt. Simultaneously under pressure from the FDA, the company upgraded the warning with a bold black heading, "Discontinuation of Treatment with PAXIL." The label now summarizes reports that it has received concerning withdrawal reactions:[12]

Dysphoria [painful] mood, irritability, agitation, dizziness, sensory disturbances (e.g., parethesias such as electric shock sensations), anxiety, confusion, headache, lethargy, emotional lability, insomnia, and hypomania.
While these events are generally self-limiting, there have been reports of
serious discontinuation symptoms.

The new antidepressant label notes that the withdrawal symptoms can
become "intolerable." Consistent with our earlier suggestions in the first
edition of this book, GlaxoSmithKline now recommends slow withdrawal
with resumption of the previous dose if the suffering becomes intolerable.

Do Antidepressants Have Any Positive Effects?

In *Toxic Psychiatry* in 1991 and again in more detail in *Talking Back to
Prozac* in 1994, I documented that antidepressants are so ineffective
that even drug company–rigged studies have difficulty showing any
positive effects. I pointed out that the drugs are little better than sugar
pills and that the slightly better performance of the antidepressants in
short-term clinical trials is due to many extraneous factors including
investigator bias and the manipulation of data. Recent research has
confirmed these observations.

In 2002 a team led by psychologist Irving Kirsch at the University of
Connecticut published an analysis of efficacy data submitted to the
FDA between 1987–1999 for Prozac, Paxil, Zoloft, Effexor, Serzone, and
Celexa.[13] In order to approve a drug, the FDA requires only two positive
studies, but drug companies invariably have to conduct many clinical
trials before they can come up with a couple of positive clinical trials.
Kirsch and his colleagues looked at all the studies conducted by the
companies—not merely those used to get approval by the FDA. After
analyzing the entire group of antidepressant clinical trials conducted by
the drug companies, Kirsch and his colleagues concluded that there was
little or no evidence that the drugs worked. Their research demonstrated
that any beneficial or positive effects in comparison to placebo were
"negligible."

In 2006 Joanna Moncrieff and Kirsch published another review and
analysis of antidepressant efficacy in the *BMJ* (*British Medical Journal*)
focusing on SSRIs such as Prozac, Zoloft, and Paxil. They concluded that
these drugs "do not have a clinically meaningful advantage over placebo."

New FDA Disclosures about Stimulant Drugs
for Treating ADHD in Children

The first edition of *Your Drug May Be Your Problem* also emphasized the dangers associated with the stimulant drugs used to treat Attention Deficit Hyperactivity Disorder (ADHD). As Brian Kean (2005 and 2006) has amply documented, a worldwide marketing campaign continues to expand the number of children whose basic human rights are being trampled by unscientific diagnoses and toxic treatments. Meanwhile, the FDA has admitted that these medications are far more dangerous than previously admitted. The relatively benign FDA-approved labels for stimulant drugs such as Adderall, Dexedrine, Ritalin, and Concerta have misled physicians and the public into underestimating their hazards. Few professionals or consumers realize how addictive the drugs can be and even fewer realize that they frequently cause serious psychiatric side effects such as psychosis, mania, aggression, and suicide.

In 2005 the FDA finally acknowledged that it was receiving numerous reports of stimulant-induced harmful psychiatric effects such as psychosis, visual hallucinations, suicidal ideation, aggression, and violence.[14] Then in early in 2006 the FDA's Division of Drug Risk Evaluation issued an alarming report that declared: [15]

> The most important finding of this review is that signs and symptoms of psychosis or mania, particularly hallucinations, can occur in some patients with no identifiable risk factors, at usual doses of any of the drugs currently used to treated ADHD. Current labeling for drug treatments of ADHD does not clearly address the risk of drug-induced signs or symptoms of psychosis or mania (such as hallucinations) . . . A substantial proportion of psychosis related cases were reported to occur in children age ten years or less, a population in which hallucinations are not common.

Their data was derived from all the drugs involved in treating ADHD, including Strattera, amphetamine (Adderall and Dexedrine) and methylphenidate (Focalin, Concerta, Metadate, Methylin, Ritalin, and methylphenidate skin patches). It also included Provigil, a drug sometimes used as a stimulant. A complete list can be found in the Appendix.

The FDA's report also identified stimulant-induced aggression, including many cases that were "considered life-threatening or required hospital admission." It noted that the FDA had already placed a suicide warning in the Strattera label[16] and it warned with less conviction that the other stimulants showed signals of causing suicidality.

With these observations and warnings about stimulant drugs, the FDA began to catch up with warnings I had first issued in 1998 as the scientific presenter on adverse drug effects in children at the Consensus Development Conference on the Diagnosis and Treatment of Attention Deficit Hyperactivity Disorder, a highly publicized meeting sponsored by the National Institutes of Health (NIH).[17] In my published report and my presentations to the conference I specifically warned about an unexpectedly high number of cases of stimulant-induced psychosis, aggression, and suicidality. Using an earlier version of the same data that the FDA recently relied upon—reports sent to it from various sources— by 1998 I had already found hundreds of psychiatric adverse drug reactions such as agitation, hostility, depression, psychotic depression, psychosis, hallucinations, emotional lability, and abnormal thinking. I also reported on finding many cases listed as overdose, intentional overdose, and suicide attempt. I enlarged upon this warning in "Psychostimulants in the treatment of children diagnosed with ADHD: Risks and mechanism of action" (1999) and in *Talking Back to Ritalin* (2001).[18]

Why was I able to pick up the signal in 1998, while the drug companies never found it and the FDA only became aware in 2005? I was looking for potential problems from the drugs while the drug companies and the FDA were looking away from them.

Ultimately the FDA failed in its initial promises to seriously upgrade its warnings about the newly recognized adverse psychiatric effects of stimulants. In September 2006 the agency held hearings on the subject and decided not to "scare" parents by putting a black box warning in the label concerning either cardiovascular or psychiatric side effects. In February 2007 the FDA issued a news release announcing its intentions to warn about the risk of cardiovascular adverse events including sudden death in patients with underlying serious heart problems or defects and stroke and heart attack in adults with unspecified risk factors. It then went on to minimize findings of psychiatric adverse events, citing "a slight increased risk (about 1 per 1,000) for drug-related psychiatric adverse events, such as hearing voices, becoming suspicious for no reason, or becoming manic, even in patients who did not have previous psychiatric problems." The cited rate of one event per 1,000 is unconscionably small. One retrospective review of clinic records, for example, found that nearly 10 percent of children, or 100 per 1,000, developed signs of psychosis including cases of "paranoia," "visual hallucinations," and "auditory hallucinations; aggressive, agitated behavior." [19]

A New Concept: Spellbound by Psychiatric Drugs

Why do so many people take such harmful drugs? Why do they persist in taking them long after the drugs have begun to do more harm than good?

The persistent use of harmful drugs is not limited to psychiatric drugs. People frequently abuse non-prescription drugs such as alcohol and marijuana despite their obviously harmful mental and emotional effects. In the extreme, alcoholics ruin their lives and the lives of their families as they drink themselves to death. Alcohol, of course, causes dependence (the new name for addiction). But even in the absence of addiction, people often take drugs to their obvious personal detriment and frequently to the detriment of others as well.

Over the years I have evaluated many dozens of clinical and legal cases in which individuals have endured severe and sometimes lasting mental impairment from taking psychiatric drugs. In many of these cases, the individuals committed horrendous acts that were wholly out of character for them. Recently when re-evaluating my extensive experience with these cases, I realized that all psychoactive drugs produce an effect that can be called medication spellbinding or, more technically, intoxication anosognosia.[20] Anosognosia means the inability to recognize illness in oneself. Drugs that impair mental function at the same time impair the individual's ability to recognize that dysfunction.

All psychoactive drugs—that is, all drugs that affect the brain and mind—tend hide or to mask their harmful mental effects from the individuals who use them. Often these drugs make spellbound individuals feel that they are mentally improved when they are in reality mentally impaired. In extreme drug spellbinding, they compel people toward thoughts and actions such as violence and suicide that they would ordinarily find appalling.

Every class of psychiatric drugs—antidepressants, stimulants, tranquilizers, mood stabilizers, and antipsychotics—causes mental impairments that often go unrecognized by the victim, even when they are severe. (The drugs in these categories are listed in the Appendix.) This misleads medicated patients into believing that they are doing better even when they are getting worse. As a result, people often feel they cannot live without psychiatric drugs when a careful history reveals that their lives have deteriorated during the time they have been exposed to them.

Antidepressants, stimulants and tranquilizers (especially Xanax) frequently cause unrecognized over-stimulation that can lead to acts of aggression or suicide. Mood stabilizers like lithium and antipsychotic drugs like Zyprexa, Risperdal, Seroquel, and Geodon often lead to a flattening of emotions that the patient and doctor alike overlook or mistake for clinical depression. The concept of medication spellbinding helps to explain how adverse reactions go unrecognized or unappreciated, and why so many people feel compelled to take so many drugs that cause them mental impairment. The concept of medication spellbinding clarifies the destructive compulsion to persist in taking harmful drugs. The subject of spellbinding will be expanded and documented with dozens of cases in my forthcoming book, *Medication Madness: True Stories of Mayhem, Murder, and Suicide Caused by Psychiatric Drugs*.

In conclusion, a great deal has happened in the past eight years that confirms our concerns and warnings expressed in first edition of this book. The reader can be reassured that the observations made in this book are based on sound scientific data, even if some of these observations remain ahead of their time.

Peter R. Breggin, M.D.
Ithaca, New York
www.breggin.com

The first edition of *Your Drug May Be Your Problem* appeared at the height of a period of "biopsychiatric hubris"—the excessive pride and arrogance linked to the view that people who suffer emotionally or misbehave have defective brains and genes and should take psychiatric drugs.

It seemed to me then that this viewpoint resembled a cult. It was impervious to reason or evidence, hostile to counter-arguments, and locked its adherents in a strange chemical embrace. At the time, to argue that prolonged psychotropic drug use had no scientific justifications and was potentially very dangerous, and to suggest how to stop taking drugs, went so straight against conventional thinking and practice that it could have seemed foolhardy.

In the intervening eight years, however, the basic arguments set out in this book have been shown to be prescient, well founded, and useful to patients and clinicians alike. This may have occurred partly because of the following:

- the Internet changed the usual methods of creating and disseminating information about drugs, partly by allowing direct and uncensored expression of patients' voices on issues that matter to them rather than to experts with ties to the drug industry;
- scores of media reports discussed how drug companies—aided and abetted by their paid "academic" researchers, medical journal editors, and even the FDA itself—actively suppress unfavorable findings about medications;
- the FDA required makers of antidepressants to include prominent warnings on the official drug labels concerning the emergence of suicidal thinking in children and adolescents;
- even *Newsweek* carried a story on August 3, 2005, on the hardships of coming off antidepressants, and more people realized that *all* psychotropic drugs may be associated with withdrawal effects that can produce enough impairment to overshadow all previously perceived benefits;
- results of several large, long-term drug treatment studies conducted without drug industry funding squarely denied the oft-repeated claims about psychiatric drugs' effectiveness;
- the realization that doctors prescribe the most dangerous psychiatric medications to hundreds of thousands of children, some as young as two and three years of age, without tested evidence, makes more people wonder if the biopsychiatric approach has any fail-safe mechanism.

Let me discuss briefly some of these changes and what they could mean for you as a consumer or potential consumer of psychiatric drugs, or as someone contemplating coming off psychiatric drugs.

The Internet and Drug Information

When we drafted *Your Drug May Be Your Problem* back in 1998, the Internet helped us mostly to search for bibliographic sources and to peruse a few hundred postings from individuals discussing their withdrawal reactions online. However, when I typed "antidepressant withdrawal" on a popular Web search engine while writing this introduction in early 2007, the startling result was 1.2 million hits. The few listings I consulted offered general advice from professionals and laypersons on discontinuing drugs, how-to-taper strategies, users' daily withdrawal logs, summaries of published case reports, ways to cut pills or divide capsules, advertisements for antidepressants or for "herbal detoxification" products, legal briefs, online discussions between consumers, as well as other varied material including some extremely sophisticated analyses of drug effects from laypersons. Of course, just like information about drugs from experts, information on the Internet must be evaluated critically, and we offer in Chapter 7 some guidelines to assess the quality of Web sites offering withdrawal-related advice.

To me, however, this content illustrates how the creation of knowledge about psychiatric drugs has moved and will continue to move far beyond the traditional confines set by credentialed experts. Withdrawal reactions and dependence on antidepressants did not emerge from observations by experts. Rather, experts could no longer ignore these problems when they were described without intermediary by tens of thousands of patients.

The Drug Industry Exposed and Re-Exposed

How extensively the pharmaceutical industry shapes medical and psychiatric research and practice and how it thwarts drug regulation to the industry's advantage has now become a mainstream topic of study.

In its relentless pursuit of profits, the drug industry uses every means at its disposal to shape how people think about disease, health, and treatment. This means, notably, that it carefully orchestrates the production of infomercials that are passed off to policymakers, clinicians, and consumers as scientific studies, to the detriment of patients' health and of the integrity of scientific research.

In 2004 and 2005 alone, the following titles, among others, documented this depressing reality in detail: *The Truth About the Drug Companies: How They Deceive Us and What to Do About It*, by Marcia Angell, former editor-in-chief of the *New England Journal of Medicine* and a professor at Harvard Medical School; *On the Take: How Medicine's Complicity with Big Business Can Endanger Your Health*, by Jerome Kassirer, also a former editor-in-chief of the *New England Journal of Medicine* and professor at the Tufts University School of Medicine; *Let Them Eat Prozac: The Unhealthy Relationship Between the Pharmaceutical Industry and Depression*, by David Healy, psychopharmacologist and historian of psychiatry; *Selling Sickness: How the World's Biggest Pharmaceutical Companies Are Turning Us All Into Patients*, by medical journalists Ray Moynihan and Alan Cassels; *Medicines Out of Control? Antidepressants and the Conspiracy of Goodwill*, by Charles Medawar, founder of the U.K. organization Social Audit, and Professor Anita Hardon; *Overdo$ed America: The Broken Promise of American Medicine*, by John Abramson, clinical instructor at Harvard Medical School; *The $800 Million-Dollar Pill: The Truth About the Cost of New Drugs*, by Merrill Goozner, journalist; and *Generation Rx: How Prescription Drugs are Altering American Lives, Minds, and Bodies*, by Greg Critser, author and journalist.

If I had to choose one take-home message to extract from the sum of these compelling works, it's the following: The personal, individual choices that both you and your doctor make with respect to your treatment for emotional distress are, more often than not, simply the end result of well-organized marketing campaigns by the industry to sell its products.

Drugs for Schizophrenia, Depression, and Bipolar Disorder—A Bust

Despite the decades-long barrage of reports of industry-funded clinical trials presumably demonstrating the superiority and safety of psychiatric drugs, the National Institute of Mental Health (NIMH) was prompted to support, at a combined cost of $100 million, three large studies to test the latest drug treatments for the major psychiatric disorders.

The studies were unusual in that they enrolled several thousand patients, most of whom would have been excluded from most short-term clinical trials. Under more "real-world" treatment conditions and using more real-world outcomes than those from conventional clinical trials, many of these patients were followed for more than a year. Main findings from the studies began appearing in late 2005 and continue as of this writing.

The Clinical Antipsychotic Trials of Intervention Effectiveness (CATIE) project recruited nearly 1,500 individuals diagnosed with schizophrenia and randomly assigned them to receive one of five different antipsychotic drugs (four newer "atypical" drugs, Zyprexa, Risperdal,

Seroquel, Abilify, and one old antipsychotic rarely used today, Trilafon). After eighteen months, across the five groups, between 64 percent and 82 percent of patients had quit their treatment because of "intolerable side effects or lack of efficacy or other reasons." [21] Most observers were taken by surprise, having accepted as scientific facts the drug industry's promotional messages that atypical antipsychotics were basically magic potions. I wasn't surprised, having shown earlier how studies of the atypical antipsychotics were so rigged with systematic biases and manipulations that few of their claims could stand critical scrutiny.[22]

The Sequenced Treatment Alternatives to Relieve Depression (STAR*D) project recruited nearly 2,900 patients diagnosed with nonpsychotic major depression and subjected them to what modern psychiatry considers to be the best treatment for depression. In the first sequence, all these patients were treated with the SSRI antidepressant Celexa. Their doctors could tailor doses individually based on patients' feedback and, on average, each patient was medicated for about twelve weeks. The result: less than 30 percent had a remission of symptoms during the entire study period (20 months).[23] The study continued, with different medication strategies—such as augmentation with other antidepressants or switching to other antidepressants—applied as the pool of subjects who did not drop out got smaller and smaller. In one particular sequence, among 727 people initially medicated with Celexa with no success and then agreeing to take either Wellbutrin, Zoloft, or Effexor for up to fourteen weeks, an average of only 21 percent experienced a remission—less than the percentage of those who dropped out because of intolerable side effects (23 percent). And more than half of all participants reported that they experienced moderate to severe side effects *more than half of the time*.[24]

Finally, results of the Systematic Treatment Enhancement Program for Bipolar Disorder (STEP-BD), described as the largest treatment study of bipolar disorder ever performed, also appeared recently. The study claimed to use a "best-treatment-available" approach (mostly anticonvulsants, antipsychotics, lithium, and benzodiazepines), and as in the other treatment studies just described, recruited a broadly representative sample of almost 1,500 patients from across the country who underwent a full two years of treatment. The results: only 28 percent of treated individuals achieved full remission and experienced no recurrence during the two years.[25]

Keep in mind that there were no placebo-treated groups in these three studies. Conservatively, one could estimate that at least half of subjects who responded to the drugs would have responded to placebos—which would have revealed "net" desired drug effects as even less impressive. Keep in mind also that subjects in all studies might have received several medications. In the STAR*D study, for example, in addition to Celexa, additional drugs to counteract sleep, anxiety, and agitation problems, as well as Celexa-induced sexual dysfunction, were given at physicians' discretion.

It remains to be seen just how doctors seeking to obtain informed consent from their patients to receive psychiatric drugs for depression, psychosis, or bipolar disorder will discuss these latest findings with their patients. Commenting on the CATIE findings, the lead investigator candidly admitted that "The claims of superiority for the [newer antipsychotics] were greatly exaggerated. This may have been encouraged by an overly expectant community of clinicians and patients eager to believe in the power of new medications. At the same time, the aggressive marketing of these drugs may have contributed to this enhanced perception of their effectiveness in the absence of empirical information."[26]

Disseminating greatly exaggerated claims of superiority, in the absence of empirical information—is this science, or propaganda?

Medications and Prescribers Out of Control

Many practitioners, recognizing that results from these major treatment studies directly challenge practice-as-usual, suggest that the best guideline still remains to "use medication wisely." But, as this book argues, this is not so simple as it might sound. It's difficult to find a doctor admitting that he or she does not prescribe medication wisely, yet it's disconcertingly easy to identify harmful, scientifically unsupported, involuntarily imposed, or plainly excessive psychotropic drug prescription practices.

In one recent case in which I reviewed medical records, a ten-year-old child in the middle of a custody dispute was receiving, from the same doctor, six psychotropic drugs simultaneously, belonging to five different drug classes. Over the past few years, the child has been placed on and withdrawn from over fifteen different drugs. The case notes and discharge summaries were filled with descriptions of behaviors that might reasonably be attributed to the mental confusion and emotional and physical roller coaster to which this unbelievably irrational drug cocktail was probably subjecting the child. Yet neither the child's doctors, nor the judge overseeing the case, nor an experienced clinical psychologist appointed by the court to make recommendations, voiced that anything might be wrong with this picture.

The bigger picture includes the following: The number of antipsychotic prescriptions to children two to eighteen years increased from under 500,000 in 1995–1996 to almost 2.5 million in 2001–2002.[27] Most of these prescriptions were for indications for which antipsychotics have not been studied in children. Even more dramatic trends are being reported about the prescription of anticonvulsants to youths.[28] Yet the psychiatric journals reporting these findings merely call for more well-controlled studies of antipsychotics or anticonvulsants in children.

Arguably, "better" evidence is not likely to slow this engine running out of control. The *absence* of evidence did not prevent doctors (not only psychiatrists but pediatricians, family medicine physicians, emergency department physicians, and other types of providers) from experimenting with antipsychotics and anticonvulsants. It is difficult to see how any self-corrective mechanisms might come into play to bring sanity back to caring for children in distress.

Conclusion

In sum, now more than probably any time before, I believe that most people are able to avail themselves of better quality, unbiased information and critical perspectives to help them decide whether, when, and for how long to take psychiatric medications, and how to safely come off them.

However, the playing field remains quite uneven, with most consumers and even clinicians deeply in the dark about the common pitfalls of using psychiatric drugs, with increasing numbers of children subjected to the most powerful and harmful drugs, and with most sources of information on drugs still controlled by the drug industry and vested medical interests.

We are gratified by the response from readers of the first edition of *Your Drug May Be Your Problem*, and we are hopeful that this second edition will continue to meet their needs and answer their questions.

David Cohen, Ph.D.
Miami Beach, Florida
www.davidcohenphd.com

Introduction:
What Is Your
Ultimate Resource?

This book is filled with technical and scientific information about psychiatric drugs (especially their dangers) and how to withdraw from them. However, it is also important to understand the underlying psychological, social, and ethical principles that may affect your decision to use or not use psychiatric drugs.

We can learn a great deal about ourselves and how we view life by asking, "Where do we turn when we feel emotionally upset or despairing? Where do we go when life seems unendurable and we have little or no hope left? What are our ultimate resources in life—the places and persons to whom we turn for help, direction, and inspiration?"

Our Final Resort

All people seem to need faith, but the varieties of faith seem infinite. For many individuals, the ultimate resort or resource is religious or spiritual: God and prayer, or other beliefs and practices, and perhaps a trusted minister, priest, rabbi, or counselor. For others, the ultimate resort may be a loved one—a husband or wife, a parent, a friend. Still others may believe that they themselves are the ultimate resource. They may turn to creative work, nature, pets, hobbies, sports, or some other more seemingly individual or personal pursuit. Increasingly, people nowadays also turn to science to find answers about how to live life. Probably for most people, the final resort is a combination of these resources: God, nature, science, other people, and oneself. Ultimately, all human resources are related. Commitment to a loving, zestful, rational, principled life becomes the cornerstone of life and the final resource.

Resort to Drugs

Many people, however, rely on another, more limited resource when they face psychological or social crises. They turn to psychoactive or mind-altering substances. Although they may believe or hope that they are relying on seemingly objective science, in reality they are placing their faith in drug company marketing—and so are their doctors.

Consider the seemingly different situation with respect to recreational or illicit drugs. For untold millions throughout the world, the last resort is alcohol, tobacco, or substances such as marijuana and cocaine. Many turn to them whenever they feel on the verge of experiencing painful emotions. In the extreme, they become addicted to these substances and build their lives around them. When they eventually try to give up their addiction, they may discover that they have no other resources left and nowhere else to turn. Their lives have been emptied by their reliance on drugs. They must rebuild from scratch their faith in God or other ethical convictions, their trust in other people, and their reliance on themselves and their love of creative work or nature.

Seeking Relief

If people do feel better when drinking alcohol or smoking marijuana, it is because they feel better when their brain is impaired. Psychiatric drugs are no different. The people who take such drugs may feel less of their emotional suffering. They may even reach a state of relative anesthesia. But to the degree that they feel better, it is because they are experiencing intoxication with the drugs.[1]

Most of us can empathize with people who are willing to sacrifice brain function in return for a blunting of emotional suffering, but should therapists or doctors offer this alternative? Should we ourselves turn to this alternative in our own lives? Is the cost too great in terms of brain dysfunction and the failure to deal with the real issues in our lives?

The resort to psychoactive substances, whether legal or illegal, recreational or psychiatric, involves a compulsive narrowing of focus in the search for solutions to life's problems. Almost always the emphasis is on obtaining relief from painful emotions, too often regardless of the potential cost.

What Suffering Tells Us

Emotional suffering is inevitable in life. But it has a meaning—a purpose. Suffering is a signal that life matters. Specifically, it is usually a signal that something in our lives that matters a great deal needs to be addressed. Depression, guilt, anxiety, shame, chronic anger, emotional numbing—all of these reactions signal that something is amiss and requires special attention. The depth of suffering is a sign of the soul's desire for a better, more creative, more principled life.

For example, when faced with a patient in deep depression, should we immediately focus on relief of the pain? On the contrary, we should respond by saying that the pain is a signal of the intensity of the person's spirit: "The strength and intensity of your suffering indicates the strength and intensity of your spirit. Your discomfort shows how alive you are. Now imagine if you could learn to turn all that self-destructive energy into creative energy and a love of life."

The degree to which we suffer indicates the degree to which we are alive. When we take drugs to ease our suffering, we stifle our psychological and spiritual life. Instead, we need to find a way to untangle that twisted energy and to redirect it more creatively. Sometimes this process of personal and psychological growth can be helped by insightful psychotherapy or other therapeutic and educational techniques—including those that facilitate our understanding of early childhood sources of the suffering. At other times, the process is helped by our understanding of the problems in our immediate lives, such as an unhappy marriage, a frustrating job, or a difficult financial situation. Sometimes this understanding involves learning new principles of living with which to guide ourselves more effectively, which, in turn, may entail a recommitment or a new commitment to spiritual or philosophical ideas, and especially love for ourselves, for other people, and for life or some other guiding ideal. Sometimes it involves a therapist who cares so much about the client that the client can begin to care about himself or herself.

The New Ultimate Resource

The last ten to twenty years have seen a drastic change in viewpoint regarding the ultimate resource of moral and psychological guidance:

Regardless of their religion or philosophy, many educated and informed people have come to believe that psychiatry and psychiatric drugs provide the best last resort for themselves when in psychological distress. Indeed, such drugs are increasingly the *first* resort. It appears that we have replaced reliance on God, other people, and ourselves with reliance on medical doctors and psychiatric drugs. The ultimate source of guidance and inspiration is no longer life itself with its infinite resources but biopsychiatry with its narrow view of human nature.

This view of ourselves is a most astonishing one. It suggests that most if not all of our psychological, emotional, and spiritual problems are "psychiatric disorders" best treated by specialists who prescribe psychoactive drugs. Our emotional and spiritual problems are not only seen as psychiatric disorders, they are declared to be biological and genetic in origin.

The propaganda for this remarkable perspective is financed by drug companies and spread by the media, by organized psychiatry and individual doctors, by "consumer" lobbies, and even by government agencies such as the National Institute of Mental Health (NIMH). As a result, many educated Americans take for granted that "science" and "research" have shown that emotional upsets or "behavior problems" have biological and genetic causes and require psychiatric drugs. Indeed, they believe they are "informed" about scientific research. Few if any people realize that they are being subjected to one of the most successful public relations campaigns in history.[2]

These days, your doctor is likely to suggest medication for relatively mild degrees of emotional upset or distress; even a few weeks of moderate sadness or anxiety are apt to lead to a prescription. If your child has been difficult to deal with for a few weeks at home or in school, that, too, is likely to bring out the prescription pad. The problem may have lasted for only a short period, but the drug treatment may go on for years or even for a lifetime.

Psychiatric diagnosis has become so widespread that it is almost impossible to mention any kind of "feeling" to a medical doctor without being assigned a psychiatric label and prescribed the latest psychiatric drug. And this scenario is not limited to strong emotions or serious distress. Feeling fatigued? Take Prozac. Feeling as though you've lost your enthusiasm or direction? Take Paxil or Zoloft, especially if Prozac hasn't worked. Feeling trapped in an abusive relationship? Take Effexor, Luvox, or lithium. Feeling a little nervous? Take Xanax, Klonopin, or Ativan. Having trouble disciplining your child? Give the child Ritalin, or Dexedrine, or Adderall. Having trouble focusing on work that bores you?

Try Ritalin for yourself. Having ups and downs of any kind? Take any number of psychiatric drugs.

What Do We Really Know About How Our Brains Work?

Do we know what we are doing to our brains and minds when we take psychiatric drugs? Do we know what we are doing to our children when we give them these substances?

Consider this extraordinary reality. The human brain has more individual cells (neurons) than there are stars in the sky. Billions! And each neuron may have 10,000 or more connections (synapses) to other brain cells, creating a network with trillions of interconnections. In fact, the brain is considered to be the most complex organ in the entire universe. With its billions of neurons and trillions of synapses, it is more complex than the entire physical universe of planets, stars, and galaxies.

Scientists have well-developed ideas about how the physical universe works. They possess mathematical formulae for describing the various forces that control the relationships among physical entities from black holes to subatomic particles. All these forces also affect the human brain. However, the living processes of the brain add complexities unknown in the physical universe. Those trillions of interconnections between brain cells, for example, are mediated by hundreds of chemical messengers (neurotransmitters), as well as by hormones, proteins, tiny ions such as sodium and potassium, and other substances. We have limited knowledge about how a few of these chemical messengers work but little or no idea as to how they combine to produce brain function.

The Science Behind Psychiatric Drugs

The public is told that a great deal of science is involved in the prescription of psychiatric drugs, but this is not so—given that we know so little about how the brain works. The knowledge that we do have about the effects of psychiatric drugs on the brain is largely limited to test-tube studies of biochemical reactions utilizing ground-up pieces of animal brain. We simply do not understand the overall impact of drugs on the brain.

Nor do we have a clear idea about the relationship between brain function and mental phenomena such as "moods" or "emotions" like depression or anxiety. We don't even know where to begin looking because we don't fully understand how the brain functions.

Some theoreticians would urge us to focus on the molecular level by looking for biochemical imbalances. But that's sheer speculation. Why would a biochemical imbalance be at the root of feeling very depressed any more than it would be at the root of feeling very happy? And if there were biochemical substrates for extreme sadness and extreme happiness, would that fact make them *diseases*? The idea of individual biochemical imbalances is wholly at odds with the complexity of the brain.

Besides, whose biochemical imbalance are we looking for? That of the child who is out of control or the caregiver who has difficulty disciplining? That of the child who isn't learning or the teacher who hasn't figured out how to reach this child? That of the individual who becomes anxious in dealing with people or the adult who abused the individual as a child? That of the person who is deeply depressed over a lost loved one or the doctor who recommends electroshock? That of the person who feels insecure or anxious or the doctor who thinks that the person's problems require drugs? In short, whose brain isn't working right?

Are There Biochemical Imbalances?

As one of our colleagues recently said, "Biochemical imbalances are the only diseases spread by word of mouth." Individually, we must all use our own intuitive understanding of life to determine the likelihood that our problems are caused by some as-yet-undetected brain dysfunction rather than by conflicts in the home, at work, or in society, painful life experiences, confused values, a lack of direction, or other aspects of human life.

Of course, our bodies *can* affect our emotional outlook. We all find it much easier to maintain a bright and enthusiastic attitude when physically healthy than when physically ill. And anything from lack of sleep to the common cold can affect our moods.

However, doctors commonly give people psychiatric drugs without checking for obvious signs of serious physical disorder, such as hypothyroidism, estrogen deficiency, or head injury from a car accident. Moreover, they seem particularly prone to overlooking the importance of physical symptoms in women. Some women with obvious signs of a hormonal disorder or heart condition are put on antidepressants and antianxiety drugs without first being required by their internists or psychiatrists to undergo a physical evaluation.

It is therefore theoretically possible that some anxious or depressed people may be afflicted with an as-yet-undetected physical dysfunction. But this speculation doesn't justify the unfounded conclusion that people in emotional distress are beset by specific biochemical imbalances or that such imbalances can be corrected with drugs.

In our own experience, most people with depression and anxiety have obvious *reasons* for how they feel. These reasons are often apparent in their everyday lives and may be complicated by past experiences in childhood or earlier adult life. But even if some people do turn out to have subtle, undetected biochemical imbalances, there is no reason to give them drugs like Prozac or Xanax that *cause* biochemical imbalances and disrupt brain function.

Let us again consider the final resort. Is it defined by our values, our family and friends, and ourselves—or by a medical doctor with a prescription pad?

What Do We Really Know About Psychiatric Drugs and the Brain?

Almost all psychiatric drug research is done on the *normal* brains of animals, usually rats. As noted earlier, much of this research involves grinding up brain tissues to investigate the gross effects of a drug on one or more limited biochemical reactions in the brain. More sophisticated research involves micro-instrumentation that injects small amounts of drugs into the living brain and measures the firing of brain cells. Yet even these more refined methods are gross compared to the actual molecular activity in the brain. For example, we have no techniques for measuring the actual levels of neurotransmitters in the synapses between the cells. Thus all the talk about biochemical imbalances is pure guesswork. More important, what's actually being studied is the disruption of normal processes by the intrusion of foreign substances.

This research in no way bolsters the idea that psychiatric drugs correct imbalances. Rather, it shows that psychiatric drugs *create* imbalances. In modern psychiatric treatment, we take the single most complicated known creation in the universe—the human brain—and pour drugs into it in the hope of "improving" its function when in reality we are disrupting its function.

The notion that Prozac corrects biochemical imbalances is sheer speculation—propaganda from the biological psychiatric industry. But disruption of biochemical reactions in the brain, causing severe bio-chemical imbalances and abnormal rates of firing among brain cells, is a proven fact about Prozac that cannot honestly be disputed by anyone who knows the research.

How does the brain react to the intrusion of psychiatric drugs such as Prozac, Ritalin, or Xanax?

The brain reacts as if it is being invaded by toxic substances; it tries to overcome, or compensate for, the harmful drug effects. In the process, the brain literally destroys its own capacity to respond to the drug. It numbs itself to the drug and, in so doing, actually kills some of its own functions. So when a doctor tells us that Prozac is putting our biochem-icals into balance, we are being badly misled. In actuality, Prozac is pro-foundly disrupting the function of the brain.

Prozac, Ritalin, and Xanax, like most psychiatric drugs, overstimulate particular neurotransmitter systems either by increasing the output of a neurotransmitter or by preventing its removal from the synapses be-tween nerve cells. Prozac, for example, overstimulates a chemical mes-senger called serotonin by blocking its removal from the synapse. The brain reacts initially by shutting down the release of serotonin and then by reducing the number of receptors that can respond to the serotonin.[3]

These self-destructive processes in the brain are relatively easy to re-search. They were demonstrated in the private laboratories of Eli Lilly—the manufacturer of Prozac—even before the drug was approved for marketing by the Food and Drug Administration (FDA). Long before the marketing of Prozac, the drug was known to routinely cause drastic bio-chemical imbalances rather than to correct them.

How long does it take the brain to recover from the imbalances caused by Prozac? We don't have an answer to this critical question. Why not? Because drug companies and the scientific community have never car-ried out the relatively simple and inexpensive research that would be re-quired. Yet we should suspect that the brain does not always recover from Prozac or similar antidepressants such as Paxil and Zoloft.

We already know that the brain's recovery from exposure to many psy-chiatric drugs can be prolonged and that full recovery may never take place. Studies have demonstrated this outcome for stimulant drugs such as the amphetamines, including Dexedrine and Adderall, that are pre-scribed for children. Although the final verdict concerning Ritalin isn't in, its similarity to the other stimulants is such that we should be con-cerned about its capacity to cause irreversible changes. We also know that irreversible changes can occur in response to the drugs used to treat schizophrenia, such as Haldol, Prolixin, and Risperdal. These drugs can cause permanent, severe impairments of brain function. Indeed, we should suspect that any psychoactive drug—any drug that affects mental function—tends to produce irreversible changes in some if not most people.

What hope can we have that bathing the brain in a psychiatric drug will actually improve the overall function of this mysterious organ? Almost none. In fact, as already noted, most of what we know about the various neurotransmitters has been gathered by studying how psychiatric drugs disrupt or spoil their functioning.

What If We Treated Our Computers the Way We Treat the Brain?

Imagine what would happen if we treated our much simpler computers in the same way as we treat the brain in psychiatry. Consider the case of a computer that is "crashing" too often. With considerable poetic license, we can compare this mechanical dysfunction to the human tendency to become "overwhelmed" or "overloaded" with depression, anxiety, or obsessions and compulsions, and unable to function easily in everyday life.

Perhaps the computer is crashing for reasons having to do with its hardware. For example, the computer may need more memory or a new hard drive. Alternatively, the problem may be traceable to its software— to one or more of the programs installed in the computer. Then again, the operator of the computer and its programs may be responsible. Or the source of the problem could lie outside the computer and even outside the office, as in the case of power surges.

When troubleshooting such a problem, computer experts routinely take all of these factors into consideration—the computer, the program, the operator, and the power source. If the cause of the problem isn't immediately apparent, they may run experimental tests or programs in order to diagnose the problem.

The approach taken by psychiatrists and other medical doctors, by contrast, is both simple-minded and destructive. In contemporary psychiatry, the doctor almost always assumes that the problem lies in the "hardware" of the brain (i.e., in "biochemical imbalances"). In the words of one well-known psychiatrist, emotional and behavioral difficulties are caused by a "broken brain."

Modern psychiatrists seem to consider themselves brain consultants, but they have little knowledge with which to establish that expertise. Unlike computer consultants, psychiatrists have no way of identifying or locating the source of the problem in a patient's brain. So the patient must take their "expert" assertions on faith.

How would you react if your computer consultant treated your computer the way psychiatrists treat patients and their brains? Suppose your consultant invariably concluded that the problem must lie in the hardware of your machine rather than in the program, the operator, or some external factor such as the power source. Suppose your consultant always began by pouring toxic agents into your computer. Further suppose that your consultant never guaranteed you a good result while continuing to pour toxic agents into your machine without regard for the consequences—and, when pressed for an explanation, made vague references to "crossed wires" or "electrical imbalances" in your computer but never looked inside, conducted any tests, or provided a definitive physical diagnosis.

How long would you put up with such nonsense from your computer consultant? Not very long. If computer consultants behaved like psychiatrists, we would fire them. Yet, tens of millions of people put up with even more slipshod, irrational treatments involving their far more complex and vulnerable brains and minds.

What This Viewpoint Does to Us

What happens when we start viewing a human being as an object? We lose our own capacity for rationality and for love. It is impossible to reduce a person's emotional suffering to biochemical aberrations without doing something psychologically and morally destructive to that person. We reduce the reality of that individual's life to a narrowly focused speculation about brain chemistry.

In taking such a distorted view of the person, doctors also do harm to themselves. They suppress their natural tendency to be empathic toward other human beings. Thus, in their efforts to be "objective" and "scientific," biological psychiatrists and doctors end up doing very destructive things to people, including themselves.

Herbal and "Natural" Remedies

Although this book is about psychiatric medications that are approved by the FDA, many readers may have questions about psychoactive *herbal* remedies that can be obtained over the counter (OTC). They may wonder if these more "natural" substances can be used instead of psychiatric drugs during the withdrawal process or as a general substitute. In brief, we do not recommend the use of psychoactive herbs for these purposes.

Many people believe that such natural remedies are likely to be safer than prescription drugs. This is the implication conveyed by many books that evaluate herbal medicines, such as *PDR for Herbal Medicines* (1998) and *Alternative Medicine* (1994).[4] Both list far fewer adverse effects for typical herbal remedies (such as St. John's Wort as an antidepressant or ginseng as a stimulant) than are usually described in the literature for psychiatric drugs used for corresponding purposes (such as Prozac or Ritalin).

Nonetheless, anyone who uses psychoactive herbs should do so with caution. Some of these herbs have recognized adverse effects. For example, ginseng, in large doses, can cause dependence with serious adverse effects. The scientific citations typically listed for herbs are mainly non-English language reports not readily accessible to the ordinary reader in the United States. The composition of many of these substances, including St. John's Wort and ginseng, is very complex, with numerous active agents that have been little studied. Preparations from different manufacturers—or even from the same manufacturer—may not be standardized. And, finally, even though the FDA often fails to live up to its mandate, FDA-approved drugs are usually more thoroughly studied than herbal remedies in regard to adverse effects.

Some people might believe that a long history of use without known ill effects is in itself a good indication of a psychoactive herb's safety. However, consider two of the most widely used natural psychoactive substances, alcohol and tobacco: Both were once recommended by physicians for medicinal purposes, and both have been heavily promoted by government and corporate interests. Alcohol has been used for many reasons by untold millions of human beings since before recorded history, but only in the last few decades have the harmful effects of chronic excessive alcohol use been generally recognized. Society has also become increasingly aware of the association between acute alcohol use and many forms of violence and accidents. Likewise, tobacco has an ancient history of ritual use in Native American societies and, in more recent centuries, of widespread chronic use in Western society. But the dangerousness of smoking did not gain widespread recognition until a few decades ago.

Any drug that affects the brain and mind should be viewed with caution, especially in the context of daily or persistent use. And any person who decides to use herbal remedies should read as much as possible about them. To use these agents is, to some extent, to step into the unknown. By contrast, all psychiatric drugs have well-documented, serious hazards.

Even if psychoactive substances were harmless, we would question their use for "therapeutic" or "psychiatric" purposes—that is, to overcome psychological and social problems. The use of a psychoactive substance for such purposes is wrong in principle because it represents an attempt to fix the brain instead of the problems that lie within the person's internal life, relationships, and environment.

It is understandable, of course, that people want relief from emotional suffering, just as they tend to take aspirin, ibuprofen, or other drugs for head, muscle, and joint pains. The latter treatments play a valuable role, especially if they are administered over the short term. However, both aspirin and ibuprofen also have many potentially serious adverse effects, ranging from stomach ulcers to stroke.

The use of "emotional painkillers" is more questionable. If a person gets headaches because of the stress of a conflicted marriage or a frustrating workplace, it would ultimately be self-defeating to rely on pills instead of dealing with the issues involved. Besides, *all* psychiatric drugs have far more negative effects on brain and mind function than do aspirin or ibuprofen. Psychiatric medications are, first and foremost, psychoactive or psychotropic drugs: They influence the way a person feels, thinks, and acts. Like cocaine and heroin, they change the emotional response capacity of the brain. If used to solve emotional problems, they end up shoving those problems under the rug of drug intoxication while creating additional drug-induced problems.

There is another lesson to be gained from how long it has taken us to recognize the dangers of tobacco and alcohol. Because it has taken centuries to grasp the damaging effects of these natural substances on individuals, families, and society, we cannot blithely assume that we can learn about the dangers of psychiatric drugs in a matter of months or years.

Many drugs are effective in bringing about the short-term relief of emotional suffering. Alcohol, for example, affects the same general neurotransmitter system as tranquilizers like Xanax, Valium, Klonopin, and Ativan. It has similar clinical effects, too. Millions of people "take a drink" to relax or calm down, to relieve anxiety or even depression, and to fall asleep more easily. Yet alcohol, much like the tranquilizers, has many negative effects on behavior, tends to worsen the very problems it is used to treat, and can become addictive.

The question, then, is not "Do drugs affect mental processes?" Many drugs are called "psychoactive" precisely because they have effects on the mind. Rather, the question is, "Should they be prescribed as treatments?"

This book is aimed at helping people understand some of the medical and psychological dangers of relying on psychiatric drugs, but it can only hint at the psychological and social void created by such reliance on mind-altering agents. The book also offers approaches to coming off psychiatric drugs, but, in this context too, it can only hint at the kinds of resources to which people must turn to live a meaningful and satisfying life. The choice is not between psychiatric drugs and some other "therapy" but between psychiatric drugs and all the resources that life can offer us.

— *I* —

Psychiatric Drugs— Much Easier to Start Than to Stop

The use of psychiatric drugs has continued to increase in recent years among all age groups, men and women, and members of minority groups. Society is becoming increasingly dependent on prescription drugs to solve psychological and social problems. Drugs like Paxil and Ritalin are advertised directly to the consumer through magazines and newspapers. Other advertisements in mass media urge people to wonder whether they are suffering from the latest popular psychiatric disorder, often encouraging them to ask their doctors about a specific medication and sometimes offering a free sample. TV news magazines frequently paint rosy pictures of the latest "miracle drug." Innumerable books continue to be written for the layperson extolling the virtues of psychiatric drugs for myriad psychological or emotional problems in children and adults.

Even psychotherapists who favor "talking therapy" often recommend a visit to a psychiatrist for medication, sometimes in the hope that these drugs will facilitate their clients' progress or help them handle painful and overwhelming emotions. Indeed, many therapists have been led to believe that psychiatric drugs are required as part of the treatment of emotional problems such as "anxiety" or "depression."

Health maintenance organizations (HMOs) and other health care insurers encourage and sometimes insist on the use of psychiatric drugs as a supposedly cheaper alternative to talking therapy. Physicians in almost every specialty—from surgery and obstetrics and gynecology to pediatrics and family practice—are quick to prescribe psychiatric medications for problems such as insomnia, anxiety, depression, obsessions and phobias, and even "stress."

A Few Minutes That Can Become a Lifetime

In today's prodrug environment, a doctor often takes only a few minutes to make an evaluation before writing a prescription for an antidepressant, anticonvulsant, antipsychotic, or tranquilizer. But your decision to accept medication may lead to a lifetime of drug use, including exposure to long-term harmful effects. Furthermore, whereas it was easy to find a doctor to start you on psychiatric drugs, it may be very hard to find one who is willing to help you stop.

When you start taking a psychiatric drug, you may not experience any serious negative effects. But what happens when you want to stop taking it? All psychiatric drugs can cause problems during withdrawal. You also need to be aware of those unusual circumstances when the abrupt discontinuation of a psychiatric drug can produce potentially dangerous physical or psychological reactions.

Reasons to Stop Taking Psychiatric Drugs

Even if you and your doctor don't realize it, the psychiatric drugs that you are taking could be causing you serious mental, emotional, or physical harm. Your doctor may fail to appreciate that some of your problems are being caused by the prescribed medication and, instead, mistakenly increase your dose or add another drug to your regimen. This prescription cycle—a common occurrence—could expose you to increased risks of adverse drug effects.

When you reduce or skip your medication, you may experience painful emotional or physical reactions as the effects of your drug wear off. This is due to drug withdrawal between the doses. But if you don't realize that you are undergoing interdose withdrawal, you may wrongly assume that you will *always* feel that uncomfortable if you stop the medication. Similarly, your doctor may mistakenly insist that your discomfort is proof that you need to take *more* of the drug or additional drugs to control your discomfort.

Some of us have relatives who are taking psychiatric drugs. Often we watch with concern and frustration as our husband or wife, or perhaps a parent, takes medications that seem to be doing them more harm than good. Meanwhile, millions of children are being prescribed stimulant drugs such as Ritalin and Adderall, and many other youngsters are being given adult psychiatric drugs that have never been approved for children, such as Paxil, Catapres, Tenex, or Zyprexa. Parents are often told that these drugs are very safe when in fact they can be extremely dangerous to a child.

Perhaps you can see yourself, a relative, or a friend in one of the stories that follow.

Amanda started taking Zoloft when she became depressed during a period of conflicts at work and in her marriage. After explaining that she had a "biochemical imbalance" in her brain, Amanda's psychiatrist encouraged her to stay on antidepressants "indefinitely." But after three years on Zoloft, Amanda decided she didn't want to "take pills forever."

Amanda skipped two days of Zoloft and "crashed." It was like falling into a black hole; she wanted to die. Perhaps unaware that withdrawal from antidepressants can cause depression, her doctor responded by writing a prescription that doubled her original dose.

Amanda wanted to find another psychiatrist who could help her withdraw from the medication, but each new doctor urged her to stay on Zoloft or to start another medication. So she took matters into her own hands and tapered off the Zoloft over a several-week period, fortunately without lapsing into depression.

As she became drug-free, Amanda realized how stagnant her life had been during the time she was taking the medication. The emotional pain of her conflicts at work and at home had been dulled by the drugs, but her circumstances and the quality of her life had not improved. She found a psychotherapist who would help her to begin the process of taking charge of her life without drugs.

Robert had been taking one or another psychiatric drug for ten years, including tranquilizers like Xanax and Ativan, antidepressants like Prozac and Paxil, and mood stabilizers like lithium and Depakote. He often found himself saying, "I don't feel like myself anymore." He was even unsure what he would be like if he weren't on drugs. His daily experience was one of tinkering with his biochemistry. His moods seemed to go up and down depending on how much time had transpired between doses. Although his diagnosis was changed every year or two, his psychiatrist remained certain that Robert had a genetic and biological disorder that made him anxious and depressed. He assured Robert that he would need medications for the rest of his life. But Robert didn't like the idea of being forever dependent on drugs. He wished he had some guidance about how to stop taking them. But he could not seem to make up his mind about what to do.

Robert's indecisiveness was partly due to the medications themselves. From alcohol to stimulants to antidepressants, all medications that affect the mind tend to impair judgment, making it difficult for people to know whether they are being harmed by the drug they are taking. Most people are well aware that alcohol can impair judgment. They know that friends who are "drunk" cannot judge their ability to competently drive a car or to control their temper in a conflict situation.

Eventually Robert sought help from a psychiatrist known to be willing to help patients withdraw from drugs. While Robert worked with a psychotherapist who included his family in the treatment, the psychiatrist slowly withdrew Robert from the drugs he was taking. Because Robert had been using psychiatric drugs for many years, it took him more than a year to complete the withdrawal. But with a brain and mind free of drugs, Robert realized that his suspicions had been correct. He was better able to manage his life and to fulfill his potential without mind-altering drugs. Although his life still had its ups and downs, it felt wonderful to know that they were *his* ups and downs rather than those induced by drugs.

Pamela began taking an antidepressant, Elavil, thirty years ago when she was in her teens. She had been depressed as far back as she could remember and always lacked confidence in herself. Now she suspected that years of taking the antidepressant had cost her some of her mental sharpness, especially her ability to focus and concentrate. Her psychiatrist, whom she saw every few months to renew her prescriptions, wanted to add Ritalin to her drug regimen for what he deemed to be "adult attention deficit disorder."

Pamela suspected that her increasing mental difficulties were due to years of taking Elavil rather than to "adult ADD," so she tried on her own to stop taking the drug. Within twenty-four hours, she underwent the worst attack of "the flu" in her entire life. She was overcome with vomiting and diarrhea, her body ached, her head felt as though it was caught in a vise, and a dreadful sense of impending doom overcame her.

Pamela experienced immediate relief upon restarting the Elavil. Her stomach and gut settled down, her muscles stopped aching, the headache and feeling of dread went away. What did this mean? Did she have a bad case of the flu? Or did she need Elavil to keep her from going crazy? She called her psychiatrist who said she had probably contracted a viral flu. He urged her to continue on Elavil. The next day, Pamela looked up the drug on the Internet and found out that "flu-like" symptoms and depression are commonly associated with withdrawal from Elavil and many other antidepressants.

With the help of a psychotherapist who did not advocate psychiatric drugs, Pamela was able to plan a withdrawal that ended her dependence on the drugs she had been taking. Because she had been using them for so many years, she spent several months tapering down her doses. To her relief, her mental sharpness gradually returned.

As she came off the drugs, Pamela began to discover the sources of her lifelong depression. Like many persistently depressed and anxious people, she had endured an extremely abusive childhood. Many dreadful memories and painful feelings surfaced in therapy, but she was glad to be facing her history of abuse with a clear, more focused drug-free mind.

Pamela also joined an incest survivor group at her church. At first it was an act of faith—believing that a group of survivors could help to encourage and empower her. But she found that sharing her experiences with them gave her new faith in herself and her ability to grow. Over time, Pamela gained great support from the church community and from her rekindled faith in God.

Marvin became depressed during the beginning of his senior year of high school. He did not think that anything in his life was causing these negative feelings, so he never sought counseling. Hoping for medication, he went to a psychiatrist who diagnosed him as suffering from "clinical" and "biochemical" depression and put him on Prozac. Within a few days, Marvin felt a "lift" in his mood. The drug really seemed to work.

Within a few more weeks Marvin's somewhat shy personality began to undergo a dramatic transformation. He now felt "super—better than ever" and "very outgoing." But his parents became concerned about the changes. He was sleeping too little, talking a mile a minute, wearing outlandish clothing, and losing weight. He also stopped studying and, wholly unlike himself, skipped classes on a whim.

Although the effects of Prozac are described in the package insert that comes with this substance, as well as in the *Physicians' Desk Reference*, the psychiatrist did not realize that Prozac could be causing Marvin's symptoms of extreme energy and elation. Instead, the doctor changed Marvin's diagnosis from "clinical depression" to "manic depression" or "bipolar disorder" (severe mood swings). He told Marvin and his parents that Marvin was suffering from a "genetic" and "biochemical" disorder. The doctor added lithium to the Prozac and stated that Marvin would have to stay on both drugs for the rest of his life.

During his first year of college, Marvin began to feel sluggish and lifeless. He also began having trouble focusing his mind on his studies. He phoned his psychiatrist and asked, "Could the lithium or Prozac be causing me problems?" "No," the doctor said. "Since you have a biochemical imbalance, the drugs improve your mental functioning."

During the summer break, Marvin sought help from another psychiatrist who confirmed his suspicion that the drugs could be suppressing his vitality and his mental processes rather than improving them. The new psychiatrist also informed Marvin that his episode of "mania" during high school was probably caused by the Prozac. Marvin felt betrayed by his previous doctor who had never mentioned this possibility to him or to his parents.

During the summer, Marvin was weaned off both Prozac and lithium. For the first time since starting Prozac, he felt "like myself" again.

Marvin also began psychotherapy with his new psychiatrist and quickly began sharing experiences he had been previously ashamed to tell anyone. He recalled that at the time he became depressed in high school, he had repeatedly witnessed severe yelling and screaming matches between his parents that usually left his mother depressed and in tears. Marvin's psychiatrist helped him to understand how these family conflicts had played a prominent role in the initial development of his depression. More recently, several family therapy sessions with his mother and father helped Marvin to separate himself emotionally from their problems. They in turn sought help for themselves. Marvin did well emotionally and academically without psychiatric drugs throughout the remainder of college.

Marjorie was having trouble coping with the isolation and stress of raising two children, as well as with her husband's extreme preoccupation with "making money for the children's future." She felt so lonely and hopeless about her situation that she tried not to think about it during the day. Instead, she lay awake worrying at night. When she told her family doctor about her "difficulty sleeping," he prescribed the tranquilizer Klonopin before bed each night.

For the first few nights, Marjorie slept much better. But within a few weeks, she was having more difficulty falling asleep and experienced increased nervousness and tension upon awakening in the mornings. She became short-tempered with her children and nearly violent with her husband. He in turn feared that she needed to go to a mental hospital but knew that he couldn't afford to pay someone to take care of the children in her absence. It never occurred to either Marjorie or her husband that the "sleeping pill" could be causing or contributing to her emotional upsets during the daytime.

Instead of explaining that Marjorie might be experiencing "rebound anxiety" as the Klonopin wore off each morning, her doctor prescribed yet another tranquilizer, Xanax, for her daytime distress. He instructed Marjorie to take one or two tablets of Xanax three or four times a day for "anxiety," depending on how she felt. Like too many doctors, he may have not fully appreciated the dangers of these drugs, including "rebound anxiety" between doses.

Marjorie was now in a constantly unstable emotional state. Shortly after taking each Xanax tablet, she would feel calmer. But she would also feel lethargic and apathetic from the sedation. Sometimes she unintentionally fell asleep in the middle of the day while trying to care for her children. Then, as the drug effect wore off later in the afternoon, she would become "hyper" and agitated. Sometimes she had "panic attacks" in between doses. Her memory was also affected; on a "bad day," she would lose track of the number of Xanax tablets she had taken. No matter how many sleeping pills she took, she never had a restful night and never felt refreshed in the morning.

By the time Marjorie sought help in withdrawing from these drugs, she had lost faith in her ability to handle her life without medication. Her weaning from the drugs over a several-month period was combined with psychotherapy.

In therapy, Marjorie learned more about the balance that she needed in her life between raising children and being with other adults in more intellectually stimulating activities. She volunteered at church and then went to work and to school part-time.

Marjorie's husband eventually agreed to join her in couples counseling. He learned that he was very much a part of Marjorie's problems in that he had emotionally abandoned his wife and children in his efforts to earn a living.

Andy's mom and dad didn't want to give him Ritalin. They believed that their child was normal and that with proper discipline and consistent love he would outgrow his problems adjusting to school. But the school psychologist said that Andy suffered from attention deficit-hyperactivity disorder (ADHD). He warned that Andy would need special classes if he didn't go to a physician to get Ritalin.

After a ten-minute discussion with Andy's mom, the family pediatrician prescribed two doses of Ritalin each day, one before school and one at lunch break to be given by the school nurse. Within a week, Mom noticed that Andy was more "hyperactive" than ever in the evening. Because no one had warned her that Andy's brain might "bounce back" from the medication, resulting in increased hyperactivity later in the day, she thought that her son's condition must be getting worse.

The pediatrician may not have known that Ritalin and other stimulants commonly make children more agitated and excited as they wear off in the evening. In response to a brief phone call from Andy's mother, he added a late-afternoon dose of Ritalin for a total of three per day.

The third dose of Ritalin seemed to work. According to the afternoon babysitter, when Andy got home from school he took his Ritalin right away and then went upstairs to watch TV or to do his homework. But within a week, the parents discovered that Andy was staying up all night. Now the doctor added Dalmane as a sleeping pill.

One morning, Andy's mom and dad looked with dismay at their son at the breakfast table. Their hearts sank at the sight of the listless, sad-faced little fellow. They decided to stop all his medications but didn't know how to go about it. After a consultation with a second pediatrician who wanted to put Andy on another stimulant, Adderall, Andy's mom and dad decided to seek help from a doctor who was critical of the practice of giving stimulants to children and who supported the parents' efforts to wean Andy from prescription medications.

The new pediatrician explained the various Ritalin withdrawal effects to both Andy and his parents, encouraged them to stay in close touch, and tapered the boy from Ritalin. As the dose was reduced, Andy no longer needed the Dalmane to sleep. Within a couple weeks, Andy's mom and dad felt that their child had been restored to them.

Instead of sending Andy back to the public school, his parents enrolled him in a small private school that prided itself in individualizing its programs to the needs of its students. To their joy, the child who "needed Ritalin" in the public school did fine in the private school from the very first day of class. In retrospect, they were appalled at how close they had come to subjecting their child to years of drugging in order to make him conform to the local school system.

Nowadays the drug companies are marketing a whole new array of timed-release or long-acting forms of stimulant drugs (See Appendix A). While today Andy would probably have been prescribed one of these, or perhaps Strattera, the outcome for him would have remained unchanged. All stimulant drugs share essentially the same adverse effects. They work by producing short-term suppression of spontaneous behavior, combined with enforcement of obsessive-compulsive behavior, all of which is then mistaken for an improvement. None of the drugs have any proven long-term effectiveness, even in regard to the suppression of behavior. And none of them have been shown to improve a child's learning, scholastic work, social life or psychological outlook (see Chapter 2). In addition, the longer-acting preparations have two disadvantages: First, they make it less bothersome to adults to administer the drugs, thereby further encouraging their use; and second, when an adverse reaction develops, it will last longer because the body cannot as quickly rid itself of the drug. The reader may assume that these negative reactions to psychiatric drugs are rare, but, in reality, they are quite common. Moreover, the harm they cause often goes unrecognized or is attributed to something other than the medications. The stories you've just read illustrate several potentially serious problems that you are likely to face when you or a family member are prescribed psychiatric medications:

- You will probably not be given the information you need about a drug's negative effects before making an informed decision about taking it. This lack of information will also make it more difficult for you to recognize any adverse effects that develop after you start taking it.
- If you do develop an adverse reaction to the psychiatric drug, your doctor may overlook it, deny that it is possible, or decide that you need more of the same or another medication.
- If you stop the psychiatric drug abruptly, serious withdrawal reactions may follow. This outcome may lead your doctor to increase the drug dose when, in fact, you need to withdraw from it more gradually.

The above stories also illustrate some important aspects of the drug withdrawal process that your doctor may fail to communicate to you:

- Probably the most common mistake made by doctors and patients is to withdraw the psychiatric drug too rapidly. Especially if you have been taking medication for several weeks or more, or if you are taking large doses, it is almost always preferable to withdraw slowly.

- Even though many people manage to stop taking most kinds of psychiatric medication without difficulty, keep in mind the possibility that you may undergo severe emotional and physical reactions as you attempt to stop.
- When attempting to wean yourself from psychiatric drugs, you need to pay close attention to your emotional reactions. You will also benefit from a support network of family and friends who understand what you are going through. Often, therapy or counseling can help you with underlying problems that may resurface as you start to become drug-free. Therapy can also help you with any problems that have developed as a result of your taking the drugs.

How This Book Can Help

If you are considering taking a psychiatric drug but remain unsure about doing so, this book can provide the information you need to make up your mind. For instance, you may be wondering whether the use of mind-altering drugs is the wrong way to go about handling stress, conflict, or psychological problems. You may be concerned about becoming dependent on drugs in a way that undermines your self-confidence. Or you may have read or been told many good things about psychiatric drugs but wonder if the claims are exaggerated or if there is a hidden downside. All of these circumstances, and more, are considered in the chapters that follow.

This book can also be of use if you are concerned about *stopping* psychiatric drugs. Even if you feel that medications have improved your life, you may eventually want to become drug-free. You may wonder if the improvement you felt after taking a drug was due to your own personal efforts rather than to any drug effect. You may sense that there is a cost to taking drugs—a dulling of your emotions, a slowing of your thinking processes or memory, a lackluster attitude toward life in general.

Perhaps you also want to stop taking psychiatric drugs in order to feel in control of yourself rather than at the mercy of a medication, to properly assess your mental state while free from mind-altering substances, to tap your deeper psychological resources, and to define for yourself the kind of life worth living and to go after it with a clearer brain and mind. You may feel that taking psychoactive drugs isn't consistent with the healthier, less artificial lifestyle that you desire. This book will encourage you to make the changes that you want to make.

Without attributing your problems to your drug intake, you may be suffering from one or more of the many symptoms that are identified in Chapter 4 as commonly caused by psychiatric drugs, including poor memory or concentration, headaches, blurred vision or other difficulties with reading or seeing, insomnia, stomachaches, problems with bladder or bowel function, sexual problems, excessive weight loss or gain, fatigue and lethargy, lack of coordination, tremors or clumsiness, irritability, impatience, anxiety, and depression. Alternatively, you may have developed a facial tic or muscle twitch that could possibly worsen and become permanent.

Perhaps you want to understand why you have been feeling worse in some ways since starting on certain psychiatric drugs. Could the drugs themselves be making you emotionally dull or blunted, hypersensitive, uninterested in sex or other pleasures, withdrawn from loved ones, or stressed? Indeed, many adverse drug effects are difficult to distinguish from emotional problems. This book can help you decide whether the drugs, rather than your psychological difficulties, are responsible for making you feel worse.

Or perhaps your doctor wants you to stay on certain medications while trying higher doses or new combinations, but you suspect that stopping the drugs is the only way to find out if they're doing more harm than good. In fact, stopping is often the only way to discover that psychiatric drugs have been the source of your persistent symptoms. This book can help you and your doctor reach the decision to come off drugs in order to more accurately evaluate their effects.

You may have tried to stop taking psychiatric drugs in the past and failed because of your emotional or physical response in the days, weeks, or even months afterward. You will learn in this book that your reactions might have been caused by drug withdrawal rather than by your psychiatric or psychological problems.

More Reasons to Stop Taking Drugs

Your doctor may have heard or read that taking psychiatric drugs is supposed to help in psychotherapy by making it easier for patients to handle their feelings and to communicate. The authors' experience is very different. We have found that psychiatric drugs suppress feelings and estrange people from themselves. This makes it more difficult to explore, identify, and channel emotions. Weaning off psychiatric drugs can improve your ability to benefit from any personal or educational relationship, including therapy.

You may have been taking drugs for a long time and can no longer tell if they are doing much good. Very few studies show a positive effect from psychiatric drugs beyond more than four to six weeks' duration. Important recent studies reviewed in David Cohen's introduction reveal that less than a third of people taking drug treatments for depression, schizophrenia, or bipolar disorder experience sustained remissions even after two years of treatment. Furthermore, there is too little information available about drugs' long-term dangers.[1]

Even if you don't plan to completely stop taking psychiatric drugs, you may want to cut back to the minimum effective dose for you. Psychiatric drugs are often given in doses that exceed recommended or approved levels, thus substantially adding to their dangers. Similarly, you may wish to reduce the number of psychiatric drugs that you are taking. Too often doctors prescribe psychiatric drugs in dangerous combinations. And since very few drugs have been tested or approved for use in combination with others, you essentially become an experimental subject when given two or more psychiatric drugs at the same time. Meanwhile, it is commonplace for patients to get worse and worse, while increasing numbers of drugs are being prescribed, without any question from their doctors as to whether the drugs themselves have become the problem.

Doctors often tell patients not to worry about adverse drug effects because they are being prescribed "small doses" of the drug. But keep in mind that people vary enormously in terms of how sensitive they are to drug effects. Thus you could have a serious, even life-threatening reaction to a relatively small dose of a drug.

Although you may often have wanted to stop taking psychiatric drugs, you may realize that there can be dangers involved in doing so. Evidence suggests that all psychiatric drugs can produce withdrawal reactions. Some of these may be quite distressing or even disabling. In most cases, psychiatric drugs should be withdrawn slowly, preferably under experienced clinical supervision and, especially, with careful attention to how you are feeling and reacting to the change.

During pregnancy and breast-feeding, women should make every possible effort to stop taking psychiatric drugs in order to avoid harming the fetus or baby. All psychiatric drugs have the capacity to cross what is called the blood-brain barrier in order to enter the brain. The same capacity enables these drugs to cross the placenta to circulate in the fetal bloodstream and, from there, to enter the unborn infant's brain. Similarly, psychiatric drugs enter the mother's milk and thus also affect the nursing infant's brain. Also, antidepressants cause distinct withdrawal and distress reactions in neonates whose mothers were medicated during the last trimester of pregnancy. Accordingly, all psychiatric drugs can impair the brain function of both the fetus and the nursing infant. Although few studies have attempted to measure any potential lasting effects on the brain that may result from this early drug exposure, enough is known in the field of developmental neurotoxicity that parents should be warned to avoid taking psychiatric drugs during pregnancy and while nursing.[2]

In addition, some psychiatric drugs are known to cause obvious physical abnormalities as a result of fetal exposure. For example, women who take lithium or Depakote during pregnancy expose their infants to an increased rate of heart defects. Information about known birth defects caused by individual psychiatric drugs can be found in many standard sources, including the *Physicians' Desk Reference*.

This book provides a review of the withdrawal reactions associated with individual psychiatric drugs and describes methods for coming off them as safely as possible.

If Someone You Care About Is Taking Psychiatric Drugs

You may initially have encouraged your husband or wife to take psychiatric drugs to combat a psychological or emotional problem. Perhaps your doctor said that lithium or Depakote would "smooth out" your spouse's moods and make him or her easier to live with. Or perhaps you went along with having stimulants prescribed for behavioral control of your child. But, then, after a few weeks or months of apparent improvement, you have begun to notice negative changes in this individual's behavior.

The drugs may seem to be making your loved one less sensitive, less in touch, less interested in enjoying the company of friends and family, even less loving. He or she may seem more cranky or distant. In some instances, especially when medical supervision has been inadequate, people have developed toxic psychoses—severe drug-induced states of brain dysfunction with loss of touch with reality and bizarre behavior.

Too often doctors dismiss warning signs, such as communications from the family that the patient "isn't acting right," "seems more irritable and impatient," or is "getting quiet and withdrawn." Failing to stop the offending drug at the earliest signs of an adverse emotional reaction can lead to disastrous consequences such as a severe drug-induced personality change or psychosis. Drugs such Paxil, Prozac, Effexor, Zoloft, Xanax, Strattera, and Ritalin have been implicated in many cases in producing or aggravating depression, suicidal ideation, and aggressive behavior.[3]

Perhaps you are a school teacher whose students have been taking Ritalin or other stimulant drugs. School policy encourages you to recommend difficult children for referral for evaluation and possible medication. Although some of the children do become quieter and easier to manage on medication, the "sparkle" seems gone from their eyes. They look vacant or dulled. What is being sacrificed for the convenience of the school? You need more facts about what the drugs are really doing to these children.

Alternatively, you might be a health professional, such as a pediatrician or psychologist, who has been involved with diagnosing or prescribing drugs for children or adults. You've always taken for granted what you've read or been told about how safe and effective they are, but your own clinical experience is raising doubts. Could you have been misled by the drug companies and the "experts"? You wish you had more information about adverse effects and techniques for helping your patients or clients withdraw from medication. With the possible exception of the more notoriously addictive drugs, such as tranquilizers like Xanax and Valium, even medical doctors are rarely taught much about how to help their patients withdraw from psychiatric drugs.

Sources that advocate the use of psychiatric drugs are readily available in libraries and bookstores, so we shall not take up space here by repeating the standard arguments in favor of them. Rather, we believe that the benefits of psychiatric drugs are vastly exaggerated, that their disadvantages are too often minimized, and that there is far too little information about how to *stop* taking them. This book is, in fact, the first and only one to focus on the overall problem of why and how to stop taking psychiatric medications. We are not, however, trying to convince anyone not to take prescription drugs. We are simply providing a more critical viewpoint than is readily available. For more thoroughly documented critiques of biological psychiatry and psychiatric drugs, see the following: Breggin (1991, 1997a, 1998a); Breggin and Breggin (1994); Cohen

(1990, 1994, 1997a); Fisher and Greenberg (1989, 1997); Jacobs (1995); Mender (1994); and Mosher and Burti (1994).[4]

An Independent Decision

Choosing whether or not to take psychiatric drugs should be an independent, personal decision. Law and ethics support the right of competent adults to make such a decision.

In recent years, the virtues of psychiatric drugs have been widely extolled, but an informed decision can be made only when people also have access to both a more critical view of drugs and a frank analysis of their hazards. The law also supports the right of people to be fully informed about potential hazards before agreeing to a doctor's recommendation for a drug.

Ideally, withdrawal should be a collaborative effort involving the individual who wishes to stop the medication, a competent consultant or therapist, and family or friends when necessary. Of course, many patients stop taking psychiatric drugs on their own. In fact, whereas many doctors encourage patients to take drugs for seemingly endless periods of time, most patients stop on their own. Often they do so without any difficulty. But sometimes they run into serious withdrawal problems.

It can be difficult to predict who will have an easy time and who may experience profound distress during drug withdrawal. However, clinical experience confirms that the larger the doses and the longer the exposure to the drug, the more distress you can expect during withdrawal.

Stopping the long-term use of "antipsychotic" drugs such as Risperdal and Zyprexa can be emotionally and physically difficult and should be done very slowly with a great deal of social support. Stopping the long-term use of lithium can lead to severe emotional reactions, including mania. Stopping the short-term use of minor tranquilizers, such as Xanax, Klonopin, Valium, and Ativan, can cause anxiety, agitation, insomnia, or even seizures. And stopping almost any antidepressant, including the newer ones, can lead to depression and even suicidal feelings.

This book reviews the hazards of psychiatric drugs in general, examines the potential withdrawal reactions from most classes of psychiatric drugs currently in use, and makes specific suggestions on how to withdraw as safely as possible. It concludes with a discussion of how you and your therapist can handle emotional crises without resort to drugs.

Do not let anyone pressure you into starting or continuing psychiatric drugs. As a competent adult, you have the ethical and legal right to make your own decisions about taking psychiatric drugs. You also have the legal right to be completely informed in advance about the dangers of any psychiatric drug, including its withdrawal effects.

No matter how many doctors favor one or another psychiatric drug, you can and should decide for yourself. Your decisions about taking or rejecting drugs need to be made without coercive pressure from doctors and in the absence of exaggeration, misinformation, and deception.

Similarly, don't let anyone push you into *stopping* psychiatric drugs before you're ready. This decision, too, has to be your own. If you have already begun to withdraw from drugs, don't let anyone hurry you. You are the best judge of how much you can handle during drug withdrawal, and you have the right to go at your own pace.

— 2 —

The Limits of
Psychiatric Drugs

Pharmaceutical companies and organized psychiatry have conducted a worldwide campaign to convince ever greater numbers of people to take psychiatric drugs. At the 1998 annual meeting of the American Psychiatric Association, an alliance of "mental illness advocates" announced the results of its international survey: Two-thirds of people "with psychiatric disorders" often wait two to five years or more before seeking treatment. This survey was funded by a grant from Bristol-Myers Squibb Company, which manufactures both an antidepressant and an antianxiety drug.[1] The results were presented and discussed at the world's most prestigious psychiatric meeting by professors from Harvard Medical School, the New York University Medical School, and the University of Toronto.

The survey unintentionally confirmed a major reason that so many people don't seek treatment: The treatment frequently does more harm than good. More than 50 percent of patients drop out of psychiatric drug treatment "due to side effects," including drug-induced "sleep problems, anxiety and agitation, and sexual dysfunction." These results confirm the obvious limits of drug treatment; yet the survey director announced the need for a "worldwide" campaign to *encourage* more people to seek psychiatric treatment. A more recent survey found that 42 percent of American adults prescribed an antidepressant between 1996 and 2001 stopped taking it within one month; only 28 percent remained on the drug past three months.[2]

The National Institute of Mental Health (NIMH) and pharmaceutical companies have been placing increasing emphasis on marketing psychiatric drugs to children.[3] Consistent with this strategy, the survey urged "aggressive treatment in childhood and adolescence." Children, of course, have less power than adults to reject the drugs, no matter how bad the adverse effects become.

Claims that "mental illness" is caused by "biochemical imbalances" is the major public relations thrust of current drug promotion. In magazine advertisements and during consultations with doctors in their offices, potential patients are repeatedly told that psychiatric drugs "work" by correcting known "biochemical imbalances" in the brains.[4] Media reports treat these claims as the gospel truth, and the American Psychiatric Association reports that 75 percent of Americans believe in them.[5] What is the basis for them?

How We Learn What Drugs Do

During the FDA approval process, new drugs are first tested on healthy animals to see if they have effects similar to those already in use, such as other antidepressants or stimulants. They are sorted out for future testing on humans on the basis of how they affect animals. Thus, if they cause loss of appetite, weight loss, and hyperactivity in animals, they will be tested on people as "stimulants" or perhaps as "antidepressants"; and if they produce a calming effect, slowed reflexes, and sleep in animals, they will be tested on people as sleeping pills or tranquilizers.

After being screened for their effects on animals, the drugs are tested on healthy volunteers to make a gross estimate of safety and to determine the doses needed to achieve a therapeutic impact. Only then are they tried on specific diagnostic groups of patients. The drug effects, which are the same in healthy animals, healthy volunteers, and diagnosed psychiatric patients, result from the drugs' impact on these animals, volunteers, and patients.

The process of testing drugs for FDA approval thus confirms, step by step, that psychiatric drugs have the same effects on healthy animals, healthy people, and patients with psychiatric diagnoses.

How Current Drugs Affect
Animals and People

Not all drugs were first discovered through the process of screening their effects on animals. Sometimes the effects were accidentally discovered in people. Nonetheless, it turns out that the drugs have the same effects on healthy animals and volunteers as on patients.

For example, so-called antianxiety drugs such as Xanax, Ativan, and Klonopin have the same calming effects on healthy animals and volunteers as on anxious people. As the dose increases, these drugs will put all creatures to sleep and eventually into a potentially fatal coma. The drugs also bring about the same adverse effects, such as memory loss, in healthy animals, healthy volunteers, and diagnosed patients.

Stimulants also affect animals and people in the same characteristic ways. They produce "good caged rats" much as they produce "good school children."[6] The drugged animals, like compliant school children, lose their motivation to explore, to innovate, to socialize, and to escape. Instead, they sit around in their cages performing meaningless tasks, such as repetitive grooming or chewing on the bars.

Even antipsychotic agents have the same effects on animals and people alike, producing apathy, indifference, docility, and movement disorders in all creatures.[7]

Can We Test for Biochemical Imbalances?

Because of ethical and legal restraints, researchers cannot conduct studies that are certain to cause brain damage in human subjects. For example, they are not allowed to implant electrodes or to inject minute amounts of drugs into the brain tissue of living patients to test the effects of experimental drugs. Because there is no other way to do it, the basic biochemical research on drug effects is carried out on animals rather than on humans. Most of the information about a psychiatric drug's biochemical effect is deduced from conducting tests on living animal brains or, more often, from killing the animals in order to study their brain tissue following exposure to drugs. Furthermore, the animals almost never have anything wrong with them; the drug effects are being studied in *healthy* mammalian brains.

In short, when explaining how a psychiatric drug like Prozac or lithium affects the biochemistry of the human brain, researchers are drawing almost entirely on animal research conducted on normal mammalian brains rather than from studies involving people with supposed biochemical imbalances in their brains!

The concept of biochemical imbalances in people diagnosed with depression, anxiety, or other "disorders" remains highly speculative and even suspect. Although we have ample reason to doubt the validity of this concept, there is at present no way to prove its validity. Specifically, we lack the technical capacity to measure biochemical concentrations in the synapses between nerve cells. Although medication advocates often speak with seeming confidence about how psychiatric drugs can correct biochemical imbalances in the brain, they are merely indulging in pure speculation or using figures of speech that they know will resonate with their audiences. There's little evidence for the existence of any such imbalances and absolutely no way to demonstrate how the drugs would affect them if they did exist.

Causing, Not Curing, Biochemical Imbalances

As confirmed in animal research, all psychiatric drugs directly affect the brain's *normal* chemistry by disrupting it. Ritalin, for example, is known to produce overactivity in three of the brain's neurotransmitter systems: dopamine, norepinephrine, and serotonin. However, the fact that a drug increases *brain cell* activity by no means indicates that it will increase *behavioral* activity.

In the case of stimulants such as Ritalin or amphetamine, the effects on people are very complex, variable even in the same user at different times, and sometimes inconsistent. Often these drugs subdue or numb those who take them, making them more docile and manageable. This is precisely why they are used to treat behavior problems in children. At other times, however, stimulants produce opposite effects, making some children and adults hyperactive and impulsive.

Prozac, Zoloft, Paxil, and Luvox produce hyperactivity in the serotonin system; but since serotonin nerves spread throughout the entire brain, the effects are widespread and ultimately involve other neurotransmitter systems such as dopamine. The minor tranquilizers, such as Xanax, Valium, Klonopin, and Ativan, produce hyperactivity in yet another neurotransmitter system, GABA; but GABA activation produces a suppressive effect on the overall functioning of the brain.

It is important to keep this in mind: The brain is *always* impaired by psychiatric drugs.[8] If a drug is strong enough to have a supposedly positive effect, then it is disrupting normal brain function. Although this conclusion may seem controversial, it is supported by common sense and an enormous amount of scientific research detailing the biochemical imbalances in the brain created by psychiatric medication.[9] These drug-induced biochemical imbalances commonly cause psychiatric disorders in routine psychiatric practice. An egregious example of how far researchers can go to deny damage caused by psychotropic drugs is illustrated by a report in which researchers found gliosis—scarring tissue around neurons that is a hallmark sign of cell death and degeneration—in healthy rhesus monkeys after they received antipsychotic drugs. The researchers nonetheless proposed that gliosis "may be beneficial to cortical function despite the negative connotation of the term 'gliosis' due to long-established association with neurodegenerative processes"![10]

More Flaws in the Myth of Biochemical Imbalances

Even if some emotional problems turned out to be caused by subtle, as-yet-undetected biochemical imbalances, this finding would not be a rational justification for using any of the psychiatric drugs that are currently available. Because they impair normal brain function, such drugs only add to any existing brain malfunction. When psychiatric drugs are given to patients who do have known brain dysfunctions such as head injury or hormonal disorder, psychiatric drugs add to their brain dysfunction, frequently causing further mental deterioration. Experienced clinicians who work with brain-injured patients, for example, avoid prescribing brain-altering chemicals to them. And endocrinologists try to correct actual hormonal problems instead of suppressing their symptoms with psychiatric drugs. Unfortunately, the psychiatric literature is also replete with examples of the opposite practice: prescribing multiple psychiatric drugs to persons with traumatic brain injuries, despite a dearth of evidence that these treatments reduce behavioral problems in such patients.

If psychiatric drugs could correct specific biochemical imbalances, specific types of drugs for specific disorders would be available. But this is not the case. For example, even though Prozac mainly affects just one neurotransmitter system, it is used with supposed success for a broad range of difficulties, from anxiety to depression to behavior problems in children. The same has been true of other psychiatric drugs. Even the first "antipsychotics," such as Thorazine, were originally marketed for nearly every possible human problem, from behavioral difficulties in children to insomnia and anxiety in adults, as well as for a variety of supposed psychosomatic disorders, including skin and digestive problems. Similarly, the stimulants, such as Ritalin and amphetamine, were originally advertised not only for behavioral control of children but also for stress and depression—and even for energizing old people.

Furthermore, many psychiatric disorders are treated with a variety of drugs with widely varying biochemical effects. The treatment for depression, for example, involves drugs that affect the serotonin, norepinephrine, acetylcholine, dopamine, and GABA systems.

No psychiatric drug has ever been tailored to a known biochemical derangement. Instead, the drugs are marketed on the basis of whether they "work" in short clinical trials on one particular diagnostic group—although subjects in that group typically carry other diagnoses as well and may have little in common with each other.[11] The drug companies, followed by drug advocates, then construct an argument that the medications must be correcting a biochemical imbalance in this group of patients.

At the same time, no biochemical imbalances have ever been documented with certainty in association with any psychiatric diagnosis. The hunt goes on for these elusive imbalances; but their existence is pure speculation, inspired by those who advocate drugs.[12]

Anesthesia of the Soul

Arguing that psychiatric drugs "work" by correcting a biochemical imbalance in patients is similar to arguing that surgical anesthesia renders patients unconscious by correcting a biochemical imbalance in them. The comparison is not farfetched. Some psychiatric drugs, such as the benzodiazepines, can be and are given in higher doses to produce surgical anesthesia. And the original "antipsychotic" drug, Thorazine, was first used by a French surgeon who noticed that it was useful in making surgical patients indifferent or apathetic toward the pain that they were undergoing.[13] There is also evidence that the SSRIs may produce a particular sort of emotional blunting, apathy, and unconcern.[14] Scientific evidence can be marshaled to support the hypothesis that most psychiatric drugs "work" by producing a kind of anesthesia of the mind, spirit, or feelings.[15]

What Does "Improvement" Mean in the Context of Psychiatric Drugs?

If a person falls asleep more quickly due to the chemical effects of a sleeping pill such as Ambien or becomes more calm after taking a tranquilizer such as Valium, the effect is due to a suppression of brain function. The impact of the drugs, in fact, is very similar to that of alcohol. All three agents—Ambien, Valium, and alcohol—activate an inhibitory system in the brain called GABA. This inhibitory system, when made hyperactive by a drug, causes varying degrees of brain suppression that, following high enough doses, will produce sleep and then coma. The abnormalities caused in the GABA system can be studied in animal brains. Various abnormalities in brain waves in humans demonstrate how the drugs disrupt normal awake/asleep patterns in people, regardless of whether they have a sleep problem or anxiety.

Similarly, in cases where an individual's mood swings seem to be "smoothed out" on lithium, the drug has suppressed the normal electrical transmission of brain cells, limiting the individual's *capacity* to feel or to react. Lithium literally replaces basic elements in the brain's electrical transmission system, including sodium and potassium ions, thereby slowing down nerve conduction. This intrusion produces a grossly abnormal condition in any animal or person quite apart from any supposed biochemical imbalance.

When a person's emotions are altered by drugs, the effect is not limited to the emotion-regulating centers of the brain. Indeed, since the brain is a highly integrated organ, and since the drugs cause widespread disruptions within it, emotional suffering cannot be dulled without harming other functions such as concentration, alertness, sensitivity, and self-awareness.[16]

The Limits of Psychiatric Drugs in General

Despite a hugely successful promotional campaign by drug companies and biological psychiatry, the effectiveness of most or all psychiatric drugs remains difficult to demonstrate. The drugs often prove no more effective than sugar pills, or placebos[17]—and to accomplish even these limited positive results, the clinical trials and data that they generate typically have to be statistically manipulated. Furthermore, no psychiatric drugs have consistently demonstrated effectiveness in studies lasting more than a few weeks or months.[18]

Concerning antidepressants, for example, meta-analyses (overviews) of hundreds of published clinical trials are challenging the idea that such drugs, including Prozac, have any genuine antidepressant effect.[19] Studies show that at least 80 percent of the antidepressant effect is a placebo effect—the positive response that people have to any treatment that they hope or think will work. But the remaining 20 percent of the positive result may be caused by the "active placebo" effect—which is related to the fact that the antidepressants, unlike placebos, have noticeable side effects that convince the subjects that they are getting "strong" or "real" medicine.

Ideally, clinical trials involving drugs are "double-blind," so that both the researchers and the patients are unaware of who is getting the real drug and who is getting the placebo. This research design is supposed to maintain the objectivity of both the investigators and the patients. Otherwise, both are likely to give higher ratings of improvement to the new "miracle drug" than to the sugar pill.

Unfortunately, the ideal of the double-blind is rarely attained. The side effects of psychiatric drugs—including antidepressants, stimulants, and tranquilizers—are usually very noticeable. In short, they let the investigators and the patients know who is taking a real drug rather than a sugar pill. This knowledge destroys the double-blind and allows bias in favor of the drug to affect the outcome of drug studies.[20] Still, despite these advantages in favor of drugs, recent clinical trials of SSRI antidepressants consistently show these drugs to be equaled or outperformed by placebos.[21]

Regarding antianxiety drugs such as Xanax, researchers have even greater difficulty establishing any effectiveness because the rebound and withdrawal effects often leave the patients worse off than before they started taking the drugs. Marginal positive results are erased by the eighth week, at which time many or most patients experience more anxiety than before they began taking the drugs.[22]

Psychostimulants, such as Ritalin and Adderall, can also leave children worse off than before they began receiving the drugs. In addition, they have never been shown to have any long-term positive effects at all. Their impact is limited to subduing the behavior of children for a period ranging from seven to twelve weeks. Even in the short term, stimulants have not been shown to improve a child's mental state, academic performance, or learning. Prescription of these drugs is strictly a method for short-term behavioral inhibition.[23]

The Limits of Drugs for Helping in Emotional Crises

Despite their almost universal use as a first resort, often the use of psychiatric drugs is justified as a "last resort" or as a means of "saving a life" from suicide or violence. Yet there is no scientific evidence that drugs are useful to people during acute emotional crises. The testing employed for the approval of psychiatric drugs by the FDA usually excludes people who are suicidal or violent.[24] And, in any case, the FDA has never approved a drug specifically for the prevention or control of suicide or violence.

More generally, there is no convincing evidence that any psychiatric medication can reduce the suicide rate or curtail violence. But there is substantial evidence that many classes of psychiatric drugs—including neuroleptics (antipsychotics), antidepressants, stimulants, and minor tranquilizers—can cause or exacerbate depression, suicide, paranoia, and violence.

Most people are aware that psychiatrists commonly tell their patients, "It can take eight weeks or more for the drug to take full effect." Yet there is little evidence in support of this assertion, given that clinical trials seldom last beyond four to six weeks. Because the brain compensates for drug effects, drugs often *stop* having their anticipated effects after four to six weeks. Moreover, many patients drop out after a few weeks because of diminishing positive effects and increasing adverse effects, so there aren't enough left to draw any statistical conclusions beyond the short term. Thus it's very difficult to conduct a clinical trial that will last for more than a few weeks.[25]

It's also difficult to show any good effect from psychiatric drugs during the first one or two weeks. This is another reason that drugs should not be relied upon to provide immediate relief to people who are in crisis or acute distress. For example, the FDA requires antidepressants to carry a warning about the danger of suicide during the first few weeks before the drug effect kicks in. The warning is misleading, however, since there's no evidence that the antidepressants reduce the suicide rate even after they achieve their maximum effect.

Movies about mental hospitals or psychiatric treatment sometimes accurately depict how psychiatric drugs can turn people into zombies. In *The Dream Team*, a comedy starring Michael Keaton, mental patients successfully masquerade as doctors. The patients manage to escape by prescribing enforced medication for the psychiatrists themselves, who are last seen staring in a drugged stupor at the TV on a hospital ward.

To some extent, at least, this zombie effect can render people temporarily unable to harm themselves or others. For instance, "antipsychotic" drugs, which can be injected into the muscles to quickly subdue resistant patients, are used in this way in emergency rooms, hospitals, and prisons. The resistant patients are chemically controlled by the numbing effect on the brain. This procedure has accurately been called a "chemical lobotomy." "Antipsychotic" drugs also suppress the brain centers that control voluntary movement, rendering the person unable to respond with any speed, agility, or determination—thus warranting the descriptive phrase "pharmacological straitjacket."[26]

The use of such drugs should be viewed not as "therapy" but as chemical restraint—as a seemingly easy, inexpensive, and efficient way to temporarily subdue a person. Unfortunately, doctors often fail to implement the best way to calm disturbed and disturbing individuals—by spending time with them in a confident, caring, and skillful manner.[27]

Chemical force is sometimes used as a police method for controlling people, much as straitjackets, shackles, and "quiet rooms" are used for the same purpose. In fact, a good case can be made for the greater safety of physical restraint compared to chemical restraint; the former restrains the limbs, the latter can harm the brain. Furthermore, the use of drugs for short-term control does not empower patients to handle their own emotions and their lives more effectively. To the contrary, holding people down in order to inject them with paralyzing drugs adds to their sense of personal shame, resentment, and helplessness. In any case, skilled individuals using sound therapeutic approaches are almost always able to calm down upset and menacing patients without the use of drugs.

People Are Better Than Pills—
Even for the Most Disturbed Patients

There is a great deal of discussion in the media and in professional journals about the relative merits of medication and psychotherapy. Claims are usually made for the superiority of medication; it is supposedly faster, more economical, and more effective. In reality, however, the comparable or superior efficacy of psychotherapeutic interventions, even for severely disturbed persons, is much better documented than most therapists or the public realize.[28]

It is also misleading and futile to compare drugs to talk therapy. Drugs and psychotherapy don't have the same effects. Both their immediate effects and their outcomes are different. Their "efficacy" cannot be measured by the same standards. Drugs can suppress "symptoms," such as intense emotions, but they may also impair overall brain function. Psychotherapy can strengthen and liberate individuals to respond to their emotions in a rational way and to live better, more fulfilling lives.

Even emotionally disabled, institutionalized individuals respond better to personal attention than to drugs. Peter Breggin's "clinical" experience began in the 1950s when, as a college student volunteer, he worked with very disturbed and disturbing inmates in a dilapidated state mental hospital.[29] While still an undergraduate college student, he became director of the Harvard-Radcliffe Mental Hospital Volunteer Program.[30] He and his fellow students developed a special project that allowed more than a dozen of them to work with their own individual patients under the group supervision of a therapist. Each of the students was assigned a "chronic inmate" who had little hope of release from the hospital. They were able to help almost every patient to leave the hospital.

There was no need for a special control group of untreated patients to show what would have happened without the intervention of the Harvard-Radcliffe student volunteers in their lives. The whole hospital was the control group! In the mid-1950s, the patients from the "back wards" were almost never discharged. Even after the "miracle drugs" were introduced, no large-scale increase in discharges occurred until a decade later, when hospital admission and discharge polices were changed for political and economic reasons.[31] Without the help of the volunteers as caring therapists and case aides, few if any of the patients would have left the state hospital for many years, if ever.

Therapy has also been shown to be more effective than drugs in helping patients diagnosed with their first "schizophrenic" break. Nowadays it is argued that these people must have drugs and that psychotherapy is futile; yet nothing could be further from the truth. In controlled studies, untrained therapists in a home-like setting have proven more successful than drugs and mental hospitals in treating patients diagnosed with their first episode of schizophrenia.[32] A key factor was the caring, noncoercive approach of these therapists.

According to an international study by the World Health Organization (WHO), less industrialized cultures characterized by extended families have a very positive effect on the recovery of individuals who are diagnosed as schizophrenic—in contrast to their counterparts in Western cultures, where isolated families are more common. In cultures with extended families, a large proportion of very disturbed individuals labeled schizophrenic had complete recoveries. Tragically, this study also showed that the availability of modern psychiatric treatment with drugs has a negative effect on the outcome for people diagnosed as schizophrenic.[33] This finding corroborates our own assertion that biological psychiatry does more harm than good.

If nondrug, caring approaches work better for severely disturbed people, they are clearly even more effective with less impaired people who can benefit from relationships and "talk therapy."

Conclusion

Virtually everyone today recognizes that the public has been subjected to a high-power selling campaign for psychiatric drugs. This campaign, conducted by drug companies and organized psychiatry, has convinced most people that psychiatric drugs are much safer and more valuable than they really are.[34]

Psychiatric drugs do not work by correcting anything wrong in the brain. We can be sure of this because such drugs affect animals and humans, as well as healthy people and diagnosed patients, in exactly the same way. There are no known biochemical imbalances and no tests for them. That's why psychiatrists do not draw blood or perform spinal taps to determine the presence of a biochemical imbalance in patients. They merely observe the patients and announce the existence of the imbalances. The purpose is to encourage patients to take drugs.

Ironically, psychiatric drugs cause rather than cure biochemical imbalances in the brain. In fact, the only known biochemical imbalances in the brains of patients routinely seen by mental health professionals are brought about through the prescription of mind-altering drugs.

Psychiatric drugs "work" precisely by causing imbalances in the brain—by producing enough brain malfunction to dull the emotions and judgment or to produce an artificial high. Some people may choose this alternative because they do not know that other options exist or because they have lost faith in themselves and in the ability of other people to help them, or because they have been taught to believe that their brain is defective and that a drug will temporarily fix the problem.

In the experience of the authors, when people are caught in emotional crises and are suffering from extreme emotional pain, the most important therapeutic intervention is a caring individual or group willing to create a safe space and a safe relationship. We further discuss this point in the final chapter, after examining in more detail the hazards of taking psychiatric drugs and the process of stopping them.

— 3 —

Your Drug May Be
Your Problem—
But You May Be the
Last to Know

If you or a loved one are taking psychiatric drugs, you may be dismayed to discover how many "psychiatric symptoms" can be caused or worsened by the drugs themselves. In fact, nearly all psychiatric symptoms, including the most severe ones such as hallucinations and delusions, can be produced by these drugs. The present chapter describes the overall ways in which psychiatric medications can adversely affect how you think, feel, and act. Chapter 4 provides detailed information on the adverse effects of specific drugs.

The Variability of Individual Responses to Drugs

Do not be misled by a doctor or friend who tells you that you're taking only a "small dose" of a psychiatric drug. Although the risk of harmful drug effects does usually increase with the size of the dose, some people are very sensitive to mind-altering drugs and can suffer bad reactions even from small doses. One of the most important observations in psychopharmacology is that all psychotropic drugs have complex and variable effects, and will not affect everyone the same way. A drug's effect commonly varies within the same person over time, and among different people. Severe adverse reactions often occur when the dose has been changed up or down or when another drug has been added but they can appear for the first time at any time during the treatment.

Consider the wide variety of responses that people have to caffeine, a relatively mild stimulant. Some individuals can drink six or more cups a day without any dramatic effect on their psyche. But others are so sensitive that even the small amount of caffeine in decaffeinated coffee can make them feel jittery and anxious. For them, a full cup of coffee would be a prescription for physical symptoms that feel like a spontaneous "panic attack."

Likewise, some people cannot drink coffee late in the day without being kept awake all night by the stimulant effects, while others routinely have coffee with dinner, or even later in the evening, without experiencing any apparent interference with their sleep. Some people suffer a stomachache from drinking one or two cups of coffee, while others never experience any stomach upset from much greater amounts. Some people can stop drinking coffee without any major withdrawal effects, while others develop headaches and become temporarily fatigued and lethargic, even depressed.

The effects of psychiatric drugs are similarly variable. One person may "feel nothing" after a 10–20 mg dose of Prozac, while another person may develop severe agitation and insomnia, and even become psychotic. One person with insomnia may hardly notice the impact of 5 mg of Valium taken before bedtime, while another will sleep like a log and feel "sluggish" and "irritable" for a day or two afterward. Some children may seem unaffected by a 5 mg dose of Ritalin; others become zombie-like.

Individual responses to psychiatric drugs also vary over time. Some effects tend to appear after a week or two, while others may not appear for months or years. Similarly, a person may react to a drug one way and then in an entirely different fashion at a later date after restarting it.

"Creeping" Adverse Effects

Unfortunately, drugs that affect the brain and mind can seriously impair your mental function before you recognize that anything is the matter. You may not realize that your thinking is slowed, your emotions dulled, or your coordination impaired. You may believe that your newly developed feelings of anxiety or depression are due to events in your life rather than to the drug you are taking. If you feel euphoric or "high" from taking the drug, you may think that you are doing "better than ever" when, in fact, your judgment has been impaired.

Your doctor may fail to notice these drug side effects or mistakenly attribute them to something else such as your psychological problems. Family or friends may become increasingly dismayed by the deterioration in your memory, attention span, sensitivity, or emotional responsiveness, while you and your doctor remain seemingly unaware that anything is wrong.

Patients often suffer from common adverse drug effects that their doctors have never warned them about. In order to encourage their patients to start drugs or to stay on them, doctors frequently misinform their patients by inflating the benefits and minimizing the hazards of psychiatric medications. Many doctors nowadays feel that they should cajole or push their patients to take these medications against the patients' better judgment.

Even when patients develop serious drug-induced adverse reactions—such as depression or psychosis, weight loss and fatigue, or abnormal movements of the body—doctors tend to attribute the effects to something other than the drug. On a particular occasion, one of us was presenting grand rounds—a special educational seminar for doctors at a hospital—when a case history came to our attention. It concerned a middle-aged business executive who became violent for the first time while taking Prozac.[1] In a minor altercation at a gas station, he assaulted a stranger with a crowbar.

Experience, prudence, and reason suggest that the drug should be suspected as the cause of the problem when unusual, irrational behavior erupts for the first time after the patient has started taking it. Yet some of the doctors at the grand rounds totally rejected the possibility that the patient's unprecedented, extreme, and bizarre violence had been caused or exacerbated by Prozac. They recommended *raising* his dose of Prozac instead of stopping it.[2]

Too many health professionals are reluctant or resistant to recognizing adverse drug effects, especially those that affect the patient's emotional state. They find it easier, apparently, to blame the effects on the patient's "mental illness." Yet a doctor's refusal to face the dangers of medication can lead to irreversible and ultimately tragic adverse drug reactions.

In our consultations, we find that patients are rarely told all they need to know about the psychiatric drugs they are taking. Of course, some patients are reluctant to know in advance about the dangers to which they are being exposed; but it remains the doctor's responsibility to insist on informing them. But physicians are not alone in withholding facts about drug hazards; printed handouts from doctors' offices or pharmacies, as well as textbooks and drug advertisements, also often fail to give sufficient emphasis to the dangerous effects of psychiatric drugs.[3] (See Chapter 6 for a discussion of the possible motivations that lead some health professionals to minimize the risks of these drugs.)

The Risk of Permanent Brain Dysfunction Caused by Psychiatric Drugs

Very few studies have examined the danger of potentially permanent changes in brain chemistry caused by long-term use of psychiatric medication. However, enough is known and suspected about these dangers to make a thoughtful person cautious about using any psychiatric drug.

Prozac, Zoloft, Paxil, and Luvox are recent examples of drugs tailor-made in the laboratory to stimulate the activity of the serotonin system. In the case of Prozac, the brain's compensatory mechanisms were documented from the beginning of the research involving this drug.

All four drugs, known as selective serotonin reuptake inhibitors (SSRIs), block the normal removal of the neurotransmitter serotonin from the synaptic cleft—the space between nerve cells. The resultant overabundance of serotonin then causes the system to become hyperactive. But the brain reacts against this drug-induced overactivity by destroying its capacity to react to stimulation by serotonin. This compensatory process is known as "downregulation." Some of the receptors for serotonin actually disappear or die off.

To further compensate for the drug effect, the brain tries to reduce its output of serotonin. This mechanism is active for approximately ten days and then begins to fail, whereas downregulation continues indefinitely and may become permanent. Thus we know in some detail about two of the ways in which the brain tries to counterbalance the effects of psychiatric drugs. There are other compensatory mechanisms about which we know less, including counterbalancing adjustments in other neurotransmitter systems. But, overall, the brain places itself in a state of imbalance in an attempt to prevent or overcome overstimulation by the drugs.

The brain probably has compensatory mechanisms to ward off or reverse the effects of all psychiatric drugs. Some of these mechanisms have already been recognized and studied. For instance, downregulation of overstimulated neurotransmitter systems occurs with all of the older "tricyclic" antidepressants such as amitriptyline (Elavil) and imipramine (Tofranil). Downregulation also takes place with stimulant drugs such as Ritalin and the amphetamines Dexedrine and Adderall.

Psychiatric drugs do not always overstimulate neurotransmitter systems. Some drugs inhibit or block nerve transmission in the brain. When this happens, the brain again tries to compensate by reacting in the opposite direction—this time by "upregulation" of the suppressed neurotransmitter system. The "antipsychotic" drugs—such as Thorazine, Haldol, Prolixin, Risperdal, and Zyprexa—tend to suppress the dopamine system. The brain tries to overcome this effect by making the dopamine system hypersensitive. As discussed below, this upregulation can lead to severe, even permanent neurological disorders.

In its attempts to overcome the effects of psychiatric drugs, the brain becomes distorted in its functioning. And as already emphasized, the brain cannot immediately recover its original functions once the drugs are stopped. In some cases, the brain may never recover.

Physicians Urge Long-Term Use
Without Justification

Physicians who prescribe psychiatric drugs for long-term use *believe* that the drugs are useful, but their views are based on personal impressions and unproven assumptions rather than on scientific evidence. Medical doctors rely heavily on medications and tend to be very biased in favor of their use. For example, many doctors who prescribe psychiatric drugs recommend them for *long-term* use as soon as they become available on the market. They recommend that patients take a new psychiatric drug for months or years, even though the studies used for FDA approval typically last for only a few weeks.[4]

The widespread use of Zyprexa exemplifies how new and potentially dangerous drugs are often prescribed with unjustified enthusiasm for their safety and efficacy. In 1996 Zyprexa was approved by the FDA for the treatment of psychosis and a few years later for the treatment of bipolar disorder. Drugs approved for such manifestations are called neuroleptics or antipsychotics. All are extremely dangerous.

As required by the FDA, all neuroleptic drugs, including the newer ones like Zyprexa, must carry a "class warning" about the dangers of tardive dyskinesia (TD).[5] Tardive dyskinesia is a disfiguring and potentially disabling, usually permanent neurological disorder characterized by tics, spasms, and abnormal movements. These drugs also cause neuroleptic malignant syndrome (NMS), a potentially fatal disease of the brain with effects similar to those associated with severe viral encephalitis.[6] For the neuroleptics that have been extensively studied, as we document in Chapter 4, the rates of tardive dyskinesia and neuroleptic malignant syndrome are very high.

The controlled trials used for the approval of Zyprexa lasted only six weeks and were conducted on adults diagnosed with schizophrenia. Yet immediately after Zyprexa became available on the market, doctors began recommending it for indefinite, even lifetime usage. Doctors also began prescribing it for people with no psychotic symptoms, even for children with behavior problems.

Despite the absence of long-term studies and the newness of the drug, doctors accepted the drug manufacturer's promotional pitch that Zyprexa is safer than other drugs used for the same purpose. In fact, almost all psychiatric drugs start out amid claims of being "safer" and "more effective." Rarely in psychiatry is this enthusiasm confirmed by more sober, realistic appraisals based on time and experience.

In the case of Zyprexa and other newer antipsychotics, long-term use revealed that many patients were at higher risk of developing elevated blood sugar, diabetes, pancreatitis, elevated cholesterol, and considerable weight gain. Some patients gained over 60 pounds a year, and several died from these complications. In his clinical and forensic practice Peter Breggin has evaluated several cases of rapid death caused by acute Zyprexa-induced diabetes and pancreatitis.

In 2004, the FDA mandated that newer antipsychotics carry a warning about the risk of hyperglycemia and diabetes. Moreover, a systematic analysis had also revealed that older, frail patients with dementia prescribed atypical antipsychotics had nearly double the risk of dying, and here again the FDA in 2002 ordered a "black box" warning about the risk of premature death from such drugs. Some recent reviews find that older antipsychotics also appear to significantly increase this risk of premature death among the frail elderly, and we believe that the FDA "black box" warning should be applied equally to this entire class of drugs.[7]

Even when drugs later prove to be useless or highly dangerous when prescribed over the long term, many doctors continue to push patients to take them for many months or years at a time. Regarding Ritalin and other stimulants, for example, there is no substantial evidence for positive effects on any behavior, including hyperactivity, beyond the first several weeks.[8] These drugs can temporarily subdue the behavior of children and make them more obedient, conforming, and quiet in the classroom. But they are routinely prescribed for months and years, even over entire lifetimes. Similarly, although Ritalin is known to disrupt growth hormone production, causing significant growth inhibition, it is routinely prescribed throughout childhood.

All the so-called antianxiety drugs—such as Xanax, Ativan, Klonopin, Valium, and Librium—are known to be highly addictive. After only a few weeks of treatment with Xanax, many patients suffer from severe withdrawal symptoms when they cease taking the drug. Others feel unable to stop without help.[9] Indeed, after several weeks of treatment, many Xanax patients develop anxiety that is more severe than before their treatment began.

Despite these limits on the long-term use of drugs such as stimulants and minor tranquilizers, large numbers of physicians continue to prescribe them for months or even years at a time. Some doctors trust their "clinical judgment" more than the scientific data; others simply haven't kept up with the scientific literature. In addition, most of the seminars that doctors attend are sponsored by drug companies and too often provide opinions that are biased toward the long-term use of drugs. The doctors never see negative comments about the long term use of drugs in the eye-catching pharmaceutical advertising that they read in almost every professional journal. Nor are they likely to hear this kind of critical information from the drug salespersons who regularly visit them in their offices. Doctors may also fail to realize that their patients have become addicted and want to stay on their drugs in order to avoid withdrawal reactions. Overall, doctors often take the easy route of writing prescriptions rather than the more arduous route of helping their patients to find more complex long-term solutions to their emotional difficulties.

Meanwhile, as noted, the patients themselves may feel compelled to take the drugs to avoid painful and frightening withdrawal reactions such as anxiety, agitation, insomnia, depression, fatigue, and abnormal sensations in the head or body. Depending on the drug, one or more withdrawal symptoms can develop within hours or days of cutting back on the medication. These reactions can become severe enough that patients begin to pressure their doctor into continuing to prescribe drugs. In effect, the prescribing physician maintains or "enables" the patients' drug dependence.

Some drug advocates believe that years of clinical use by thousands of patients can prove a drug's long-term usefulness and safety. And some individual doctors feel that their own prescription of a drug over many years can demonstrate its safety. These beliefs have led to tragic outcomes for millions of patients. One of these has already been described—millions of patients suffering from lifelong dependence on addictive tranquilizing drugs such as Xanax, Valium, Ativan, Klonopin, and Librium.

Overconfidence in clinical judgment concerning the long-term safety of drugs has led to an even more tragic outcome. Millions of patients have been afflicted with gross neurological disorders from taking antipsychotic drugs. This class of drugs—starting with Thorazine, and now including many others such as Haldol, Prolixin, Navane, Risperdal, Clozaril, and Zyprexa—was used for two decades before it was generally recognized that the entire group frequently causes tardive dyskinesia and neuroleptic malignant syndrome. Even today, fifty-five years after the first neuroleptics were introduced, many doctors fail to realize the frequency or severity of these dangers and prescribe the drugs without adequately monitoring their use or warning patients and their families.

The Special Danger of Psychiatric Drugs

The brain is the "target organ" for psychiatric drugs. All drugs approved for psychiatric purposes directly affect the brain, causing a variety of mental or psychiatric symptoms. Commonly reported effects include confusion, memory difficulties, dulled emotions, artificial feelings of euphoria, depression, anxiety, agitation, personality changes, and psychosis. A review of handbooks or textbooks, as well as the discussions in Chapter 4, will confirm that *any* psychiatric symptom or disorder can also be caused by psychiatric drugs.

By law, every psychiatric drug must have an FDA-approved label listing all mental and behavioral side effects, sometimes including suicide and violence. This information is based on reports of adverse effects made during the drug testing process as well as after the drug has been marketed. However, in its efforts to be politically accommodating, and partly owing to its administrative limitations, the FDA often fails to force the drug companies to list well-known serious adverse effects in a drug's official label. Not until 1986 did the FDA require drug companies to include neuroleptic malignant syndrome in the labels (and package inserts) for all antipsychotic or neuroleptic drugs—nearly three decades after this disorder was initially described.[10]

Adverse Effects on How You Think, Feel, and Act

As we have been emphasizing, any psychiatric drug can and will impair mental function. The impairments associated with most psychiatric drugs can also be caused by an endless variety of other kinds of trauma, including head injury, extreme fatigue, chronic illness or stress, lack of oxygen to the brain, chronic use of alcohol, or exposure to toxins such as lead or carbon monoxide.

Sometimes these symptoms of mental dysfunction are aggravated by emotional problems. However, if problems develop for the first time or worsen after you have started a psychiatric drug, you should suspect the drug. Even in cases where the symptoms seem to get worse when you're upset, the underlying cause may be the psychiatric drug. Many drug-induced adverse reactions, from agitation to memory problems and neurological tremors, can worsen under stress. Conversely, they can improve during rest and relaxation.

Drug-Induced Toxic Psychoses

The term *toxic psychosis* or, more simply, *psychosis* is often used to describe the extreme negative impact that psychiatric drugs frequently have on the brain. Although *psychosis* has many meanings, in general it refers to a loss of touch with reality, often accompanied by hallucinations or delusions.[11]

Drug-induced impairment of overall brain function may also be called *confusion* or *delirium*. Delirium is a disturbance of consciousness and cognition (thinking processes) that usually develops over a short period of time.[12] Related terms are *organic brain syndrome* and *dementia*. Finally, the term *mania* is often used to describe an especially dangerous psychosis that is commonly caused by psychiatric drugs (as further discussed below and in Chapter 4).

Initially, these disorders often manifest as memory problems and disorientation, but they eventually involve impairments of all higher mental functions such as judgment, insight, and abstract reasoning. Mood or feelings may be unstable, disturbed, or inappropriate. Hallucinations and delusions may develop.

A significant percentage of patients who take psychiatric drugs will develop full-blown toxic psychoses or deliriums, but many more will develop milder variations of these drug-induced symptoms.

Trust Your Own Perception of Yourself—Up to a Point

In trying to decide if you have a drug-induced symptom—such as memory problems, slowed thinking, or dulled feelings—your own perception of yourself is the most sensitive instrument there is for detecting when your brain and mind aren't working right. If you sense that a drug is interfering with your normal mental processes, take your perceptions seriously. You could be mistaken—and other people may try to reassure you that "nothing's the matter" or that "you're doing fine." But you could also be right about suffering from the ill effects of medication.

Keeping track of your changing mental responses soon after you take a dose of medication, compared to when the drug effect is wearing off, may help you to determine if you are having a drug-induced problem. If the symptoms become worse soon after taking the drug, you may be suffering from a drug toxic effect. If they grow worse when the drug effect is wearing off, you may be suffering from withdrawal symptoms. It can be difficult, of course, to distinguish between drug effects and your own psychological reactions.

On the other hand, psychiatric drugs can confuse your reasoning and judgment, leading you to believe that you are being helped when in fact you are being mentally impaired.

Common Adverse Effects on Your Thinking, Feeling, and Behaving

If you are taking a psychiatric drug, you may eventually find yourself experiencing one or more of the following drug-induced mental abnormalities:

Impaired Concentration.   Almost any psychiatric drug can make it harder for you to pay attention to conversations, to focus on reading anything complicated, or to work consistently on a project. The subjective awareness of impaired concentration is a subtle but important sign of drug-induced toxicity.

Poor Memory.   Psychiatric drugs can make it difficult for you to re-member things such as a list of items to get at the grocery, the time your children said they were coming for dinner, or the name of the person who just left a phone message for your wife or husband. You may find it harder to recall recipes or simple operations on your computer, to find the word or phrase you want, or to remember the name of some familiar object. As in the case of impaired concentration, you may notice your poor memory before your family or psychiatrist do, and even before it can be detected by psychological testing.

Confusion or Disorientation.   This is a more serious sign of brain dys-function caused by psychiatric drugs. It may be harder for you to find your way around buildings or within places you've been before. You may discover that you've walked or driven by a familiar place without realiz-ing it or that you have difficulty driving somewhere using written direc-tions. Malls and other large spaces are more confusing than they used to be. You may lose your bearings more easily.

Slowed or Simplified Mental Functioning.   You may find it harder to follow complicated questions or directions, to think about more than one thing at a time, or to carry out a logical sequence of thought. You may find yourself wishing that people would slow down and not expect such quick responses. While you used to think of yourself as "quick," you now seem "slow." You may become baffled by conversations involving more than one person, or you may be unable to carry out more than one task at a time, such as talking on the phone while you prepare dinner.

Exaggerated Responses to Stress.   You may find yourself increasingly less able to handle everyday stresses, such as getting the children ready for school, trying to arrive at work on time, having a conflict with friends or co-workers, being late for an appointment, falling behind in a project, or being interrupted.

Increased Irritability, Anger, or Aggressivity.   To your embarrassment, you find yourself getting unusually annoyed, frustrated, or irritable, and sometimes you hurt people's feelings without meaning to. You may also find yourself becoming unexpectedly angry or aggressive. In the worst-case scenario, you may do something dangerous or harmful that you would otherwise never do, landing you in trouble at work, at home, or on the street. These drug-induced problems are called "paradoxical reactions" or "disinhibition."

Sleep Difficulties.   You may have trouble falling asleep or staying asleep. Overall, you may not be sleeping as deeply as before; and when you do sleep, you may not wake up refreshed. Some psychiatric drugs can make you sleepy during the daytime, impairing your daily activities. Other psychiatric drugs can stimulate you at night, keeping you awake and leaving you sleepy and exhausted the next day.

Emotional Blunting and Insensitivity.   The highs and the lows of your emotions may have been leveled off by the drug you are taking. You don't care about anyone or anything as much as you used to; your feelings often seem blunted; your internal landscape is bland and less colorful; you feel "blah." This drug-induced diminished responsiveness and loss of vitality is given many different labels in the medical literature, including indifference, apathy, lethargy, and diminished or blunted affect. Other labels for this overall flattening of the mind, spirit, and energy level include fatigue, malaise, and depression.

Fatigue.   You find that you don't have the same amount of mental or physical energy that you once did and that you get tired and discouraged much more easily. You may be sluggish or lethargic when you get up in the morning and exhausted by the evening.

Malaise.   You feel not just lethargic or fatigued but "ill," "worn out," "blah"—as if you have the flu or some other debilitating physical ailment. These drug-induced reactions are sometimes referred to as "flu-like symptoms" in the medical literature.

Depression.   Many psychiatric drugs can lead to depression, involving a loss of enjoyment of life, feelings of gloom and hopelessness, and even suicidal feelings or attempts. The final draft of the label for Prozac—the description included on the package insert—initially said that "depression" was "frequently" reported as an adverse effect of the drug. However, the reference to depression was edited out at the last minute. Secret documents in the files of Eli Lilly, the manufacturer of Prozac, reveal that, in comparison to placebos and other antidepressants, the drug caused an increased rate of suicide attempts in controlled clinical trials.[13]

Patients often become more depressed on antidepressants, but doctors then mistakenly increase the dose.

Almost all psychiatric drugs—from the minor tranquilizers to stimulants like Ritalin—can cause depression.[14] For example, depression is generally recognized as a potential result of taking Antabuse, anticonvulsants, antidepressants, barbiturates, benzodiazepine tranquilizers, beta-blockers, calcium channel blockers, narcotics, neuroleptics, and stimulants.

Reduced Imagination and Creativity.   You feel as if you've lost your old "spark" when it comes to thinking about solutions to problems, new ways of looking at things, or even what to do with your time on a free Saturday afternoon. Too often, you feel bored.

Impaired Self-Insight, Self-Understanding, or Self-Awareness.   You no longer feel confident about your appraisals of your own behavior, and other people give hints or signals that they think you're not behaving as appropriately as you think you are. You have trouble figuring out how you're feeling and why you're feeling that way, and you're not sure whether the drug is helping you or causing you problems. Friends or family may comment that you're not looking well, or may inquire whether you're feeling ill, when you haven't even noticed anything wrong.

Feeling "Out of Touch" with Yourself or Others.   You feel disconnected, remote, or out of touch with yourself and your feelings, and perhaps with the feelings of other people as well. It's as if there's a dark glass or a great distance between you and other people, such that you're not quite the same person you used to be. These reactions are called "depersonalization" or "derealization."

Personality Changes.   Even if you don't notice it, other people who care about you may say that you are not acting like yourself. You may have become moody, less sensitive, more irritable, more careless, withdrawn, "high" or mildly euphoric, or somewhat "out of it." In drug-reaction reports, this symptom of toxicity is often called "personality disorder."

Emotional Instability.   Your feelings seem to go up and down without any reason, and you have more trouble controlling what you feel and when and how you show it. This condition is sometimes referred to as "increased lability" in reports of adverse drug reactions.

Anxiety.   Many different drugs can make you feel agitation, anxiety, and panic. To add to your confusion, these symptoms are commonly caused by drugs used to treat anxiety and panic disorder. Relatively short-acting tranquilizers such as Xanax or Ativan can cause episodes of anxiety when the drug effect wears off and the brain rebounds several hours after each dose.[15] Most antidepressants and stimulants can also cause anxiety and agitation. And Prozac-like drugs, as well as antipsychotic drugs, can cause a particularly distressing syndrome known as akathisia, which involves anxiety or inner irritability that leads to a compulsive need to move about. It can feel like being tortured from the inside out.

Euphoria and Mania.   If you feel "wonderful" while taking a psychiatric drug, the feeling may not be realistic. Instead, you may be so "high" that your judgment is impaired. Many psychiatric drugs can produce unrealistic feelings of well-being and confidence. When this effect becomes obviously abnormal, it is called *euphoria* or *hypomania* (*mild mania*). Temporary euphoria can be followed by its opposites, despair and depression.

Drug-induced euphoria sometimes progresses into a psychosis called *mania*. Probably all antidepressants and stimulants are capable of causing mania, which is characterized by exaggerated or unrealistic feelings of being happy or "high," excitability, insomnia, boundless energy, racing thoughts, grandiose schemes, and feelings of extreme self-importance and omnipotence. Irritability, insensitivity to others, paranoia, and aggression often go along with being manic. During mania, a person can become "physically assaultive or suicidal."[16]

Mania can ruin anyone's life. Manic people can become very paranoid and react with violence toward innocent victims, including loved ones. They have been known to offend important people, quit jobs, leave marriages, commit criminal acts, or do something so bizarre or harmful that it results in jail or involuntary commitment to a mental hospital.

Mania, depression, and other abnormalities of emotional control commonly result from taking psychiatric drugs. These drug-induced "mood disorders" are mentioned many times in the *Diagnostic and Statistical Manual of Mental Disorders, 4th edition (DSM-IV),* which is the source of all official diagnoses in psychiatry. The manual makes clear that a number of psychiatric drugs, including antidepressants, can cause mania.[17]

Rates of mania caused by antidepressants frequently reach or surpass 1 percent of patients. They are probably several times higher for children receiving psychiatric drugs.[18]

Neurological Problems, Including Spasms and Seizures.   Most psychiatric drugs can cause a variety of neurological and muscular abnormalities, including headaches, impaired sleep, abnormal dreams and nightmares, incoordination or awkwardness, weakness, muscle spasms (sometimes called myoclonic spasms), tics, tremors, abnormal visual or auditory perceptions, and strange discomforts in the skin or head. Many psychiatric drugs can also cause a variety of seizures or convulsions. The most serious seizures are grand mal convulsions with loss of consciousness. Seizures can be caused by the direct action on the brain of drugs such as antidepressants, stimulants, and antipsychotic agents, as well as by withdrawal from many drugs, especially those that calm or sedate the brain, such as antianxiety drugs (benzodiazepine minor tranquilizers), sleeping pills, and antiepileptic medications.

All of the psychiatric symptoms caused by the chemical effects of psychiatric drugs can also be considered to be neurological symptoms, since they are caused by impairments of brain function.

Withdrawal and Rebound.   Most if not all psychiatric drugs can cause withdrawal reactions. Usually the withdrawal effect is the opposite of the drug's direct effect. Withdrawing from sedative minor tranquilizers such as Xanax will typically produce anxiety, agitation, insomnia, and, in extreme cases, seizures. Withdrawal from stimulants such as Ritalin and Adderall can produce fatigue, excessive sleep, and depression, but also opposite effects such as hyperactivity, agitation, and insomnia. In Chapter 9 we consider the kinds of withdrawal reactions that are typical of individual drugs or classes of drugs.

You May Be the Last to Know

Most of us know that recreational drugs can impair the ability of individuals to assess how they are really doing. We've seen or heard of cases in which alcohol drinkers or cocaine users show no judgment about how impaired they have become. Similarly, psychiatric drugs can compromise a person's ability to evaluate how he or she is doing.

Georgia was taking antidepressants for years and felt that they were "life-saving." She doubted if she could survive without them. But her husband was concerned that they were making her less emotionally present. He urged her to see a doctor who would be willing to offer psychotherapy

while trying to reduce or eliminate her use of drugs. She reluctantly decided to try.

Four months later, no longer taking antidepressants, Georgia felt like she
was "alive" for the first time in years. She had completely forgotten how
much zest she had for living. The drug had been suppressing her vitality
without her realizing it. She had mistakenly thought she was chronically
depressed and in desperate need of continued medication.

A more extreme example is tardive dyskinesia, the disorder involving
permanent twitches and spasms caused by neuroleptic or antipsychotic
drugs such as Haldol and Risperdal. Numerous studies have shown that
most patients with these drug-induced twitches deny that they are having any such problem, especially while they are taking the drugs.[19]

Prozac, Zoloft, Paxil, Luvox, Effexor, and other drugs that overstimulate the serotonin system often produce personality changes such as irritability, aggressiveness, mood instability, and varying degrees of
euphoria. The person taking the drug may feel "better than ever,"
whereas members of the family may feel that the individual has become
a "different person" with many negative personality traits.

Patients may become dependent on minor tranquilizers, such as Xanax
or Valium, without realizing what is happening to them until months or
years have gone by. They may believe that they need to take more and
more of the drug to control their anxiety and insomnia when, in fact, the
drugs are actually worsening their condition. Even when they realize that
they have become addicted, people often find the problem too difficult
to face. They often end up denying that they have an addiction while
continuing to take the drugs.

Many patients on psychiatric drugs may find that they have lost the
sharpness of their memory function. This outcome is commonly associated with lithium, tranquilizers, and a variety of antidepressants. Both
patients and doctors may mistakenly attribute the problem to "depression" rather than to the drug and, in the case of older patients, may mistakenly attribute the memory difficulties to aging. It is worth
emphasizing that the psychiatric drug you are taking may be impairing
your alertness, mental acuity, emotional awareness, social sensitivity, or
creativity without your realizing it. It may be causing adverse physical or
mental effects that you are unable to recognize or appreciate. Furthermore, since these drug-induced symptoms resemble the impairments

associated with psychiatric problems, it's easy for you, your doctor, or your family to mistakenly blame them on emotional problems.

The impairment of judgment caused by brain dysfunction is called *anosognosia*,[20] a condition that was first noticed in stroke patients who denied they were suffering from partial paralysis. From a more psychological perspective, it is called *denial*—the rejection of obvious mental impairment.

Psychiatric drugs are especially dangerous because they can render you unable to recognize their harmful effects. You can become seriously harmed without realizing what is happening. In many cases, people do not become aware of the damaging effects of drugs until after recovering from taking them.

You have now learned about how psychiatric drugs in general can impair your brain and mind. The next chapter focuses on the specific effects of individual drugs. If you or someone you care about is taking a psychiatric drug, you may want to learn all you can about its potential adverse effects.

— 4 —

Adverse Effects of
Specific Psychiatric Drugs

Psychoactive drugs—those that affect the brain and mind—can cause harm in two different ways.[1] Most obviously, they cause *direct* adverse effects by impairing the function of the brain or body. Drinking alcohol, for example, can result in an intoxication characterized by slurred speech, incoordination, and impaired mental processes. Many psychiatric drugs, especially sedative tranquilizers, have similar effects.

Psychoactive drugs can have equally harmful *indirect* effects that usually begin to develop after days or weeks of exposure to them. These indirect, delayed effects are caused by the brain's attempt to overcome the original drug effect. In essence, by "fighting back" the brain creates its own problems. For example, when a person has been drinking, the brain becomes more excited or energetic in order to overcome the effects of the alcohol. If an alcoholic suddenly stops drinking, he or she can go into a state of withdrawal involving agitation, anxiety, tremors, and, in extreme cases, psychosis and seizures. Again, many psychiatric drugs produce similar withdrawal effects.

All psychiatric drugs produce both direct and indirect adverse effects. This chapter focuses on the *direct* effects, whereas Chapter 9 concentrates on the indirect effects that often manifest themselves between doses or during and after withdrawal.

Growing Recognition of the
Dangers of Psychiatric Drugs

The use of psychiatric drugs, especially stimulants, antipsychotics, and anticonvulsants for children and antidepressants for all age groups, has been escalating in recent years.[2] At the same time, there has been growing concern about the adverse effects of prescription medications in general.

A recent study in the *Journal of the American Medical Association* (*JAMA*) concluded that the frequency of severe and fatal reactions to prescribed drugs in the United States is "extremely high."[3] More than 100,000 people a year are estimated to die in hospitals from drug reactions, implicating medications as one of the nation's top killers. Depending on the specific estimate, drug reactions in hospitals may constitute either the fourth or the sixth leading cause of death behind heart disease, cancer, and stroke.

The actual figures for drug fatalities are much higher than the estimates in the *JAMA* report, in part because the study was limited to hospitalized patients. Many patients die of drug-related causes outside of hospitals through suicide, accidents caused by mental impairment, and acute fatal reactions such as heart attack and stroke. The *JAMA* study also excluded patients who had been given inappropriate prescriptions, such as unusually high doses and unusual drug combinations. Yet inappropriate prescriptions are a very common cause of serious harm to patients. Given the large number of patients who were excluded by the *JAMA* investigators, it is likely that many more than their estimate of 100,000 Americans die of drug reactions each year.

The data in the *JAMA* report came as a shock to doctors who, as a group, tend to minimize the dangers of the drugs they prescribe. Death and other tragic outcomes from drug treatment often go unreported in order to protect doctors and hospitals from blame and lawsuits.

The *JAMA* report found that only heart disease, cancer, and stroke likely cause more deaths than adverse drug reactions. There are, of course, famous national associations devoted to reducing the risk of harm and death from these three diseases, as well as from lung diseases, diabetes, and other disorders that may produce fewer deaths than medications. But there are no national associations to prevent death from prescription medication. Motivated by self-interest, drug manufacturers and the medical establishment have little desire to increase the public's awareness of this problem.

True to form, when the *JAMA* report came out in 1988, the Pharmaceutical Research and Manufacturers Association—an industry lobbying group—warned the public not to make too much of the ominous findings. Rather than showing concern for the safety of patients, some doctors voiced concern that patients would be scared off from taking drugs.[4]

Drug-Induced Toxic Psychosis and Toxic Delirium

We previously described how psychiatric drugs in general produce varying degrees of toxic psychoses and other severe mental abnormalities, including anxiety, depression, and mania (see especially Chapter 3). Confirming the frequency of adverse reactions to psychiatric drugs, a German study found that 11 percent of hospitalized psychiatric patients developed adverse drug-induced symptoms that were severe enough to warrant discontinuation.[5] The researchers observed that life-threatening reactions were relatively common, occurring in 1.8 percent of the patients. By far the most common severe reaction was "toxic delirium," a drug-induced state of confusion, disorientation, and generalized mental impairment.

Elderly patients are especially prone to toxic psychoses as well as to less intense mental impairments from almost any mind-altering drug. Typical effects on the elderly include stimulation, excitement, insomnia, depression, and memory problems.

Toxic psychoses, which occur in varying degrees of severity, are also diagnosed as delirium, organic brain syndrome, confusion, or mania. Sometimes a doctor, family member, or patient may notice one or two possible symptoms of toxic psychosis—such as agitation, disorientation, incoherence, disturbed concentration, memory difficulties, or hallucinations—without recognizing the severity of the overall mental dysfunction.

Anxiety and depression are frequently caused by psychiatric drugs. They can appear in either the presence or absence of toxic psychosis.

Drug-Induced Mania

Mania is a specific toxic psychosis frequently caused by drugs. Based on data gathered from all U.S. trials for the FDA approval of Prozac, the manufacturer reported a 0.7 percent rate of *hypomania/mania* among Prozac patients.[6] Internal documents from the FDA, however, show a rate for *mania* of slightly above 1 percent—a rate much higher than that for the other antidepressants used for comparison in the trials.[7]

Recall that drug-induced mania is a severe psychotic disorder whose symptoms include extreme overactivity, insomnia, racing thoughts, frantic and exhausting outbursts of energy, grandiosity and fantasies of

omnipotence that may lead to bizarre and destructive actions, paranoia, and sometimes even suicide (see Chapter 3). People undergoing
drug-induced mania have been known to throw away their life's savings
on unrealistic schemes or to ruin or quit jobs and marriages that were
previously successful. Some end up in mental hospitals or jails. Others
commit violence.[8]

If we accept the estimate that approximately 1 percent of depressed
patients treated with Prozac will develop potentially devastating manic
reactions, that works out to be a thousand people out of every million.
These figures are disastrous in themselves, but in routine clinical practice the reactions would be much more frequent and severe. In the clinical trials used for FDA approval of Prozac, individuals with a history of
mania were excluded, while in clinical practice the antidepressant is frequently prescribed to people with a history of, and a potential predispo-
sition to, mania. In the clinical trials, Prozac was not used in
combination with stimulants and other antidepressants, while in clinical
practice, these other drugs are commonly given along with Prozac,
greatly increasing the risk of psychotic mania. And finally, in the clinical
trials, patients were typically evaluated once a week by means of check-
lists and interviews, while in clinical practice, patients frequently go
many weeks or months without being seen by a doctor. With less monitoring in clinical practice, patients are likely to become much more psychotic before being detected and removed from the medication.[9]

Children at Grave Risk for
Antidepressant-Induced Mania

Prozac even more commonly induces mania in children. In a study intended to tout the drug's safety and efficacy, 6 percent of the children were
forced to drop out due to Prozac-induced mania.[10] None of the controls
became psychotic. A similar drug, Luvox, produced a 4 percent rate of
"manic reactions" in children, according to the *Physicians' Desk Reference.**

Without a doubt, Prozac and other antidepressants are causing tens of
thousands of psychotic reactions that can ruin the lives not only of the
afflicted individuals but also of their family members. With the increas-

---

*Luvox was being taken by Eric Harris at the time he committed the murders at Columbine
High School in Littleton, Colorado, on April 20, 1999.

ing prescription of such drugs to children, we expect the devastation to increase.

Estimated Rates for Drug-Induced Mental and Neurological Disorders

In their widely used drug handbook for doctors, J. S. Maxmen and M. G. Ward (1995) summarize the available data regarding estimated rates of various adverse drug effects.[11] In the sections that follow, our references to these rates for drug-induced psychiatric and neurological disorders are intended to illustrate the frequency with which such disorders are caused by psychiatric drugs.[12] Even though our own estimates are sometimes higher, the rates reported in Maxmen and Ward's handbook are likely to startle and concern the reader.

Anti-Manic Agents: Lithium

Confusion and disorientation (22.8 percent of patients, with some studies reporting nearly 40 percent) and memory impairment (32.5 percent).

Stimulants

Ritalin.   Psychosis (less than 1 percent at normal doses), confusion or dopeyness (2–10 percent), agitation and restlessness (6.7 percent), irritability and stimulation (17.3 percent), and depression (8.7 percent).

Amphetamines.   This category comprises Dexedrine and Adderall, among other drugs. Psychosis (less than 1 percent in normal doses), confusion or dopeyness (10.3 percent), agitation and restlessness (more than 10 percent), irritability and stimulation (25 percent), and depression (39 percent!).

Benzodiazepine Tranquilizers:
Xanax, Valium, Ativan, Klonopin, and Others

Confusion and disorientation (6.9 percent), hallucinations (5.5 percent), anxiety and nervousness (4.1 percent), depression (8.3 percent), and irritability, hostility, and anger (5.5 percent). According to Maxmen and Ward, mania is particularly associated with Xanax.[13]

Tricyclic Antidepressants: Elavil

Confusion and disorientation (11.3 percent) and excitement and hypomania (5.7 percent). However, evidence from other sources suggests even higher rates.[14]

Prozac-Like Antidepressants: Prozac

Confusion and disorientation (1.5 percent) and excitement and hypomania (7.3 percent; Maxmen and Ward also note rates as high as 30 percent). As already noted, 6 percent of the participants in a recent controlled clinical trial involving Prozac for depressed children were forced to drop out due to Prozac-induced mania.[15]

Monoamine Oxidase Inhibitor (MAOI) Antidepressants: Parnate

Confusion and disorientation (6.2 percent), mental anxiety and nervousness (2 percent), physical agitation and restlessness (5 percent), excitement and hypomania (17.1 percent, with a range of 10–30 percent), myoclonic jerks (i.e., muscle spasms) (7 percent).

Antipsychotics or Neuroleptics

Thorazine.   Confusion and disorientation (6.8 percent) and depression (13.9 percent).

Haldol.   Confusion and disorientation (4 percent), mental restlessness and agitation (24 percent), physical restlessness and agitation (24 percent), and excitement (12 percent). Rigidity and acute dystonia—disabling, painful muscle spasms—occur at very high rates (30 percent each). The extraordinarily high rates for tardive dyskinesia (TD), as well as the danger of neuroleptic malignant syndrome (NMS), are discussed later in this chapter.

Adverse Effects Caused by Specific Psychiatric Drugs

Our review of adverse drug effects across the spectrum of psychiatric medications focuses on neurological and mental malfunctions—that is, on malfunctions of the brain and mind—since these effects are most likely to be confusing to patients, their families, and their doctors. Too often, these effects are mistakenly blamed on the patients' "mental illness."

Stimulants

This category comprises Ritalin and Methylin (methylphenidate), as well as Ritalin SR, Ritalin LA, Concerta, Metadate CD and ER, Methylin ER, and Daytrana (long-acting), Dexedrine and DextroStat (dextroamphetamine or d-amphetamine), Adderall and Adderall XR (dexamphetamine and amphetamine mixture), Vyvanse (lisdexamphetamine), Desoxyn and Gradumet (methamphetamine).[16] Both Cylert (pemoline) and, in Canada, Adderall XR, were discontinued or removed from the market in February 2005. For a list of stimulants, see Appendix A.

We are appalled by the widespread use of stimulants to control and suppress the behavior of children diagnosed with ADHD.[17] The aim is to correct behavior described in terms of hyperactivity, impulsivity, and inattention. In actuality, however, stimulants subdue behavior by impairing mental function; they often cause the very problems they are supposed to correct.

Ritalin and the amphetamines have almost identical adverse effects. Cylert is less addictive, but it has the extreme disadvantage of causing death due to liver failure in a small number of reported cases.

Stimulants have a powerful impact on the functioning of the brain and mind. They can lead to addiction and abuse. Children may give away or sell their stimulants to older children, who use them to get high. Parents may illegally use or sell their children's Ritalin or amphetamine.

In many or most children, stimulants routinely cause rebound, involving a worsening of behavioral symptoms a few hours after the last dose. And especially with larger or more prolonged dosing, they can lead to severe withdrawal reactions such as "crashing," which is characterized by extreme fatigue, depression, and even suicidal feelings (see Chapter 9).

Stimulants can also cause the following: excessive stimulation of the brain, including insomnia and seizures; agitation, irritability, and nervousness; confusion and disorientation; personality changes; apathy, social isolation, sadness, and, very commonly, depression. The most characteristic toxic psychosis from stimulants is mania. In addition, stimulants can cause paranoia, involving fearful and even violent feelings toward others. Stimulants such as Ritalin have been used in experiments to worsen the symptoms of patients labeled schizophrenic—a practice that should be considered unethical.[18]

Furthermore, stimulants can cause a variety of emotional disturbances that are mistakenly considered "therapeutic," including flattened emotions and robotic behavior. Children who take these drugs frequently lose the sparkle in their eyes. The edge comes off their creativity and vitality. Some become zombie-like. When stimulants cause compliance, obedience, reduced initiative, and reduced autonomy, they make children easier to manage. But these "therapeutic" effects, such as compliance or increased obedience, should be viewed as adverse drug effects.

All stimulants can cause the very symptoms they are supposed to treat: hyperactivity, loss of impulse control, and diminished concentration and focus. They can worsen a child's or adult's reactions to stress or anxiety.

Stimulants also cause dizziness, headache, insomnia, palpitations, abnormally increased heart rate, increased blood pressure, cardiac arrhythmias (heart attacks due to arrhythmias have been reported to the FDA); loss of appetite, weight loss, nausea, vomiting, constipation, and stomach pain; dry mouth; blurred vision; abnormal liver function; muscle cramping; tremor; hair loss; itching and scratching; severe and life-threatening skin eruptions; bleeding problems; weakened immunity; growth hormone disruption and prolactin hormone disruption. In 2006, following a series of reports of sudden deaths of children and adults taking stimulants, the FDA ordered a warning on all stimulant labels for doctors not to prescribe these drugs to those with heart problems. Ritalin causes liver cancer in rats, but this outcome has not been reported in humans. One study published in 2004 found evidence of genetic damage, using three different measures, in each of ten children immediately following a three-month course of Ritalin treatment. All children had tested normal on these measures prior to the treatment, and had undergone no major diet, weight, or environmental changes that could have caused these chromosomal alterations.[19]

Permanent tics, sometimes categorized as Tourette's syndrome, are a serious complication. They often start in the face and neck.

Stimulants suppress the growth of the body, including height and weight. This effect is mainly due not to suppression of appetite but to a disruption of growth hormone production caused by the drug's interference with pituitary function. Because growth hormone affects all organs of the body, overall growth is suppressed, including that of the head and its contents, the brain.

Since stimulants disrupt growth hormone and suppress growth during childhood, in addition to causing multiple biochemical imbalances in the growing brain, we believe they should never be administered to children.[20]

Recently one of the authors had the opportunity to review the animal literature on brain damage and dysfunction caused by stimulant drugs.[21] All stimulant drugs can produce lasting abnormalities in the brain. The most extensive animal research has been conducted using amphetamines (Dexedrine, Adderall), which have been shown to cause permanent biochemical imbalances and cell death, even in short-term moderate doses. The high risk of permanent injury to the brain is one more reason not to prescribe these drugs to children.

Antidepressants That Especially Stimulate Serotonin

This category comprises Prozac and Sarafem (fluoxetine), Zoloft (sertraline), Paxil and Paxil CR (paroxetine), Celexa (citalopram), Lexapro (escitalopram), Luvox (fluvoxamine), and Effexor (venlafaxine). See Appendix A for a complete list of antidepressants.

Prozac was the first selective serotonin reuptake inhibitor (SSRI) approved for use in the United States. It was followed by Zoloft, Paxil, and Luvox. Luvox was approved for obsessive-compulsive disorder. Effexor is not an SSRI; its direct impact is not limited to serotonin. Nonetheless, its adverse effects are similar to those of Prozac.

Serious criticisms of these drugs have been published for nearly 15 years now.[22] Despite the great hype surrounding these drugs, and despite their widespread use, there is little scientific evidence for their efficacy as antidepressants. The promise that they would have few harmful effects has not been fulfilled. During the first 12 years after its initial marketing, over 40,000 reports of adverse effects from Prozac were submitted to the FDA. No other drug comes close.

SSRIs were tailored to block the removal of the neurotransmitter serotonin from the synapse in order to cause increased firing of serotonin nerves. However, the brain is much more complex than this description implies. When serotonergic nerves are overstimulated, they tend to become less sensitive. This "downregulation" does not return to normal immediately after the drug is stopped. Whether downregulation can become permanent in this particular system has not been studied, but we believe it poses a serious risk to the brain.

These drugs are capable of producing effects very similar to those of amphetamine or methamphetamine, including an artificial feeling of well-being or energy, anxiety, agitation, and insomnia. Prozac and Effexor are especially stimulating. The others can cause somnolence or insomnia. Like the amphetamines and all antidepressants, these drugs cause manic psychoses. As noted earlier, the first published randomized controlled trial of Prozac in children found that 6 percent of children taking it became manic and had to stop the drug.[23] Upon withdrawal, some patients may "crash" into depression and experience suicidal thoughts or commit actions similar to those associated with stimulants (see Chapter 9).[24]

We have seen patients become very disturbed and violent, especially when the dosage is changing (as when a patient starts, increases, reduces, or stops the drug). Drug-induced loss of impulse control as well as agitation and mania are among the potential causes. Prozac can also produce akathisia—characterized by a feeling of being tortured from within—which is probably one of its mechanisms for causing self-destructive or violent behavior. Jonathan O. Cole, professor of psychiatry at Harvard and a participant in studies of Prozac, has seen cases of "obsessive suicidal thoughts" related to it.[25] Cole believes that the adverse reaction is "rare" but adds, "However, some psychiatrists do consider warning patients to check in or stop the medication should new, bizarre suicidal ideation occur."

Numerous suicide and murder cases have involved patients who have taken SSRIs for a few days or longer. The first case to go to court against Eli Lilly, the manufacturer of Prozac, was secretly settled by the company during the trial in order to mislead the judge and jury into providing a verdict in its favor. Although the judge changed the jury verdict to "settled with prejudice," Lilly still publicly claims to have won a jury verdict.[26]

The first case to go to trial against GlaxoSmithKline and Paxil involved a sixty-year-old man who suffered from depression but had never before been violent or suicidal. After his second dose of Paxil, he killed his wife, daughter, and their granddaughter before killing himself. The judge found that there was scientific basis for permitting expert testimony implicating Paxil in murder and suicide, and the jury returned a verdict of $6.4 million against GlaxoSmithKline.

As documented in Peter Breggin's introduction, the FDA has finally admitted that all of the new antidepressants—including the SSRIs, Wellbutrin, Effexor, and Cymbalta—increase suicidal behavior in children and adults. The FDA's advisory committee has suggested limiting the warning about adult suicidality to "young adults," but the distinction is absurdly artificial. The data was generated by very limited controlled clinical trials and the finding must be taken seriously for all ages.

In some ways more important, the FDA now requires a warning about the stimulant or activation syndrome induced by all of the newer antidepressants. Consistent with observations first published by Breggin in a series of books and scientific articles beginning in 1991, this particular group of drug-induced symptoms includes aggression and hostility. Specifically, the antidepressant labels are now required to warn that the drugs are associated with the production of "anxiety, agitation, panic attacks, insomnia, irritability, hostility, aggressiveness, impulsivity, akathisia (psychomotor restlessness), hypomania, and mania."

As noted in the Introduction, the FDA also added a section entitled "WARNINGS—Clinical Worsening and Suicide Risk," stating that adults "should be observed similarly for clinical worsening and suicidality, especially during the initial few months of a course of drug therapy, or at times of dose changes, either increases or decreases."

There should no longer be any doubt that the antidepressants cause an increase in suicidal and violent behavior, as well as mania, and that they often lead to a general worsening of the patient's mental condition. Drastic changes leading to destructive and criminal behavior often happen shortly after starting the drug or around dose changes, up or down; but they can occur at any time.

Withdrawal reactions also occur with these drugs and can be very severe (Chapter 9). Many patients become despondent, tearful, emotionally unstable and suicidal while trying to withdraw from these drugs. A large number suffer from bizarre neurological disturbances such as shock-like pains in the head and weird sensations in the skin. A significant number decide to resume taking the drugs because the process of withdrawal feels too painful to endure.

Because this group of drugs can cause agitation and anxiety, they can lead to the increased use of alcohol and other calming drugs. We have seen recovered alcoholics resume their drinking after starting on Prozac.

Patients who take these drugs often experience flattened or dulled feelings. Families report that they are less attentive, caring, or loving. Sexual dysfunctions are common. Some patients become tired and even sleepy instead of agitated, particularly on Paxil and Zoloft.

Especially when combined with other drugs that stimulate serotonin, these drugs can produce serotonergic crises involving agitation, delirium, muscle spasms (myoclonus), various neurological abnormalities, and elevated body temperature. Some reports submitted to the FDA concern Prozac-induced tardive dyskinesia.

Many patients initially experience weight loss when taking SSRIs. While some people may welcome this effect, it can be harmful to those already suffering from lack of appetite and excessive weight loss. Furthermore, over a period of months this drug effect tends to reverse, and many people experience weight gain leading to obesity.

The blunting effects of SSRIs on libido and sexual functioning are now well established. In large surveys of thousands of patients in the United States and abroad, rates of SSRI-induced induced sexual dysfunctions reach upwards of 40 percent,[27] and in smaller studies, up to 70 percent of patients on Paxil and Zoloft reported sexual dysfunctions.[28] Yet, the authors of one such survey concluded that "Physicians consistently underestimated the prevalence of antidepressant-associated sexual dysfunction."[29] Recently, reports of sexual adverse effects—total libido loss, loss of genital sensitivity, and genital anesthesia—persisting months and years after cessation of SSRIs have begun to surface, leading some to suggest that these drugs may be permanently altering gene expression.[30]

Tricyclic Antidepressants

This category comprises imipramine (Tofranil, Imavate, Presamine, SK-Pramine, Janimine), desipramine (Pertofrane, Norpramin), amitriptyline (Elavil), nortriptyline (Aventyl, Pamelor), protriptyline (Vivactil), doxepin (Sinequan, Adapin), trimipramine (Surmontil), and Anafranil (clomipramine).

Probably all antidepressants are capable of causing seizures and manic psychoses. Even relatively small doses can result in dulled and flattened feelings or agitated and "wired" feelings. Most tricyclic antidepressants have a variety of anticholinergic effects including blurred vision, dry mouth, constipation, difficulty urinating, and cardiac arrhythmias that sometimes prove fatal, especially among adults with heart problems and among children and the elderly. They frequently cause serious withdrawal reactions (see Chapter 9).

Atypical Antidepressants

This category comprises Asendin (amoxapine), Desyrel (trazodone), Effexor (venlafaxine), Ludiomil (maprotiline), Remeron, Remeron Sol Tab, Remeron RD, Cymbalta (duloxetine), and Wellbutrin, Wellbutrin SR, Wellbutrin XL or Zyban (buproprion). See Appendix A for a complete list. Following an unexpectedly high number of reports of severe liver injuries, Serzone was withdrawn from the Canadian market in November 2003 and from the United States in May 2004.

Of extreme importance is the fact that the antidepressant Asendin is converted into a neuroleptic within the body, producing the same problems as those associated with other neuroleptics, including tardive dyskinesia and neuroleptic malignant syndrome (see below). For this drug, the FDA requires class warnings regarding TD and NMS.

Ludiomil and Remeron are classified along with Asendin as tetracyclic compounds. Seizures and involuntary abnormal movements (extrapyramidal symptoms) have been reported in association with Ludiomil. Remeron is relatively new; hence its profile of adverse effects is less understood. Many of the adverse effects of other antidepressants, including the tricyclics, should be considered in regard to these three drugs. Remeron, in particular, tends to induce sedation as well as dizziness, weight gain, and low blood pressure. Cardiovascular problems have been reported in connection with both drugs. Like all antidepressants, they can cause toxic psychoses, including mania and delirium.

Effexor (venlafaxine), mentioned earlier as a drug that stimulates serotonin, also stimulates norepinephrine neurotransmission in the brain. However, its effects are very similar to those of Prozac, including stimulation, anxiety, nervousness, insomnia, loss of appetite, and weight loss. In addition, it can cause agitation and mania, hostility, paranoid reactions, psychotic depression, toxic psychosis, and hypertension.

Serzone (nefazodone) also stimulates serotonin and norepinephrine, but it has other effects as well. It is more likely to cause sleepiness than insomnia. It can produce lightheadedness, confusion, memory impairment, and hypotension. And it can lead to hostility, paranoid reaction, suicide attempts or ideation, derealization and depersonalization, and hallucinations. As he did in regard to Effexor, T. J. Moore (1997) reviewed the FDA data generated during the approval process for Serzone. He found that suicides and suicide attempts were several times more frequent among patients on Serzone than on placebos.

Desyrel (trazodone) tends to cause sedation, dizziness, and fainting. It can lead to heart problems in cardiac patients. And among men it can cause a potentially serious adverse reaction called priapism—uncontrolled, irreversible penile erection that sometimes requires surgical correction.

Wellbutrin (buproprion) produces an unusually high rate of seizures. It is known to be very stimulating and agitating, causing anxiety, nightmares, and manic psychoses. In 1997, this very same drug, marketed as Zyban, was approved by the FDA as an aid for smoking cessation.

Duloxetine (Cymbalta) arrived on the antidepressant market in August 2004, when it was also approved for the treatment of diabetic neuropathic pain. A recent review summarized its most frequently observed adverse effects as "nausea, dry mouth, constipation, diarrhea, decreased appetite, weight loss, feeling of fatigue, dizziness, somnolence, hypohidrosis [lack of sweating], decreased libido and erectile dysfunction."[31] A systematic review of its clinical trials by the independent medical journal *Prescrire International* concluded that "In practice, duloxetine currently has no place in the treatment of depression or diabetic neuropathy. Its efficacy has not yet been demonstrated to be even equivalent to that of other available drugs, and it has too many adverse effects, given this degree of uncertainty."[32] Another independent newsletter, noting that the manufacturer Eli Lilly claims that Cymbalta has special value in managing the painful symptoms of depression, concluded, "At this time, any claim that duloxetine is useful for managing pain is groundless."[33] Even more ominous, in 2004–2005 Cymbalta received considerable negative press surrounding the suicide of nineteen-year-old Tracy Johnson and several other volunteers who took the drug in the initial clinical trials for depression.[34] Nonetheless, undoubtedly as a result of Eli Lilly's vigorous marketing and advertising campaign to doctors and the public, sales of Cymbalta jumped 85 percent in 2006.[35]

Monoamine Oxidase Inhibitor (MAOI) Antidepressants

This category comprises Parnate (tranylcypromine), Marplan (isocarboxazid), Nardil (phenelzine), Eldepryl (selegiline), and Manerix (moclobemide, available in Canada).

Parnate is chemically similar to amphetamine and is very stimulating. Eldepryl was approved for the treatment of Parkinson's disease, and not for depression.

Although all antidepressants can cause toxic psychoses including mania, the MAOIs are particularly prone to these potentially life-ruining adverse reactions. They often produce mental abnormalities such as dulling of feelings or delirium. Especially when combined with certain foods and drugs, they can also cause life-threatening hypertensive crises (involving violent headaches and possible strokes) as well as serotonergic crises (involving agitation, delirium, muscle spasms, various neurological abnormalities, and elevated body temperature). These food and drug reactions can lead to coma or death. Patients and families should be warned about such problems in advance.[36] MAOIs interact especially dangerously with stimulants and antidepressants.

MAOIs have many of the same side effects as those typically associated with other antidepressants, but they also include hypertensive crises, low blood pressure, extreme fevers (hyperpyretic reactions), sexual dysfunction, daytime sedation, nighttime insomnia, excessive stimulation, muscle pain, and muscle spasms.

Years ago these drugs went out of favor because of their dangers and questionable efficacy. With the resurgence of biological psychiatry and the disappointing results obtained with other antidepressants, they are again in vogue.

Manerix is currently available in Canada but not in the United States. Although it does not suppress monoamine oxidase for as long as the other drugs in this class and is considered less of a risk for producing hypertensive crises when combined with certain foods, it shares a similar adverse reaction profile with the other MAOIs, including stimulation, insomnia, anxiety and agitation, and occasionally aggressive behavior. Liver problems have been reported in a small percentage of patients.

Benzodiazepines Prescribed for Anxiety and Insomnia

This category comprises Ativan (lorazepam); Klonopin (clonazepam); Librium, Librax, and Limbitrol (chlordiazepoxide); Paxipam (halazepam); Serax (oxazepam); Tranxene (clorazepate); Valium (diazepam); and Xanax (alprazolam).[37]

These drugs are prescribed for anxiety, panic attacks, and related problems. They are also prescribed for insomnia. The benzodiazepines most commonly prescribed for insomnia are Halcion (triazolam), which is banned in England; Dalmane (flurazepam); Doral (quazepam); Prosom (estazolam); and Restoril (temazepam). Versed (midazolam) is also used in injectable form for anesthesia.

When they first came out in the 1960s, benzodiazepines were promoted as relatively safe and free of the well-known addiction problems associated with barbiturates. Nothing could be further from the truth.

Consider Xanax, for example. Most patients taking this drug for even a few weeks will develop serious withdrawal problems, and many, if not most, will have trouble discontinuing the medication. In fact, it can be dangerous to stop any benzodiazepine too abruptly (see Chapter 9).

Especially in the case of short-acting agents such as Xanax or Halcion, withdrawal symptoms can occur on a daily basis in between doses. These often manifest as a rebound worsening of the original anxiety symptoms. The individual can end up cycling between withdrawal and intoxication from dose to dose throughout the day.

In addition to addiction and withdrawal reactions, patients taking benzodiazepines face hazards similar to those who abuse alcohol. Intoxication can sneak up on users without their realizing it. They can develop slowed thinking, slurred speech, lack of coordination, clumsiness and impaired walking (ataxia), tremor, poor judgment, and drowsiness. Drugged feelings and hangovers with amnesia are not uncommon.

Benzodiazepines work by producing a continuum of suppression of the brain. Initially, for some people, this suppression is experienced as relaxation or a reduction in anxiety and tension, an effect similar to that of alcohol. As the dose increases, sleep and eventually coma are produced. The drugs work by impairing brain function, which is sometimes experienced as relief from tension or anxiety.

Because they suppress overall brain function, all drugs that are used to reduce anxiety or to induce sleep will also impair high mental functions, including thinking and memory. While only a few studies have attempted to examine this danger, the long-term use of any such drug, especially in higher doses, should be viewed as posing a risk of irreversible mental dysfunction. One review of several studies found that after withdrawal from long-term benzodiazepine use, "there remains a significant impairment in most areas of cognition in comparison to controls or normative data." The authors concluded, "there may be some permanent deficit or deficits that take longer than 6 months to completely recover."[38]

Benzodiazepines can cause severe amnesia. Students taking them in order to sleep may lose a substantial part of their memory for the material they studied that same evening. The drugs can produce confusion, paranoia, and paradoxical reactions such as excitement, agitation, and rage and violence. They can cause toxic psychosis. (Xanax is especially known to cause mania.) They commonly worsen depression and may lead to suicide. Like alcohol, they often make people irritable and impulsive. We know of individuals who have committed violence after taking just a few doses of these drugs. In cases of longer-term benzodiazepine toxicity, users may lose their judgment and perform senseless, out-of-character acts of theft or other criminal activities.[39]

Halcion, a benzodiazepine used for inducing sleep, has been banned in England because it causes so many mental abnormalities, including depression and paranoia.[40] Versed, a very short-acting benzodiazepine used for anesthesia, commonly causes behavioral abnormalities following its use for anesthesia. We have seen a case in which the emotionally disturbing effects of Versed appear to have been long-lasting. Versed should be considered a very hazardous drug.

Benzodiazepines can cause muscular twitches and other abnormal movements that are so severe as to be mistaken for seizures. Like many psychiatric drugs, benzodiazepines can also cause headache, visual problems, and a variety of gastrointestinal disturbances.

Non-Benzodiazepines Prescribed for Anxiety and Insomnia

This category comprises newer drugs such as Ambien (zolpidem), Lunesta (zopiclone), Sonata (zaleplon), as well as drugs on the market for decades, such as Atarax or Vistaril (hydroxyzine), beta-adrenergic blockers (beta-blockers) including Inderal (propranolol) and Tenormin (atenolol), BuSpar (buspirone), Miltown (meprobamate), and Trancopel (chlormezanone).

Drugs such as Lunesta, Sonata, and Ambien have been very widely advertised to the public and to doctors as safe and almost magically effective sleeping pills. Free samples are routinely offered to patients in various promotional strategies, and, as expected, the drugs have become increasingly popular, even among young persons. Unfortunately, virtually every available review of the evidence concludes that their benefits may be mostly illusory but their risks quite real. In clinical trials heavily biased in favor of these drugs, they succeed in adding mere minutes of sleep in comparison to placebo, while carrying much more risk of daytime fatigue, memory loss and other cognitive impairments, as well as morning-after difficulties with motor coordination.[41] Older people, especially those over 70 and 80 years of age, remain the most frequent and long-term users of sedatives and hypnotics, but non-drug methods to induce and maintain sleep in older persons are consistently found to be superior, safer, and more durable.[42]

A variety of non-benzodiazepines are used for sleep and for the control of anxiety. Miltown is addictive and subject to abuse, and is very much like the benzodiazepines in its profile of adverse reactions. Trancopel can cause many of the adverse effects associated with other sedative drugs, including confusion and depression. Severe skin rashes have also been reported.

Ambien, like the benzodiazepines, can cause drowsiness, confusion, awkward gait, fatigue, headache, nausea, and memory problems. It can also cause dizziness and incoordination, resulting in falls; toxic psychosis, hallucinations, and nightmares; various sensory disturbances; and disinhibition (bizarre or dangerous behavior). Occasional reports and our own clinical experience suggest that it can produce dependence. In 2003, Ambien appeared on the list of psychotropic drugs of abuse of the United Nations' Vienna convention.

Atarax or Vistaril is an antihistamine with sedative qualities. We have seen cases of abuse of this drug, usually in combination with multiple addictions.

BuSpar can cause headaches, dizziness, and nausea. It can also produce tension or anxiety, abnormal dreams, delirium, and psychotic mania.

Barbiturates, which are prescribed to induce sleep and, sometimes, to reduce anxiety, include Amytal (amobarbital), Butisol (butabarbital), Mebaral (mephobarbital), Nembutal (pentobarbital), phenobarbital (generic), and Seconal (secobarbital).

Barbiturates are highly addictive and produce toxic symptoms similar to those of alcohol and the benzodiazepines, including sedation, clumsiness, slurred speech, and poor judgment. They also produce a withdrawal syndrome similar to that of alcohol and the benzodiazepines. They can cause paradoxical reactions such as excitement, hyperactivity, and aggression. They can also cause hallucinations and depression. Extreme behavioral abnormalities are especially common among children and the elderly.

Other common problems associated with the use of barbiturates include dizziness or lightheadedness, nausea and vomiting, diarrhea, muscle cramps, and hangovers. According to one of the few studies of long-term adverse effects on mental function, relatively small doses of phenobarbital in children resulted in a measurable reduction in IQ. The drug had been administered over the long term for the prevention of seizures induced by high fevers. As emphasized earlier in the chapter, all drugs that suppress anxiety or induce sleep should be suspected of causing irreversible mental dysfunction when used over the long term.

Any drug associated with reduction of anxiety or increased sleep should also be suspected of causing tolerance—an increasing need for larger doses—as well as dependence. This is especially true of the benzodiazepines and barbiturates, but caution is suggested in cases of sedation or tranquilization from almost any drug. There is no "free ride." If the drug has a significant impact, the brain will likely try to compensate, producing the potential for rebound and withdrawal symptoms.

Beta-blockers suppress the heart rate, thereby reducing one of the most disturbing symptoms associated with acute anxiety—the pounding heart. They are also used in medicine to slow the heart rate.

Beta-blockers have more negative effects on brain function than many doctors realize. Drugs such as Inderal can cause serious depression in some patients.[43] More commonly, they can cause sedation and slow down the thinking process in a manner that physicians describe as "clouding the sensorium." They can bring about a feeling of being "washed out" or lethargic. They can cause overstimulation, delirium, anxiety, nightmares, and more extreme psychotic symptoms such as hallucinations. They can also produce impotence, gastrointestinal upsets, low blood pressure, and slowed heart rate. A dangerous possibility is the constriction of the respiratory tract (bronchospasm). Withdrawal can be a problem as well, in that it can result in rebound or increased heart rate and blood pressure.

Lithium, Anticonvulsants, and Other "Mood Stabilizers"

This category comprises several different drugs from different classes. They include Lithium (Eskalith, Lithane, Lithobid, Lithotabs) and the anti-epileptic or anticonvulsant medications, including Tegretol (carbamazepine), Depakene (valproic acid) and Depakote (divalproex sodium), Neurontin (gabapentin), Lamictal (lamotrigine), Topamax (topimarate), and Trileptal (oxcarbazepine). Other drugs prescribed as mood-stablizers include Klonopin (clonazepam), Calan (verapamil), and Catapres (clonidine). See Appendix A for a complete list.

These drugs are supposed to control mania or to reduce mood swings, which psychiatrists commonly call "bipolar disorder." Faced with disappointing results from the use of lithium, psychiatry turned to the use of anticonvulsants, three newer ones of which were approved by the FDA for the treatment of acute mania and bipolar disorder between 1994 and 2000. These drugs probably all have their effect by causing sedation and overall depression of the central nervous system. In 2006, however, as discussed in David Cohen's Introduction, there appeared several reports on the largest-ever study (nearly 1,500 patients) of the drug treatment of bipolar disorder. The study was unusual in that it was not funded by the drug industry, and it enrolled a broadly representative sample of patients diagnosed with bipolar disorder from across the country. The patients were seen as often as clinically desired, and the study claimed to use the "best available" drug treatments (mostly anticonvulsants, antipsychotics, lithium, and clonazepam) in addition to a standard psychosocial intervention. The results: only 28 percent of treated individuals achieved remission without experiencing a recurrence of major symptoms during the two-year follow-up.[44]

Lithium flattens emotions by blunting or constricting the range of feeling, resulting in varying degrees of apathy and indifference. It also slows down the thinking processes. This drug-induced mental and emotional sluggishness should be considered lithium's primary "therapeutic" effect. Lithium sometimes reduces the likelihood that a patient will become "high" or manic—but at the cost of brain dysfunction.[45]

Many people experience increasing memory problems after taking lithium for months or years. Their ability to work can become impaired.

Doctors and patients often mistakenly attribute these problems to other causes such as chronic fatigue syndrome, depression, or "old age." When the lithium is reduced or stopped, many people experience a rebirth of their cognitive and emotional capacities. Some patients, however, find that their mental faculties do not fully recover after years of lithium treatment.

Lithium can cause hypothyroidism, cardiac arrhythmias, weight gain, stomach discomfort and diarrhea, skin diseases such as severe acne and rashes, hair loss, tremor, an awkward gait, and serious disorders of the kidneys. It can cause serious, life-threatening toxicity of the brain, which may creep up on users whose judgment has become impaired by the same toxic process. For these reasons, routine blood levels are required to keep track of potential intoxication. It can cause an increased white count; concern has been expressed about its possibly causing leukemia. And, finally, lithium is known to cause birth defects, including heart malformations, and to suppress the brain of the fetus or nursing baby, leading to flaccidity and lethargy. Withdrawal from lithium commonly results in mania (see Chapter 9).

Depakote (Depakene) is somewhat similar to benzodiazepines and alcohol in that it can cause sedation, tremor, and difficulty walking. It can also cause behavioral abnormalities, including confusion or delirium.

Over the long term it may impair mental abilities, and on rare occasions it has been known to cause liver failure. It can also cause weight gain, stomach upset, hair loss, rash, pancreatitis, and blood clotting problems.

Clonidine (Catapres) is an antihypertensive drug that can cause sedation and thus has found a place in psychiatric use. If withdrawn too quickly, it can produce rebound hypertensive crises. It can also cause many psychiatric problems including insomnia, nightmares, anxiety, restlessness, depression, and, more rarely, hallucinations.

Klonopin, a benzodiazepine, can cause all the problems associated with this class of drugs, including dependence (see above). It is FDA-approved for both seizures and panic attacks.

Tegretol is closely related to the tricyclic antidepressants and can cause all of the problems associated with them (see above). It poses a special danger of bone marrow suppression, involving loss of blood cells. Patients and their families need to be alert to early signs of this condition, including fever, sore throat, and tiny bleeding spots (petechiae) in the skin. Other side effects include sedation, fatigue, nausea, and lightheadedness. Higher doses can produce signs of neurological intoxication, including lack of coordination of the muscles. When the muscles of the eyes are affected, seeing double may result. Liver functions may show up as abnormal upon testing, and, more rarely, liver toxicity may develop. Cardiac function can also be impaired. Rashes are common.

Calan, a calcium-channel blocker, is an agent used to treat cardiac disorders, but it can cause a variety of cardiovascular problems. Dizziness, headache, and nausea are common; high doses can result in sedation and lethargy. More rare are such serious adverse effects as cardiac arrhythmias that don't respond well to treatment, liver toxicity, and severe low blood pressure with fainting. The heart and blood pressure status of patients taking this drug should be checked for baseline and then for potential adverse drug effects.

Many benzodiazepines, anti-seizure medications and anti-hypertension drugs are used as mood stabilizers because of their sedating effects. The benzodiazepines and anti-seizure drugs should be gradually tapered to avoid withdrawal seizures, and the anti-hypertension drugs should be gradually tapered to avoid rebound spikes in blood pressure. An experienced health professional should be consulted about the length of time and dose schedule required for withdrawing from these drugs, many of which are listed in Appendix A.

Antipsychotic (Neuroleptic) Drugs

The available neuroleptics or antipsychotics—previously called major tranquilizers—include phenothiazines and other drugs.[46] The phenothiazines include Compazine (prochlorperazine), Etrafon (antidepressant plus Trilafon), Mellaril (thioridazine), Prolixin (fluphenazine), Serentil (mesoridazine), Stelazine (trifluoperazine), Thorazine (chlorpromazine), Tindal (acetophenazine), Trilafon (perphenazine), and Vesprin (triflupromazine).

Other neuroleptics include Haldol (haloperidol), Inapsine (droperidol), Loxitane (loxapine), Moban (molindone), Navane (thiothixene), and Taractan (chlorprothixene).

"Atypical" or "second- or third-generation" antipsychotic drugs currently include Clozaril (clozapine), Risperdal and Risperdal Consta (risperidone), Seroquel (quetiapine), Zyprexa (olanzapine), Geodon (ziprasidone), Abilify (aripriprazole), and Invega (paliperidone, approved by the FDA in December 2006). Serlect (sertindole) was approved by the FDA in 1996 but never actually marketed in the United States because of later concerns over major cardiac effects. See Appendix A for a list of most antipsychotic drugs.

Orap (pimozide) is a neuroleptic that causes an especially high rate of adverse effects. In one clinical trial involving twenty patients, reported in the 1998 *Physicians' Desk Reference*, many of the patients suffered serious neurological impairments, including sedation (fourteen patients), akathisia or inner agitation causing hyperactive movements (eight patients), akinesia or slowed movements (eight patients), adverse behavior effects (five patients), and impotence (three patients). Orap was approved by the FDA for treating tics associated with Tourette's disorder, but not for treating psychosis. Nonetheless, the manufacturer, in its drug label, refers several times to Orap as an "antipsychotic," and some doctors use it for that purpose.

Sertindole and ziprasidone are other atypical neuroleptics currently undergoing or having recently undergone the FDA approval process. These drugs are intended for use in the control of psychotic patients, usually those diagnosed with schizophrenia or acute mania.

Neuroleptics have their main impact by blunting the highest functions of the brain in the frontal lobes and the closely connected basal ganglia. They can also impair the reticular activating or "energizing" system of the brain. These impairments result in relative degrees of apathy, indifference, emotional blandness, conformity, and submissiveness, as well as a reduction in all verbalizations, including complaints or protests. It is no exaggeration to call this effect a chemical lobotomy.

Contrary to claims, neuroleptics have no specific effects on irrational ideas (delusions) or perceptions (hallucinations). Like all other psychiatric drugs, they have the same impact on healthy animals, healthy volunteers, and patients—namely, the production of apathy and indifference. They are even used in veterinary medicine to control violent animals. Most veterinarians, however, do not use them for long periods of time because they are considered too dangerous.

All neuroleptics produce an enormous variety of potentially severe and disabling neurological impairments at extraordinarily high rates of occurrence; they are among the most toxic agents ever administered to people.

Tardive Dyskinesia
Caused by Antipsychotics

Tardive dyskinesia (TD) is a common and yet potentially disastrous adverse reaction to all of the antipsychotic or neuroleptic drugs. TD involves irreversible abnormal movements of any of the voluntary muscles of the body. It commonly afflicts the face, eyes, mouth, and tongue, as well as the hands and arms, feet and legs, and torso. It can also affect breathing, swallowing, and speech. In some cases, spasms of the eyes are so severe that the person cannot see.

One variant of TD is tardive dystonia, which involves painful spasms, often of the face and neck. Tardive dystonia can be disfiguring and disabling, potentially impairing even the ability to walk.

Another variant of TD is tardive akathisia. The individual is virtually tortured from inside his or her own body as feelings of irritability and anxiety compel the person into constant motion, sometimes to the point of continuous suffering. We agree with T. van Putten and S. Marder who observe that akathisia, "in the extreme case, can drive people to suicide or to homicide."[47]

Neuroleptics actually suppress the symptoms of tardive dyskinesia while the disease is developing. As a result, the afflicted individual, the family, or the doctor may not recognize the impairment until the symptoms break through or until the drug dosage is reduced.

The rates of TD are extremely high. Many standard textbooks estimate a rate of 5 percent–7 percent per year in healthy, young adults. The rate is cumulative so that 25 percent–35 percent of patients will develop the disorder in five years of treatment. Among the elderly, rates of TD reach 20 percent or more per year.[48] For a variety of reasons, including the failure to include tardive akathisia in estimates, the actual rates are probably much higher for all patients.[49]

We have seen the lives of numerous individuals and their families wrecked by tardive dyskinesia. In many cases, patients and their families were not informed by doctors about the dangers of TD.[50] In other instances, several doctors—one after another—ignored obvious symptoms of the disorder. Often the drug dose was mistakenly increased instead of being reduced and stopped. The failure to stop the drugs at the first sign of the disorder resulted, in these cases, in painful, severely incapacitating, disfiguring twitches and spasms. The afflicted individuals were unable to work or to carry on a normal family or social life. Often they became depressed, felt humiliated by their physical appearance, and withdrew from loved ones.

Neuroleptic Malignant Syndrome

Another disastrous reaction caused by neuroleptic drugs is neuroleptic malignant syndrome (NMS). Similar to viral brain inflammation (encephalitis), NMS is characterized by severe abnormal movements, fever, sweating, unstable blood pressure and pulse, and impaired mental functioning. Delirium and coma can also develop. NMS can be fatal, especially when doctors fail to recognize it in time. Patients who recover may be left with varying degrees of irreversible mental impairment as well as permanent abnormal movements.[51] This drug reaction looks so "bizarre" that many doctors initially, and even persistently, attribute it to the patient's "mental illness." In such cases, of course, it will go untreated—with tragic results.

Although many doctors and even some textbooks say that neuroleptic malignant syndrome is "rare," others such as A. F. Schatzberg, J. O. Cole, and C. DeBattista (1997) give a more realistic estimate of 0.7 to 2.4 percent of hospital admissions treated with neuroleptics. The higher rate of 2.4 percent is probably the more accurate.[52] The FDA considers a rate of 1 percent to be "common" or "frequent." Like tardive dyskinesia, neuroleptic malignant syndrome may be caused by atypical antipsychotics. One review conducted in January 2003 located 68 published cases, most of which were caused by Clozaril, Risperdal, and Zyprexa.[53]

Using a low-end rate of 1 percent, Maxmen and Ward (1995, p. 33) estimate that 1,000–4,000 deaths occur in America each year as a result of neuroleptic malignant syndrome. The actual number is probably much greater.

If such high rates for a dangerous and disabling adverse reaction were reported in relation to drugs used in general medicine, such as antibiotics or blood pressure medication, they would probably be removed from the market. Vulnerable mental patients, by contrast, are purposely exposed to brain-damaging treatments such as electroshock, psychosurgery, and neuroleptics.

Antipsychotic Withdrawal Psychoses

A number of reports confirm that these drugs can cause very disabling withdrawal reactions, including irreversible psychosis (tardive psychosis) and irreversible deterioration of the mental processes (tardive dementia) (see Chapter 9). Tragically, individuals treated for an acute and perhaps short-lived emotional disturbance can end up with a chronic drug-induced psychosis.

Other Harmful Antipsychotic Effects

Unexplained sudden death is another adverse effect of neuroleptic drugs, especially among chronically hospitalized patients. It may be due to an increased rate of convulsions, impaired swallowing reflex, or heart attacks caused by arrhythmias. These medications also reduce the capacity to handle heat, resulting in numerous deaths in urban centers during heat waves. Because people on neuroleptics are less sensitive to signals from their body, they may become dangerously ill before they realize it.

All of the antipsychotics can cause a Parkinsonism syndrome, involving flattened emotions, stiff facial features, tremors, and a characteristic stooped and shuffling walk. The term *akinesia,* referring to the slowing down of emotions and movements, is used to describe an aspect of this syndrome. Antipsychotics can also produce acute and painful muscular spasms (dystonias) and very disturbing emotional agitation accompanied by a compulsive need to move about (akathisia). Studies indicate very high rates—sometimes exceeding 50 percent—for these acute adverse reactions. As we have described, such reactions can become permanent in a large percentage of patients.

Although there is some variation among medications in this class, all of them can cause toxic psychoses with delirium, confusion, disorientation, hallucinations, and delusions. The atypical antipsychotics are no exception. One article published at the time Abilify (aripiprazole) first appeared on the United States market in 2004 described four cases of exacerbation of psychosis after starting on this drug. The report bears the unusually informative title "Aripiprazole possibly worsens psychosis."[54] Invega (paliperidone) was recently approved by the FDA. The agency described the drug as a new molecular entity, meaning that its active substance has never been approved for marketing in the United States. Nonetheless, every person who has ever taken Risperdal has had Invega coursing through his or her body—because Invega is simply the main active metabolite of Risperdal, on the market since 1994. Invega is now described in some publications as a unique antipsychotic, but many if not all of Risperdal's adverse effects can be expected to occur with Invega.

Probably all antipsychotics can also cause depression; Prolixin, in the long-acting intramuscular form, appears to be a special offender in this regard. Most of them can cause sedation and fatigue, seizures, weight gain, dangerous cardiac problems, hypotension (especially upon the patient's attempt to stand up), a variety of gastrointestinal problems such as paralysis of the bowels, hormonal abnormalities including swelling of the breasts and even lactation, sexual dysfunctions, disfiguring facial hair growth, skin rashes and sensitivity to sunlight, eye disorders, allergic reactions that can become serious, and disorders of body temperature regulation that can lead to fatalities on hot days.

Most neuroleptics can also cause bone marrow suppression (agranulocytosis or aplastic anemia), involving immunological suppression and the risk of serious, intractable infections. Though seemingly rare, except in the case of Clozaril, these blood disorders are potentially lethal. Families need to be alert to early signs, such as elevated temperature, and immediately seek medical evaluation, including a blood count. Unfortunately, many different kinds of psychiatric drugs can cause bone marrow suppression.

Although the reader may be feeling overwhelmed by the data presented thus far, this summary has only touched on the enormous range of often serious adverse effects associated with neuroleptics. These drugs subject almost every system of the body to impairment. Research, including a recent study, indicates that these drugs are toxic to cells in general.[55]

Anyone, as well as their relatives and friends, taking these drugs should review the adverse effects listed in the *Physicians' Desk Reference* and other sources.

Loxitane, Moban, Navane, Orap, and Haldol essentially pose the same dangers as the phenothiazines, especially in regard to tardive dyskinesia and neuroleptic malignant syndrome. Haldol and Orap are especially prone to causing severe and painful neurological problems.

The atypical antipsychotics, touted for the past decade as breakthrough drugs in terms of improved efficacy and superior safety, are not so atypical after all. All of these drugs have been shown to cause the range of neurological and psychological disorders associated with the other neuroleptics (antipsychotics) including tardive dyskinesia and neuroleptic malignant syndrome (see Chapter 9). One careful review concludes that "atypical antipsychotics continue to have notable risks of [abnormal movement disorders], particularly akathisia."[56] One of their best-documented adverse effects is commonly called "metabolic syndrome," which consists of abnormal sugar and/or insulin metabolism, weight gain, elevated cholesterol levels, and high blood pressure. Approximately 50 percent of patients on atypicals gain an average of 20 percent of their weight (primarily fat), and some gain much more. Weight gain can predispose individuals to various problems, including coronary artery disease, high blood sugar, and sleep apnea. In addition, atypical drugs are relatively stimulating drugs with a tendency to cause agitation and other behavioral abnormalities.

Clozaril (clozapine) is a more sedating drug than most in this class. Many patients who take it can expect to become lethargic, subdued, and sleepy. Some reports indicate that it can cause obsessive-compulsive disorder (OCD). Among antipsychotics it also has a special reputation for causing withdrawal problems, including agitation, anxiety, and toxic psychosis (see Chapter 9).

Clozaril has many adverse effects, including low blood pressure and a 4–5 percent rate of seizures, especially at higher doses. Although we found only one published case of TD due to Clozaril, the FDA requires that the drug carry the standard class warning for TD. The drug's pharmacological actions are consistent with the production of this disorder. In addition, Clozaril is known to cause neuroleptic malignant syndrome, the more drastic and potentially lethal acute neurological impairment associated with neuroleptics.

Clozaril also poses a special danger of bone marrow suppression, which is potentially fatal. In such cases, the immune system is compromised, leading to fatal infections. Rates approach 1 out of 100 patients. Years ago, this drug was banned in some European countries because it caused so many fatalities; but the escalating power of drug companies subsequently led to its approval by the FDA. Patients and families should seek immediate medical attention if a fever or other signs of infection develop during the administration of any neuroleptic drug, especially Clozaril.

The neuroleptics or antipsychotics are extraordinarily dangerous drugs. If they were not highly profitable drugs used to control a rather helpless, stigmatized, or troubling population, often including involuntary patients, these drugs would not be so freely prescribed. They might even be taken off the market.

Medications Used to Treat Drug-Induced Abnormal Movements

This category comprises Symmetrel (amantadine), Sinemet (carbidopa-levodopa), Cogentin (benztropine), Akineton (biperiden), Kemadrin (procyclidine), Artane (trihexyphenidyl), and Parsidol (ethopropazine).

Here we describe various drugs used to treat the abnormal movements that are produced during treatment with the neuroleptics. Although they are often effective in reducing some of these *acute* neurological reactions before they become permanent, they may increase the likelihood that the neurological impairments will become permanent in the form of tardive dyskinesia. Once tardive dyskinesia develops, they can worsen it.

All of these drugs can also cause a range of effects described as anticholinergic, because they suppress the function of the neurotransmitter acetylcholine. Anticholinergic effects include potentially severe constipation with bowel obstruction and difficulty urinating, dry mouth, blurred vision, light sensitivity, dizziness, and stomach upset. The drugs can also worsen glaucoma.

The use of these drugs is hazardous in psychiatry because they can mimic symptoms of severe psychiatric disorders, including toxic psychosis, delirium, confusion, excitement, euphoria or giddiness, hallucinations and delusions, insomnia, paranoia, agitation, depression, apathy or listlessness, and bizarre behavior. They can also cause more subtle interference with memory and thinking processes. Although no studies of this phenomenon have been conducted, we agree with other clinicians who believe that these drugs may cause irreversible mental deterioration when used over the long term.

Neuroleptic malignant syndrome has been reported in connection with Symmetrel and Sinemet. Because both of these drugs bring about their impact by stimulating dopamine, they can also cause twitches, spasms, and other involuntary movements (dyskinesias).

Although it is common practice to combine these anticholinergic drugs with neuroleptics and antidepressants, which often share their anticholinergic action, we have seen severe toxic psychoses develop under these conditions. The neuroleptics with especially strong anticholinergic tendencies include Thorazine and Clozaril, followed by Serentil, Mellaril, and Orap. Tricyclic antidepressants with strong anticholinergic effects include Elavil and Vivactil, followed by Anafranil, Trazodone, Surmontil, and Tofranil.

Psychiatric Drugs During Pregnancy and Nursing

Now that we have reviewed many of the dangers associated with taking psychiatric drugs, it should be apparent that the fetus or infant needs maximum protection from these agents. Lithium, as already noted, causes heart malformations. It is contraindicated in pregnancy. But parents should be very cautious about exposing the unborn or the newborn to any psychoactive medications.

All psychiatric drugs cross the placenta and enter into the fetal blood stream. They do so "readily, rapidly, and without limitation."[57] Once the drug has entered the fetal bloodstream, it has easy access to the brain. Furthermore, after the child is born, the child's liver will have less capacity than the mother's to metabolize or break down the drug, increasing the length of time it will remain present and active in the newborn's body.[58]

Psychoactive substances can also pass to the infant through the mother's milk, although the concentrations may be higher or lower than those in the mother's blood. For example, the plasma level of clozapine in fetal blood exceeds that in the mother. But regardless of the relative tendency of the drugs to cross into the fetal blood stream, nursing mothers should avoid exposing their unborn infants to such toxic substances with their harmful effects on multiple organ systems. In addition, after birth the infant's immature liver will be less able to metabolize or break down whatever amount of drug remains in its body. Some drugs ingested by a nursing mother, such as lithium, can make the infant become flaccid. Other drugs, such as valproic acid (Depakene), can make the infant hyper-excited and may cause brain dysfunction detectable up to six years later.[59] Special caution should be shown in the first trimester, when malformations are most commonly caused by toxic agents. The use of all psychiatric drugs should be avoided during pregnancy.[60] See Chapter 9 for a discussion of drug withdrawal reactions in neonates whose mothers took antidepressants during pregnancy.

To date, the FDA has not approved any psychiatric drug for use during pregnancy or lactation. Some physicians try to reassure pregnant or nursing mothers about their baby's safety while they are taking psychiatric drugs. But there is no scientific basis for offering this reassurance in regard to any drug that affects the brain.

*   *   *

There are many reasons not to start taking psychiatric drugs and many reasons to stop taking them once you have begun. The choice to taper off or to stop a drug is a personal one; but ideally it should be made with the help of an experienced clinician who can provide advice about strategies to make withdrawal as safe as possible. Unhappily, it is often difficult to find health professionals who do not advocate such drugs and who know how to withdraw patients from them. We know that this book has helped to inform many people *and* the health professionals with whom they are working.

Our approach is based on the principle that individuals and families have the right to make their own decisions about psychiatric drug use. But, equally important, we believe that informed decisions can be made only on the basis of full disclosure, including critical viewpoints from experts who do not advocate drugs. In Chapters 3 and 4 we have examined some of the physical dangers of psychiatric drugs. In the next chapter, we look at the psychological and moral hazards of relying on these mind-altering agents.

— 5 —

Personal and Psychological Reasons for Not Using Psychiatric Drugs

We have now reviewed many of the medical hazards associated with taking psychiatric drugs. This chapter examines the personal, psychological, and philosophical reasons you may have for limiting or rejecting the therapeutic use of psychoactive agents.

A Natural Aversion to Taking Mood-Altering Drugs

In our workshops and other contacts with the public, we find that most people have a natural aversion to tampering with their brain function by ingesting psychoactive drugs, especially as a method of dealing with long-term problems. And if they do accept prescribed psychiatric medications, they generally want to limit the duration.

People who use recreational drugs do not generally view them as "therapeutic." Rather, they tend to use these substances for relaxation or socializing. Even those people who do take them to relieve anxiety, depression, or mood swings are not likely to consider this a satisfactory solution. Instead, they are likely to see their drug use as a bad habit. Most people feel the same way about using psychiatric drugs, many of which are similar or identical to recreational drugs.

Other Common Concerns About
Taking Psychiatric Drugs

You may wonder if any improvement you felt from taking drugs was caused by the drugs themselves or by personal changes you made in your life. Or you may, instead, be feeling worse and worse on the drugs and wonder if they aren't part of the problem. The title of a recent book consisting of in-depth interviews of antidepressant users says it well: *Is It Me or My Meds?*[1] In the meantime, your doctor may be suggesting that you need larger doses or additional medications, while you suspect that you need to reduce them or to get off them entirely.

You may believe that being "drug-free" will help you benefit more from therapy or other forms of help. You may also believe that it will help you to feel more in charge of yourself, to evaluate your mental state, to get in touch with your deeper spiritual resources, to live a healthier lifestyle, and to find for yourself what really matters in your life.

You may wonder if psychiatric drugs are causing some of your problems, such as memory and concentration difficulties, headaches and stomachaches, sleep problems, bladder and bowel dysfunctions of various kinds, skin problems, sexual dysfunctions, weight loss or gain, tiredness or apathy, anxious or depressed feelings, irritability, and impatience. You may need to stop taking all psychiatric drugs to sort out the causes of these problems.

You may be realizing that psychiatric drugs, like alcohol or marijuana, can interfere with your ability to appreciate your mental condition. Perhaps you are suffering less but at the cost of feeling emotionally or mentally dulled and physically fatigued.

After taking drugs for many months or even years, you may be concerned that they could be doing more harm than good. Having found that there are few studies about long-term risks, you may want to avoid the potential dangers.

You may now suspect or realize that your past failures at stopping psychiatric drugs had more to do with their withdrawal and rebound effects than with your own emotional or psychiatric problems.

If you are a woman who is preparing to become pregnant, already pregnant, or nursing, you definitely should consider stopping all psychiatric drugs. This subject was discussed in Chapter 3. Keep in mind that the absence of obvious deformities in a newborn cannot be considered proof that a particular drug was safe; modern science lacks the capacity to test for subtle kinds of damage to the growth and development of children's brains. Nevertheless, common sense and an elementary knowledge of developmental neurology indicate multiple potential dangers from exposure of the fetus to psychiatric medications.

Similarly, you should make sure that you aren't taking a drug that could damage your genes. In this respect, too, negative test results cannot be taken as proof that genetic damage won't occur. In Chapter 4 we mentioned earlier findings of genetic damage in children following treatment with Ritalin, as well as some experts' suggestion that irreversible sexual adverse effects from the use of SSRIs may reflect genetic damage.

Even if you don't plan to stop altogether, you may want to reduce your medication dose or the number of medications you are taking. As you may now realize, few drugs are approved or fully evaluated in combination with other drugs; so, by taking more than one drug at a time, you essentially become an experimental subject.

Convincing You That You're "Mentally Ill"

In recent years, the National Institute of Mental Health (NIMH) has been collaborating with drug companies to promote psychiatric medications. By calling its campaigns "Anxiety Awareness Week" or "Depression Awareness Week," it gives them a seemingly benign "educational" aura. Meanwhile, the drug companies themselves have helped to finance these activities.

Some of these companies advertise directly to the public to convince people that they are depressed or "bipolar" and thus "need" drugs. Direct-to-consumer advertising of prescription drugs (on television, in newspapers and magazines, and on the Internet) increased by almost 30 percent per year between 1996 and 2001, to a whopping $2.7 billion, and it was estimated to reach $7.5 billion in 2005.[2] As *Washington Post* writer Peter Carlson (1998) has commented:

> My favorite drug ad is for an anti-anxiety medicine called BuSpar. The headline asks, "Does your life have signs of persistent anxiety?"
> "Of course it does," I replied. "I'm the parent of a teenage girl."
> Unfortunately, BuSpar has some side effects that could tend to *cause* persistent anxiety—hallucinations, seizures, stupor, rectal bleeding, hair loss, hiccups, and a "roaring sensation in the head."

The notion that "mentally ill" people need medications is also promoted by drug company–sponsored "consumer" groups such as the National Alliance for the Mentally Ill (NAMI) and Children and Adults with Attention Deficit Disorder (CHADD), and of course by government-sponsored organizations like the National Institute of Mental Health. These groups hold national meetings that bring together drug advocates to talk directly to consumers. They also put out newsletters and other information that praise medications. Sometimes they actively suppress viewpoints that are critical of drugs—for example, by discouraging the media from airing opposing views.

One effective marketing technique involves the attempt to convince people that they now need the very product that has just been created. Indeed, just as clothing manufacturers spend millions of dollars trying to convince people that they need new clothes to remain stylish, drug companies are invested in convincing people that they need psychiatric medications—because they have "mental disorders." This is often called "disease mongering."[3]

Some people, when they first hear about a "disease," begin to fear that they are "ill." For example, it's well known that medical students tend to think that they are developing one or more of the diseases that they have read about or observed during their training. Governmental and drug company–driven "awareness" campaigns play on this natural human vulnerability. There is hardly a person alive who doesn't experience moments or even hours and days of anxiety, depression, or other emotional "symptoms," making it easy for drug advocates to claim, for example, that half of all Americans will suffer a psychiatric disorder at some time in their lives. In actuality, however, these campaigns—including the ones directed to depression and anxiety—are stigmatizing and demoralizing people, who, in turn, end up believing that they must have a mental illness.

It's all a matter of definition—of naming and labeling. When emotional discomfort or suffering is defined as a "disorder," it creates business for doctors and drug companies. The campaigns to promote "mental illness" have been so successful that, within a matter of a few years, millions of Americans have come to believe that they have "biochemical imbalances," "panic disorder," or "clinical depression," and that their children have "ADHD," and bipolar disorder, and oppositional defiant disorder.

As a result of successful marketing campaigns, consumers tend to identify trade names with generic products. We ask for a Kleenex when we mean any brand of soft facial tissue. We ask for a Xeroxed copy when we mean a "photocopy." And we speak of the "Prozac nation" when referring to antidepressants or even psychiatric drugs in general. This identification of Prozac with "antidepressants" has led doctors and patients alike to think of it as their first choice among drugs.

You may have started taking psychiatric drugs because you thought, or were told, that you had "panic disorder," "clinical depression," or some other supposed manifestation of a "biochemical imbalance." Now, however, you may be wondering if you were actually experiencing understandable reactions to stress, disappointment, loss, or frustration in your life. You may have begun to doubt the validity of national campaigns to convince Americans that they are mentally ill and in need of drug company products. And as a part of your growing skepticism, you may be questioning whether you should be taking psychiatric drugs after all.

Defining Intense or Painful Emotions as Illness

When you have tried to stop taking drugs, your emotions may have become much stronger than you anticipated. You may have felt as though you were on an emotional roller coaster. Psychiatry and the pharmaceutical industry have successfully defined intense and painful emotions as "illnesses" or "disorders." But intense and painful emotions are better understood as distress signals.

If you were marooned on an island, you might flail your arms wildly in the direction of any passing ship. You might scream and shout as well. You would probably try almost anything to draw attention to yourself— to compel a response to your desperate plight and your need for rescue. When you express anguished feelings, you are sending emergency signals that need to be heeded, not suppressed.

Phrases like "panic disorder" and "clinical depression" are intended to give a medical aura to powerful emotions. In effect, however, they stigmatize such emotions. They make strong emotions seem dangerous, pathological, unnatural, or out of control. But especially strong emotions are better seen as strong signals, sent by an especially powerful soul in need of new direction or special fulfillment.

Even when you feel overcome or swept away by an emotion, you need not do something right away to stop the emotion. You can learn to have feelings without being driven to do anything about them.

When you suppress strong feelings by rejecting them or by drugging them into oblivion, you essentially blind yourself to your own psychological or spiritual state. You are left to blunder about in the dark without direction. The feelings may later burst out of control in some grossly harmful way. Or they may remain submerged, sapping your strength. And with your distress signals suppressed, you may remain indefinitely marooned or trapped.

Many people have succumbed to the prodrug propaganda barrage. It is hard to sustain faith in one's own judgment when confronted by a public relations onslaught from the pharmaceutical industry, organized medicine and psychiatry, government agencies, private foundations, and the media. As we noted in our introductions, this tide sometimes seems to be turning, as more and more Americans realize that biological psychiatry has simply not delivered on its promises. Still, selling psychiatric drugs is huge business in America today, and we do not expect a sharp curtailment in the sale of psychiatric drugs in the near future.

How Psychiatry Takes Advantage

When people seek psychiatric or psychological help, they usually fear that their own resources are failing them. Often they feel frightened and helpless in the face of internal conflicts or external stresses. Misgivings and even embarrassment may accompany their decision to seek help. "I wanted to handle my problems on my own," new patients or clients are prone to say.

Often they believe that "there's something wrong inside my head. I can't think straight. I can't control my emotions." Irrational thoughts or feelings may seem to arise out of nowhere, making them feel vulnerable to forces beyond their control.

In psychology there is a useful concept called "locus of control." People who seek help from mental health professionals often believe that the locus of control in their lives lies outside themselves. They may feel at the mercy of their spouse or parents, or even their own children. They may feel helpless in regard to work. Or they may feel overwhelmed and no longer in charge of themselves or their lives.

Too often, all this is made worse when people seek help from a psychiatrist. First, they receive a medical-sounding diagnosis. Often they are told that they have "panic attacks" or "obsessive-compulsive disorder" or "major depression" or "manic-depressive (bipolar) disorder." Immediately, this label confirms their feelings of helplessness. The locus of control moves further away into the hands of "the doctor."

Psychiatric diagnosis, a system of thought that is alien to individuals' everyday sense of themselves, is imposed from the outside. Being diagnosed implies that the problem is a disorder or even a brain disease inside them, yet totally beyond their control. It's inside them, even a part of them, but they can't do anything about it except to take the prescribed medication. Essentially, then, they are being informed that, like a brain tumor, their painful feelings cannot be controlled or modified by personal understanding or efforts. The original feelings of helplessness and "being out of control" are now confirmed by an official medical diagnosis.

Often patients are told, "It's biological and genetic." Never mind that there's no substantial evidence that any psychiatric diagnoses have a physical basis; the pronouncement is made with such certainty and authority that the patients are likely to believe it. Besides, they have heard the claim repeated time and again in the major media.

The process of diagnosis thus takes advantage of patients' worst fears about themselves. It confirms self-destructive thoughts about "being out of control," "being sick," "being unable to help themselves," "being at the mercy of forces beyond their control." Intentionally or not, the process of psychiatric diagnosis manipulates the patients' feelings of personal helplessness.

Nowadays, a diagnosis is often immediately followed by a prescription for psychiatric medication. Unfortunately, the offer of a drug moves the locus of control further away from the individual. It is the ultimate symbolic gesture that places the authority in "the doctor" and, even more impersonally, in "the pill."

The pharmacological effect of the drug takes the dehumanizing process another giant step further. The drug impairs mental function, reinforcing the patients' sense of feeling helpless and in need of medical supervision. As a result, they become even less able to take charge of their life in new and creative ways.

Biological psychiatry takes advantage of patients' worst fear—that they are emotionally helpless. Biological psychiatry further undermines their sense of personal efficacy, replacing it with reliance on the doctor and drugs. The locus of control, already shaky in people who are seeking help, is wholly shifted to the doctor. Then, as the drugs impair the mental function of the patients, they become increasingly dependent on the doctor.[4]

Good Therapy Versus
Psychiatric Diagnosis and Medication

Good therapy or counseling does not reinforce clients' feelings of help-lessness and indecision. Instead, and in contrast to the traditions of biological psychiatry, it aims to inspire clients with the capacity to take charge of their own lives. Toward this end, nothing is more important than the therapist's ability to be empathic and caring—to bring a compassionate spirit into the therapy.[5]

Instead of emphasizing "pathology" or "mental illness," counseling and therapy should empower clients to draw on their own human potential and natural assets. Unfortunately, however, this approach is being corrupted as "talking therapists" increasingly turn to psychiatrists for medical solutions to the problems they face in working with more difficult or challenging clients.

Counselors and therapists should encourage their clients to reestablish the "locus of control" within themselves. They should also strengthen their clients' sense of personal autonomy, self-understanding, and decision making. But these ends cannot be achieved through diagnosis and medication. On the contrary, diagnosis and medication push the patient toward reliance on "expertise," on interventions that originate from the outside and lie beyond their control.

Maintaining Your Mental Faculties

When faced with emotional difficulties, we are often tempted to dull or delay our suffering by impairing our brain function. Toward this end, we may use cigarettes, alcohol, marijuana, or other substances. We may exhaust ourselves with work, sex, or sports. Or we may turn to excessive eating or television watching.

By the time we seek help from a mental health professional, we may believe we've been drained of personal resources. We may feel as though we've suffered too much or that we've exhausted our capacity to deal with life or at least with certain important problems. Or we may feel "burned out," as though we've blown a fuse or worked our minds to death. At such times it is indeed tempting to seek a solution that requires minimal mental or emotional work to dull our pain.

Yet this option, despite its short-term attractiveness, inevitably becomes self-destructive. When we are facing a personal crisis, whether acute or chronic, we need all of our brain power, all of our mental acuity, all of our ability to feel and to think. Instead of dulling our pain by suppressing our emotional signals, we need to be *more* aware of them and better able to understand them. Only then can we adopt better solutions to our conflicts and problems.

Being in Touch with Your Feelings

Many people intuitively recognize that taking psychiatric drugs can put them out of touch with their feelings. They want to have a clear brain and mind, even if it means experiencing painful emotions.

Drug effects, in lay terms, are "artificial." Many individuals understandably want to learn to conduct their lives without being under the influence of drugs that affect the mind and spirit, creating artificial tranquilization or euphoria.

Taking psychiatric drugs can make it very hard to know what you are really feeling. You may have felt better at first while taking an antidepressant, stimulant, or tranquilizer; but now you wonder if the improvement was due instead to your own personal efforts at improving your life or perhaps to changes in your circumstances or even the passage of time. Or you may feel as though you're getting worse while taking the drugs but you don't know why. Which is the culprit—the drugs themselves or the unresolved emotional problems and continuing stresses in your life? Or are the drugs preventing you from getting even worse than you already feel? Your doctor is likely to tell you that you need an increased dose, a newer drug, or a combination of several medications to help you feel better, but you have your doubts.

When you are taking psychiatric drugs, it becomes difficult to recognize your own feelings and to figure out their source. You may not even know how confused you are about your emotional ups and downs until you stop taking drugs that affect your feelings.

Feelings are the signals by which we guide our lives. If we are happy, the positive feeling can confirm that we are on the right track. If we are persistently sad, lonely, depressed, anxious, or angry, the negative feeling can be an important signal that something is the matter. Of course, it can be very difficult to know ourselves well enough to interpret and act on these signals. But without our emotional signals, we are guaranteed not to fully experience or to make progress with our lives.

Psychiatric drugs blunt and confuse these essential emotional signals. Our emotions depend on our brain function, and the brain is an intricate, delicate organ that can easily be thrown out of whack by drugs.

Sometimes drugs give us "false positive" signals, such as an artificial high or euphoria. When euphoric, we may remain stuck in unsatisfactory, frustrating situations or take unrealistic or even grandiose risks.

Sometimes drugs give us "false negative" signals, making us feel depressed, disappointed, out of sorts, or even suicidal or violent. Since the tendency is to try to attribute our negative feelings to something or someone, these false negative signals can lead us to take very irrational and destructive actions such as hurting a loved one.

Getting in better touch with our real or genuine feelings is one of the most important reasons to stop taking drugs. The concluding chapter further describes how clients and therapists can work together to overcome emotional crises without resort to drugs.

The Placebo Effect

Faith or expectation plays a key role in how we respond to medications. Regardless of the cause of our suffering or the real effectiveness of a particular drug, most of us feel better for a short time, at least, when we are given a drug that's supposed to be helpful.

Many patients with severe pain due to cancer or to physical injuries feel better for a while after an injection of plain sterile water if they are told it is a pain killer. Similarly, in clinical drug trials, forty percent or more of patients with anxiety or depression commonly feel better when given a sugar pill that they are told will be helpful to them. If the conditions are right—that is, if the patients have a lot of faith in what they are being given—a sugar pill may produce emotional improvement in 60 to 90 percent of patients. This is the placebo effect—improvement that comes from a positive expectation or faith in the drug or the doctor rather than from any chemical impact of the substance.[6]

The placebo effect can be helpful. The lowly sugar pill, which rarely causes any physical harm but can relieve physical or emotional suffering, has the best risk/benefit ratio in biopsychiatry. The placebo effect also explains much of the effectiveness of psychiatric drugs. However, when an individual attributes improvement to the physical characteristics of a pill, and to the expectation that it will work, that person's belief in his or her own psychological or spiritual power can be undermined. This experience can encourage reliance on the pill rather than on personal efforts.

Drugs like the SSRIs can become souped-up, high-power placebos. They receive so much hype from the media, and from drug company promotionals, that the expectation of help becomes enormous. The anticipation of relief can produce a relief—because of the expectation that we will feel better.

Whether the placebo effect takes place in response to a widely advertised antidepressant or to a sugar pill, it may create the false impression that emotional problems originate from physical causes and the false expectation that chemicals are the answer to personal problems. The placebo effect is complicated but it clearly demonstrates the power that people have over their own emotional state, given the proper encouragement. But people don't know that they are experiencing a placebo effect. To the extent that they think they're responding to the chemical impact of the drug upon their brains, they may become further convinced that control over their lives lies outside themselves and in the medication.

When people mistakenly believe that they are being helped by a drug's chemical effect, they develop distorted ideas about how to live their lives. Instead of recognizing the power of hope, faith, or optimism in their lives, they give false recognition to the power of drugs. Instead of developing more effective ways of living that would provide more genuine, realistic, and lasting results, they pop a pill. Bolstered by the initial placebo effect, many patients go for years trying one and then another pill to meet their needs, rather than improving their lives through self-understanding and better principles of living.

Psychological Dependence on Drugs, Doctors, and Medical Solutions to Personal Problems

Psychological dependence on drugs tends to undermine our self-esteem, confidence, will power, and sound principles of living. We turn to doctors and drugs instead of more personal resources such as self-insight, personal responsibility, love, family life, creative work, and improved principles or ethics.

As a larger problem, the use of drugs furthers dependence on physicians and on their medical approach to solving essentially psychological, social, economic, and spiritual problems such as feeling depressed or anxious. This dependence, in turn, alienates us from the most important sources of human wisdom, as well as from other human services, as sources of strength and direction.

Learning to Live Without Drugs

Advocates of psychiatric drugs often claim that the medications improve learning and the ability to benefit from psychotherapy, but the contrary is true. There are no drugs that improve mental function, self-understanding, or human relations. Any drug that affects mental processes does so by impairing them.

Once again, this principle may be best understood in relation to people who use so-called recreational drugs. Many individuals drink alcohol, smoke marijuana, or take other nonprescription drugs to "get through the day," to "handle work stress," or to "relate better." When people stop using alcohol or street drugs long enough to recover somewhat from their effects, they are likely to discover that these psychoactive substances were actually retarding their ability to handle life. While influenced by the drugs, they mistakenly accepted or adapted to a lower level of mental and social functioning. Now they must learn how to deal with life all over again with a drug-free mind. After many years of impaired functioning under the influence of marijuana or alcohol, they may need many months or even years of drug-free living to learn how to deal with life with a fully functioning brain.

Patients who have been taking psychiatric drugs for years at a time may face the same problems as recovering alcoholics or marijuana users. Under the influence of drugs, they adapted to stress, conflict, and challenge by increasing the doses of these drugs rather than by increasing their capacity to live. And when negative emotions became overwhelming, they dulled them rather than learning to harness them in creative ways. When psychiatric drugs are stopped, these emotions may soon come roaring back to life—but without the experience required to understand and to channel them.

This problem is tragically apparent in children who grow up on psychiatric drugs, such as stimulants and antidepressants, and who may never mature in a normal fashion. Much like illicit psychoactive drugs, psychiatric medications can retard the psychological and social development of children.

The long-term use of psychiatric drugs tends to teach people how to relate at a lower emotional, psychological, and cognitive level. Then, when the drugs are stopped, there is a gradual, growing realization that they have been functioning *despite* these drug-induced impairments. It can take time and help from others to learn to live with an unimpaired brain and the increased awareness and emotional responsiveness that follow.

— 6 —

Why Doctors Tell Their Patients So Little

Time and again, we are shocked at how little doctors tell their patients about the psychiatric drugs that they so freely prescribe for them. Most people are fumbling in the dark when it comes to knowing about the actual effects and hazards of these mind-altering drugs.

Encouraged Not to Tell

In fact, physicians are encouraged not to tell their patients the known dangers of psychiatric drugs. Handbooks and textbooks that document serious adverse drug effects often recommend to doctors that their patients receive extremely limited renditions of the facts. Consider *Current Psychotherapeutic Drugs*, a 1998 publication of the American Psychiatric Press.[1] This handbook for doctors lists dozens of adverse effects caused by Ritalin, the stimulant drug used to treat ADHD in children and adults. For example, it states that the drug is "contraindicated" for (and thus should not be given to) children with "marked anxiety, tension, agitation." It confirms that "frank psychotic episodes" can be caused by the drug itself and that withdrawal from it can lead to "severe depression." As the drug's "most common adverse effects," it lists "restlessness, overstimulation, insomnia, and anorexia."

After warning the physician about these and other potentially grave and confusing consequences of taking or withdrawing from Ritalin, what does *Current Psychotherapeutic Drugs* recommend telling parents? Here is the entirety of the "Patient Information" it provides:

Use caution when driving or operating hazardous machinery. Patients or their parents should record the patient's weight two times a week and report any significant loss. Any changes in mood should be reported to the physician, as should any evidence of skin rashes, fever, or pain in the joints. The sustained-release tablets should not be crushed or chewed.

Does this "Patient Information" truly inform parents about the dangers of giving Ritalin to their child? Shouldn't it mention that the drug can cause "frank psychotic episodes" and "severe depression" upon withdrawal? Don't parents need to know that Ritalin can cause or worsen the very symptoms it is supposed to cure, including "restlessness" and "overstimulation"? Shouldn't parents be told that Ritalin is contraindicated for children with "marked anxiety, tension, agitation," since these are symptoms that parents might think the drug should cure?

Fortunately, since *Current Psychotherapeutic Drugs* first appeared in 1998, the availability of drug information on the Internet has vastly increased. Also, as consumers have become more demanding of information, some professional drug guides have urged doctors to provide patients with more detailed information. Unfortunately, these guides too often minimize the risks in order to avoid causing alarm in potential consumers. For example, the 15th edition of *The Clinical Handbook of Psychotropic Drugs* (2005), written for clinicians, includes Patient Information handouts about the various drug classes. Its recommended information sheet on stimulants lists considerably more side effects than the 1998 *Current Psychotherapeutic Drugs*, but it downplays them, for example, by suggesting that they "are usually not serious and do not occur in all individuals." Although the patient handout identifies "energizing/agitated feeling, excitability" as "common" effects, it merely suggests taking the stimulant earlier in the day to lessen interference with falling asleep. In making this recommendation, it fails to take into account how the daytime occurrence of these stimulating drug effects can vastly disrupt the lives of the children, as well as their parents or caregivers. Headaches, dry mouth, loss of appetite and weight loss are also minimized as temporary effects, although weight loss in a developing child may have unforeseen consequences on development while causing psychological problems.

The *Handbook* does recommend that some effects should be reported "immediately" to the doctor, such as fast or irregular heartbeat, severe agitation or restlessness, and especially "a switch in mood to an unusual state of happiness or irritability; fluctuations in mood." Still, there is no mention of the risks of psychosis, depression, and suicidality that Peter Breggin discusses in his introduction to the book. Furthermore, there is no mention of withdrawal effects as common reactions and potentially dangerous reactions, including "crashing." Nor are patients given a sense of the relatively high frequency of most listed effects.

Under the question "How long should you take this medication?" the authors answer that "Psychostimulants are usually prescribed for a period of several years."[2] They do not warn the consumer that there is no scientific basis for prescribing these drugs long-term and that even the short-term effects are limited to the suppression of behavior and spontaneous mental activity.

Overall, we continue to detect professional attitudes in the field that encourage giving patients and their families limited information. These attitudes reflect a widespread ethical abuse in psychiatry and medicine—the failure to provide patients and their families with the necessary information to make informed decisions about taking psychiatric medications or giving them to family members. This lack of information also undoubtedly renders patients and their families unable to properly assess adverse effects when they do develop. As in the case of Ritalin, many of the drug's *common* side effects are likely to be mistaken for the patient's own problems.

Where Was the FDA?

When psychiatric drugs turn out to be harmful, the victims often tell us, "I thought FDA approval meant a drug is safe. I never thought our doctor would prescribe something so dangerous." When a loved one dies from the effects of a psychiatric drug, grieving, outraged families often demand to know, "Did the FDA know it could be lethal? Should our doctor have known it could kill?"

Especially during the drug approval process, the FDA is largely dependent on information that it receives from drug companies. Consider the following circumstances, however. The fact that a person experienced an "adverse event" (e.g., a headache or a fall) while taking a drug does not mean that this event was caused by the drug. Scientists or doctors employed by a drug company make the initial judgment that an adverse effect *may* or *may not* have been caused by a drug during testing; but management at the company headquarters makes the final decision about how to handle the data submitted to it by its paid researchers. If management decides that there's no possible connection between the company's drug and the patient's negative reaction, the data may never find its way to the FDA. Or the data may be presented to the FDA in such a disguised fashion that it fails to draw attention at the agency. For example, a drug withdrawal reaction may be recorded as "two days in duration" when in reality the patient was placed back on the drug after two days in order to stop the withdrawal reaction.[3]

At a training seminar tailored to drug company staff,[4] a drug company executive gave the following example of a death that, in his opinion, did not have to be reported to the FDA as even *possibly* drug-related: "While a subject in a clinical drug trial, a man stepped off a curb, was hit by a car, and died." According to the executive, there was no reason even to *consider* reporting this as a possible adverse drug effect.

Drug company executives are not usually scientifically qualified or sufficiently objective to play so crucial a role in regard to the safety of the drugs that their company manufactures and sells. Yet this particular executive not only played such a role in his own company but, at the seminar, trained others how to do so as well. And his assessment in this case was wrong. A drug most certainly could have contributed to or caused the death under discussion.

Many drugs impair awareness, judgment, reflexes, and balance—thus increasing the likelihood that a user will be injured or killed in an accident. Drugs can also cause a seizure or even a heart attack, either of which could have caused the drug-trial subject to fall off the curb. A more remote possibility is that the drug he was taking could have interfered with blood clotting, causing him to die from injuries that ordinarily would not have been fatal.

Looking even more deeply at the "accidental" death in this example, we might surmise that it could have been a suicide. People do intentionally kill themselves by stepping in front of cars, trucks, buses, and trains. Moreover, some drugs are associated with an increased suicide-attempt rate. Yet despite all these possibilities, the company executive was willing—on the basis of a one-line report—to dismiss this man's death as having no possible connection to an experimental drug.

Getting Information to You

If even the FDA often lacks sufficient information to get an accurate picture of a drug's dangers, individual practitioners and the public must be even less well-informed. Regularly, serious questions are raised about most drugs that occupy the coveted place of latest "miracle drug." Over the last decade, these have included Prozac, Viagra, Zyprexa, Bextra, Vioxx, Meridia, and others. Some people who have taken these drugs for their approved indications have died. Typically, the FDA acknowledges that deaths were reported during the post-marketing testing of the drugs, but it argues—as do the drug manufacturers—that the fatalities were not necessarily caused by the drug itself. How can practitioners and the public make up their own minds on this issue?

Through the Freedom of Information Act (FOIA), and increasingly through the FDA's own website, any citizen can obtain a summary of pre-marketing drug testing results for any of the recently introduced medications approved by the FDA. This material is called a Summary New Drug Application (Summary NDA). But the basic underlying data about adverse drug reactions and their interpretation are considered "proprietary"; they are the secret property of the drug company that manufactures the drug under exclusive patent. Only a product liability suit against that manufacturer would open access to the company's own research records. Even then, it would be hard for a small team of attorneys and experts (often only two or three people with limited experience) to effectively evaluate the hundreds of cartons of boxed data in the two or three days they would be allotted. And if important data were discovered, even this information would probably be kept under wraps by the courts so that the general public could not obtain it. Some drug companies actually settle product liability suits against them in order to avoid making damaging disclosures in a public trial.

This point is worth underscoring: Physicians and even key health policy planners do not have access to all the necessary data required to make an independent evaluation of a drug's safety. They must instead rely on very general information provided by the FDA, which in turn relies largely on the drug companies themselves.

FDA Approval Does Not Mean That a Drug Is Safe or Even Highly Effective

FDA records contain thousands of reports of severe and life-threatening reactions to almost every psychiatric drug in current use. With respect to each of these drugs, the agency has attempted to determine if, on balance, the drug is sufficiently useful to outweigh its potential dangers. But this evaluation does not necessarily mean that the drug is safe. Indeed, determination of whether the drug's potential benefits outweigh its potential risks is, of necessity, highly subjective. Hence FDA approval should not be interpreted as indicating that a given drug is without serious and potentially fatal adverse reactions. On the contrary, all psychiatric drugs approved by the FDA can pose enormous risks even in routine use.

Whose Risk and Whose Benefit?

Drug advocates are fond of discussing risk/benefit ratios—specifically, the relationship between the hazards and the usefulness of a drug. But who determines these ratios? Even under the best of conditions, they are rarely left up to the patient who will suffer the consequences. The patient simply doesn't have sufficient information or background knowledge to make such evaluations.

Risk/benefit analyses are initially calculated by the drug company itself, using research studies designed and carried out by doctors on its payroll. Using data prepared by the drug company, the FDA then makes its own risk/benefit analysis. In doing so, the FDA is dependent upon the drug company's analyses of the masses of data in its possession. Moreover, the FDA almost always ends up making compromises in order to accommodate industry. This process is called "negotiating" with the drug companies. It is kept entirely secret from doctors and consumers alike. Over the last several years, leaks by whistleblowers, litigation, and special investigations by reporters or lawmakers have begun to reveal some of its features—all of which lean toward concealing or distorting information from doctors and patients to present a more favorable portrait of drugs.[5]

After a drug is approved, the final risk/benefit analysis is made by individual doctors, who prescribe it to patients. For almost any drug, these prescribing physicians have almost no access to the original information generated for the approval of the drug. Increasingly, the FDA is making available on its website many of its own evaluations of the studies submitted by manufacturers to gain approval of their drugs, and this is a welcome development. However, it may take several months or more after a drug is approved for these FDA evaluations to be available. During this time, when the media, doctors, and patients first hear about the new product, the manufacturer is the only source of information about the drug. The FDA evaluations frequently add up to a few hundred pages, and most practicing physicians will never comb through them. For most practitioners, information about drugs will come from drug-industry sponsored continuing education seminars and from the glossy brochures of well-trained pharmaceutical representatives who push their wares using every possible maneuver. Moreover, FDA evaluations regularly blank out some significant information that the manufacturer believes constitutes "proprietary information." This may include, for example, the list of adverse effects observed in studies where the drug was being tested for another indication, for which the rate of adverse effects was so high that the manufacturer decided to halt the studies.

In this connection, consider again some of the facts discussed in previous chapters:

- The stimulant Ritalin disrupts growth hormone production, inhibiting the growth of the child's brain while creating severe biochemical imbalances within it. Indeed, as noted in Chapter 4, there is evidence that stimulants can cause lasting harm to the brain. From our perspective, these dangers constitute too high a risk for any child to pay. We believe that these drugs should never be given to children.

- In one controlled study, Prozac caused manic psychoses in 6 percent of the children who were participating in this research (see Chapter 4). Despite having little good effect, the drug was described by the authors of the study as useful for children. SSRI antidepressants commonly cause this potentially life-destroying mania in adults, but at a lower rate. Again, we consider the cost to be too high—especially where children are concerned.

- Antipsychotic drugs such as Abilify, Seroquel, Risperdal, Zyprexa, Haldol, and Mellaril—often used to control difficult patients—cause potentially severe neurological impairments in a large percentage of users. Most elderly patients, treated for only two or three months, develop obvious, irreversible twitches or spasms; they risk dementia as well. Once again, we think that the risk is too high.

Serious Dangers Can Surface for the First Time After Years of Use

Prozac, Zoloft, Paxil, Celexa, Luvox, Remeron, and others—the so-called selective serotonin reuptake inhibitors (SSRIs)—built their popularity as antidepressants on the mistaken belief among doctors and patients that they have fewer serious adverse effects than other antidepressants. From the very beginning, we knew this was false marketing hype created by the drug company Eli Lilly.[6] But most psychiatrists seemingly fell for it. Even now many psychiatrists and other physicians are not aware of the increasing catalog of dangers from these drugs.

To illustrate, over 10 years after Prozac was on the market, a headline in the May 1998 edition of *Clinical Psychiatry News* reported that: "Long-Term Side Effects Surface with SSRIs." The article described serious sleep and sexual dysfunctions, as well as abnormal weight gain, associated with use of SSRIs. During their disturbed sleep, patients may also suffer from periods of insomnia, nightmares, teeth grinding, sweating, and abnormal movements of their bodies.

The report mentioned a drug, Prozac, that supposedly benefits depressed people but can end up making them more depressed and even suicidal! According to the report, "With ongoing treatment [with Prozac], increasing numbers of patients report lethargy and fatigue." Lethargy and fatigue, of course, can lead to or worsen depression. Furthermore, with respect to the insomnia caused by Prozac, "there are a lot of data showing that people who sleep poorly are more likely to relapse and that suicide risk is higher."[7]

Many people have decided to use Prozac in the hope that it will help them lose weight. Eli Lilly itself tried unsuccessfully to get the drug approved by the FDA for weight control. Then it turned out that, over the long term, many patients on Prozac are *gaining* too much weight. They are becoming obese.

How did Eli Lilly respond to these newly recognized dangers of Prozac? In a full-page multicolor ad in the same issue of *Clinical Psychiatry News*, the drug company promoted Prozac as producing "*both* restful nights and productive days." But "restful nights" are a remarkable claim for a drug that was already known to produce insomnia in 20 percent of patients in the four-to-six-week studies used for FDA approval. (Because of this insomnia, many of the patients were prescribed addictive sleeping pills.) Unfortunately, the ad makes no mention of the risks of obesity, worsening depression, or suicide associated with Prozac. As required by law, however, a sentence in very fine print toward the bottom of the back page notes that there have been post-marketing reports of "suicidal ideation" as well as "violent behaviors." Though forced by the FDA to mention these possible adverse drug effects, the drug company also stated that they "may have no causal relationship with the drug." Of course, the "unexpected" weight gain issue is not limited to Prozac. One clinician writing to the *British Medical Journal* in 2003 noted: "I have observed frequent, rapid weight gain in clients using Paxil. When asking questions about the alleged anorexic effects of the drug back in 1995, I was met with skepticism. This is the first year that I've heard anything about the drugs causing weight gain. However, it's no surprise to me in my role as a therapist."[8]

Recognizing the Limits of FDA Approval

To its credit, the FDA itself has recognized and publicized that FDA approval does not rule out the danger of serious and even life-threatening adverse reactions that may surface later. Since the studies used for FDA approval of psychiatric drugs typically last only about six weeks, the FDA usually requires a warning that the drugs have not been proven safe or effective for longer use. Very few consumers appreciate this severe limitation on FDA approval. Most doctors seem to pay little or no attention to it.

Even short-term efficacy sometimes remains in doubt at the time a drug is approved. For example, internal documents from the FDA raised questions about the effectiveness of the antidepressant Zoloft right up to the moment it was approved. A high-ranking FDA official noted that the drug had been rejected by some European agencies and lamented that the FDA was loosening its approval standards to favor the drug industry.[9]

Another example concerns Prozac, which, in many of the studies used for FDA approval, turned out to be no better than a sugar pill. Making it look effective required selecting from among the studies and then doctoring them statistically to include patients who had also been treated with tranquilizers.[10] Prozac is now marketed as a generic drug and has lost popularity to other SSRIs. Predictably, interest in its effects and history has faded—which allows many of the errors and deceptions in its approval and marketing to be repeated with impunity for the drugs that follow.

How Adverse Effects Go Unreported

The many shortcomings of the FDA approval process place a great burden on the follow-up procedures that go into place after a drug is marketed. At that point, the FDA begins to rely heavily on voluntary reports sent in spontaneously, mostly by doctors and pharmacists. A pattern of reports that indicates a causal connection between a drug and serious adverse effects has often led to increased warnings in the drug's label or to removal of the drug from the market.[11] In 1990, the Government Accounting Office (GAO) reported that more than 50 percent of drugs approved by the FDA between 1976 and 1985 were found, during or after marketing, to have previously undetected "serious" negative effects. Of the fifteen psychiatric drugs approved during this period, nine were found to have additional serious risks and one was removed from the market by the FDA.[12] One antidepressant, nomifensine, was found to cause a potentially fatal blood disorder—but only after it had been marketed worldwide for eight to nine years.[13]

Spontaneous reports to the FDA have played a key role in the agency's decisions concerning these drugs. But how many serious adverse effects come to the attention of doctors, and how conscientious are the doctors about sending them in to the FDA?

Once a drug is on the market, thousands of patients may experience unpleasant or dangerous withdrawal reactions. However, only a few of them will realize that their problems were caused by the drug,[14] and even fewer will mention it to their doctors. In turn, only a fraction of doctors who become aware of even serious and unusual adverse drug reactions will actually report them to an appropriate authority such as the FDA.

In his 1998 book, Thomas Moore documents how infrequently U.S. physicians report adverse reactions. Even in the most optimistic scenario, it appears that only a tiny fraction of adverse reactions are actually reported, including cases so serious they result in hospitalization or death. Yet the FDA relies heavily on these reports to monitor drugs, to update their labels, and, if necessary, to withdraw them from the market.

In a 1998 Canadian study, fifteen hospital-affiliated primary care practitioners were queried about their personal observations of serious adverse effects of benzodiazepine tranquilizers during the previous two years.[15] Seven of these doctors described serious effects, including a fall resulting in a broken hip, a fatal overdose or suicide, a delirium requiring nine days of hospitalization, and a case of severe apathy lasting several days that disrupted all work and family activities. Yet none of the doctors had written up or reported these adverse reactions to any authority or journal.

In failing to report these admittedly serious and even life-threatening reactions, any or all of which could have resulted directly from the use of tranquilizers, the doctors withheld recognition of these dangers from the government, the public, and the medical profession. Their behavior perpetuated the unrealistic attitudes of doctors and patients alike toward the supposed safety of these drugs.

No Guarantee of Long-Term Safety

No psychiatric drug has been shown to be consistently safe and effective for more than a few weeks or months of use. Even after many years on the market, psychiatric drugs are rarely studied to the degree necessary to determine their long-term hazards or usefulness. In February 2007, the FDA indicated that from October 2005 through September 2006, pharmaceutical companies had yet to start 71 percent of outstanding "post-market" safety evaluations that these companies had committed to begin for approved products already on the market.[16] Thus, people should be very cautious about staying on any psychiatric drug for months or years at a time.

Very significant hazards may go undetected even long after a drug is marketed. As noted, the studies used for approval are very short in duration. They are also limited in scope, often excluding patients who have severe or complicated emotional problems, as well as patients who are physically ill, actively suicidal, or taking other drugs. In addition, many prodrug biases are built into the research by pharmaceutical companies that are entirely responsible for financing, planning, monitoring, and interpreting all of the studies. Drug companies typically hire doctors from whom they have learned to expect positive results. Except under unusual circumstances, the FDA relies wholly on data that the drug companies have gathered, organized, pruned, and interpreted.

Adverse drug reactions are underestimated or minimized in many different ways. During drug testing, for example, symptoms such as depression or anxiety—which can be caused by many psychiatric drugs— are often mistakenly blamed on the "mental illness" of the patient. More specifically, a worsening of depression was listed in Prozac's official label as a *commonly* reported possible adverse effect of Prozac until it was edited out on the very last day or two.[17] Who edited it out? The FDA itself. What was the explanation? The agency wanted to shorten the distracting "laundry list" of adverse reactions indicated by the drug company. Yet depression as a *common* result of taking antidepressants surely warrants emphasis rather than complete deletion from the drug label. Because of the deletion, the profession and the public remain unaware of the frequent reports by Eli Lilly's own investigators that Prozac can worsen depression.

The Media

The media have become very protective of psychiatry—especially of psychiatric drugs. Except for occasional exposés, the media tend to publish testimonials to drugs while omitting their hazards. Books critical of psychiatric drugs are rarely reviewed in major newspapers or magazines and rarely discussed on television.

In the past year, the FDA has loosened the requirements for drug company advertisements directed to the public. As a result, there has been an explosion of such ads in newspapers and magazines, and on television, accounting for a 40 percent increase in print-media ad revenues since 1997. In 1998 alone, the U.S. pharmaceutical industry spent over $1.3 billion for direct-to-consumer advertising in television, magazines, and newspapers. We anticipate that the total will continue to increase and that the media will become increasingly protective of their benefactors. Eli Lilly has clearly led the way with a mammoth campaign for Prozac, spending over $41 million in advertising this product directly to the public in 1998 (an 82 percent increase over the previous year's spending).[18]

What Do Doctors Know?

Doctors fail to inform patients about the dangers of medications in part because they themselves are not fully informed. Many doctors rely too heavily on biased drug company advertising and sales representatives, and even the more skeptical among them are bombarded with information skewed in favor of drugs. Furthermore, medical educational and scientific programs are almost always funded by drug companies and, not surprisingly, tend to promote their drug products. Psychiatrists, for example, often get phone calls from marketers asking them to accept $100 for listening on the phone to an "educational" program put on by a drug company or for attending a free dinner that includes a seminar about new drugs. In addition to the small fee or the free meal, the psychiatrists earn Continuing Medical Education (CME) credits toward maintaining their medical credentials.

Most psychiatric journals are totally dependent on drug company advertising—a relationship that influences their editorial policies. The specialty journals published by the American Medical Association (AMA), such as the *Archives of General Psychiatry* and the *Archives of Internal Medicine*, are sent free of charge to doctors in their respective specialties. How can the AMA afford this? Distribution of the journals is paid for by drug company advertising. Indeed, by offering the journals free to so many doctors, the AMA guarantees a hefty advertising investment from the companies themselves. Similarly, the American Psychiatric Association, wholly dependent on massive infusions of drug company money, is unwilling to take a critical look at either corporate practices or drug products. Ultimately, even medical and psychiatric textbooks are written by drug advocates who often minimize or ignore important and even dangerous adverse drug reactions. Only a few professionals become expert on the subject of medications without working with and for drug companies.

Doctors' Attitudes Toward Informing Patients

The failure of doctors to impart information stems partly from ignorance and partly from their attitudes toward their patients. Many doctors do not feel obliged to "tell patients everything." Instead, they control the flow of information in order to achieve certain ends, such as encouraging the acceptance of treatment. Medical education instills and reinforces this authoritarianism in young physicians. From the earliest stages of their clinical work, they must make life and death decisions, many of which are beyond their level of maturity, experience, or knowledge. If only to hide their personal insecurities about shouldering so much responsibility, doctors can become arrogant. Further encouraging their paternalistic attitudes is the almost priestly role they play within society.

Doctors also lack the time to describe the full range of adverse drug effects to each of their patients. And rather than relying on written summaries of these effects, they tend to use their unaided memory and "clinical judgment" when informing their patients. As a result, they often leave out important information about potential adverse drug effects. Doctors in managed care are especially pressed for time and probably more likely than others to skim over or omit critical facts.

Finally, some doctors purposely withhold information about the dangers of drugs for fear that their patients will refuse to take them. Because they believe that the patients need the medication, they prescribe it without providing sufficient information for the patients to make an independent decision. This unethical and potentially illegal practice is especially common among psychiatrists, many of whom harbor a patronizing attitude toward patients.

— 7 —

Plan Your
Drug Withdrawal

We can sum up the most prudent and sensible way to stop taking psychiatric drugs in one short sentence: Plan it well and go slowly. Regardless of the drug you are using and the problems it may have created in your life, a *well-planned, gradual* withdrawal has the best chance to succeed. Conversely, an unplanned, abrupt withdrawal increases the risk of undue hardship and may lead you to return, in an equally unplanned manner, to taking drugs.

In this chapter, we offer a rational, person-centered program of withdrawal from psychiatric drugs. By "rational," we mean that it rests on sound clinical principles and evidence. By "person-centered," we mean that it seeks to help individuals take charge of the withdrawal process. Anyone considering coming off psychiatric drugs, or advising a relative, a friend, a client, or a patient on this issue, should read this chapter carefully. In Chapter 8, we discuss the actual process of reducing your drug intake down to zero. Then, in Chapter 9, we review the specific withdrawal reactions associated with various types of psychiatric drugs. In Chapter 10, we discuss how to help your child come off these drugs.

The withdrawal process may be likened to a journey. Before undertaking a journey, especially one with an unfamiliar destination, you would probably find it useful to plan your steps, to make an inventory of the essentials to bring along, and to anticipate potential obstacles, allies, and resources. You wouldn't be able to predict all the difficult or pleasant surprises, but you could certainly be prepared for many of the obvious ones.

Before you take the first step, though, it would be best if you know whether you really want to undergo this journey.

Decide for Yourself

Choosing to come off psychiatric drugs should be your own personal decision. It would be unwise for anyone else to decide for you whether you should take drugs or stop taking them.

Opinions on the usefulness of drugs vary widely. As the reader knows by now, we believe that taking drugs to solve emotional, psychological, and social problems is at best a misleading, temporary, superficial solution. But other people believe that drugs are very helpful, even life saving, and some can't quite envisage ever doing without them. We have met many individuals who deeply believe in psychiatric drugs. Some have eventually come off them and found other ways to surmount life's difficulties. We believe that until people decide for themselves what course of action to take, the best we can do is to provide accurate information and share our experience.

Taking psychiatric drugs is much more than a simple medical or technical matter. Taking drugs can seem to give meaning to a person's life; if done at the urging of an authority, it may be the nearest thing to a religious ritual that you have ever experienced. Your values and ideas about human nature and personal growth, and about the sources of psychological suffering, will influence whether or not you choose to take psychiatric drugs. In turn, taking drugs will come to color your values and ideas (see Chapter 12).

As noted, the decision to take or to stop taking psychiatric drugs should be a personal one. It should not be trivialized by glib acceptance of pseudo-medical arguments from your doctor or others such as "This drug is the most effective treatment for your serious illness" or "This drug corrects biochemical imbalances in your brain" or "Never fail to take this medication; it's just like insulin for diabetes."

In the field of mental health, not a single physical explanation has been confirmed for any of the hundreds of psychiatric "disorders" listed in the *DSM-IV*. A recent editorial in the *American Journal of Psychiatry* states the case plainly: "[A]s yet, we have no identified etiological agents for psychiatric disorders."[1] Even in this age of biological quick fixes, an increasing number of researchers are documenting the observation that nondrug approaches produce equivalent or better results than drugs. This is true even for problems considered extremely serious, such as "schizophrenia."[2] Your doctor's claims to the contrary have little or no scientific basis.

Yet even well-educated people may be deeply impressed by psychiatric propaganda that appeals to their insecurities. Precisely because there is so little solid scientific backing for the use of psychiatric drugs, mystification and slogans are often communicated to doctors by drug advertising, and then to patients by doctors.[3]

Therefore, the first principle of rational psychiatric drug withdrawal is to *decide for yourself* that you want to do it. Even though taking psychiatric drugs has become a fad, pushed by drug companies and doctors, withdrawing from drugs should be a well-thought-out individual decision.

Deciding for yourself requires that you take responsibility for the outcome of your withdrawal. Regardless of the difficulties you might encounter, you should not blame others. By the same token, you should take pride in your own accomplishments. Coming off drugs in the most rational way possible often requires planning and preparation, strength and determination, and patience.

If others influenced you to take drugs in the first place, and if your own wishes were not respected, you may find it more difficult to decide for yourself to come off the drugs. If you depend on others for your economic or physical sustenance—as do many people who take neuroleptics, such as Risperdal, Seroquel, Zyprexa, and Haldol—the decision to withdraw from the drugs may be harder to make. If you've taken drugs for many years, you might not remember exactly when and why you started on them. Or if family members or your doctor are adamant that you remain on the drugs, you understandably may not wish to risk alienating these people. These are difficult circumstances, and there may be no easy solution.

Try to Get Help from an Experienced Clinician

True health emergencies only occasionally occur during a well-planned, gradual withdrawal. Our impression is that most people who come off psychiatric drugs have successfully done so *on their own*, without active clinical supervision. Yet it can sometimes be dangerous to try to withdraw without professional supervision. We believe that most people would benefit from the support of a qualified, experienced therapist or clinician who is sympathetic to their wishes. This person could be a psychiatrist, a general practitioner or other medical doctor, a pharmacist, a clinical social worker, a psychologist, a nurse, or a counselor with training or experience working with people who take prescription psychiatric drugs.

A therapist should feel free to communicate clearly to patients or clients, and often to their families, that withdrawing from psychiatric medications is a reasonable choice with great benefits for many people. The therapist should also communicate that the choice remains with the client or patient, that each person's case is unique, and that any withdrawal strategies should be tailored to the individual's needs, often with the involvement of friends and family. The emphasis always remains on the patient's right to choose whether to stay on medications or to stop them. Some people may need encouragement to break out of a destructive cycle of using medication; others may need reassurance that they will not be pressured to stop their medication unless they are facing serious risks of toxicity.[4]

We find that patients and clients often want to learn in detail about the health professional's experience in helping people withdraw from specific drugs. They should expect their health practitioners to provide in-depth answers about their knowledge and experience.

How May a Clinician Help?

Most clinicians are not well versed in the techniques for helping people to withdraw from psychiatric drugs. Some are plainly hostile to the idea, especially in cases involving neuroleptics, lithium, or antidepressants. Indeed, if you are reading this book to get help in stopping psychiatric drugs, it's possible that you've already discussed this intention with your doctor but were not able to "get through" to him or her.

An experienced therapist can be helpful precisely because he or she has observed withdrawal reactions and knows that most tend to subside within a few days or weeks. Hearing that you are experiencing a withdrawal reaction, rather than "losing your mind," may be enormously reassuring. In addition, the therapist may be able to identify a potentially severe withdrawal reaction.

A caring and empathic therapist can also work with you on the psychological and practical issues that are bound to arise as you reduce your drug intake, begin to experience your problems differently, and seek solutions for them other than drug use. One of the main challenges of drug withdrawal is not the withdrawal itself but, rather, how you live your life *after* withdrawal. A good therapist can provide you with the encouragement and advice you will probably need as you rebuild your life on more secure footing without drugs.

Having a doctor on your side may also ease the anxiety that friends or family members are feeling about your plans. And since mental health professionals are often connected to a network of colleagues who can give them advice about specific problems that arise, they are likely to have ready access to medical or psychological information and to be able to help you make sense of it.

Informing Your Doctor of Your Intentions

As a first step, you may wish to inform your doctor of your intentions concerning withdrawal. You can ask for help in developing a schedule of tapered doses and a list of likely physical and emotional reactions. If you are taking benzodiazepine tranquilizers (i.e., "antianxiety" drugs such as Ativan, Klonopin, Valium, or Xanax), your request should be easily met. Chances are that your doctor will actively support your desire to stop taking sedatives, sleeping pills, or tranquilizers. These drugs are less popular; in fact, they are viewed as decidedly dangerous by many informed physicians. Even doctors who believe that your anxiety is a chronic illness requiring lifelong medication may be sympathetic to your desire to stop taking benzodiazepines. Many physicians have seen too many patients addicted to benzodiazepines; they realize that these patients are suffering from "benzo blues"[5] rather than from their original anxiety or stress.

If your relationship with your doctor is not based on trust, you will probably find it awkward to broach the subject of drug withdrawal. If you are not used to being honest with your doctor or generally disclose only a limited amount of information about yourself for fear that your doctor will increase your dosage or add new drugs, then expressing your intention to come off drugs might strain the relationship.

If you are taking psychiatric drugs other than tranquilizers, and especially if you've had one or more psychiatric hospitalizations or a suicide attempt in the past, your doctor may be very hesitant to support you and might even become antagonistic. Try to remain calm, however. Displaying agitation over your doctor's negative reaction could be counterproductive in the planning of your withdrawal process. Instead, try to understand your doctor's perspective.

Your doctor is probably committed to believing that pills are indispensable, especially if he or she lacks knowledge about counseling and empathic listening. Chances are that most of his or her recent training or continuing education has focused on classifying patients in diagnostic categories so as to prescribe drugs for them. Moreover, if your doctor is a general practitioner, he or she probably attends annual conferences in which doctors are urged to recognize "hidden cases of depression" and "underlying anxiety" and to quickly prescribe drugs. Shifting their problem-solving abilities toward nondrug options can pose major challenges to doctors' expertise and professional identity. Many different types of mental health professionals offer psychological services, but only medical doctors prescribe drugs. If you have come to see a physician, there is a built-in expectation that you want and need—and will very likely get—a drug.[6]

Precisely because many doctors express a negative or antagonistic attitude about drug withdrawal—*especially withdrawal that the patient initiates, controls, and evaluates*—they are not likely to accept or welcome reports of positive results. Our clinical experience indicates that when patients successfully stop taking psychiatric drugs on their own, they usually do not tell their former doctors. Patients are even less likely to tell their doctors if the relationship was superficial or centered around the prescription. Frequently, patients are too angry or afraid to communicate with the doctor, or feel insufficiently cared for. Thus the doctors simply do not learn that withdrawal can be accomplished effectively and frequently results in substantial benefits.

However, if your doctor is open-minded and genuinely interested in your welfare, you should definitely discuss the issue with him or her. You will need to describe calmly the goals you are trying to reach and the nature of your withdrawal and rehabilitation program. If you detect resistance from your doctor, you might try to negotiate certain conditions under which the doctor will agree to supervise your withdrawal.

You might point out to your doctor that you have been "stable" for some time, and explain that, since drugs do not cure any problem but only help suppress some symptoms, you feel it's time for you to try to control them yourself. You could also remind your doctor that when things go well, it's your drug that gets praised; but when things go wrong, it's your "illness" that gets blamed. If you *insist* on discussing the issue, calmly but firmly, and if you share the plans you are making to ensure that the withdrawal will be successful, there's a good chance you will be able to earn your doctor's support.

Stay in Charge of the Withdrawal

This is not to say that you should let your doctor *control* the withdrawal. Even if you have been given every possible reason to believe that he or she understands the withdrawal process, it has to feel like a collaboration.

And since physicians often withdraw patients too abruptly from psychiatric drugs, above all else you must feel free to slow the process down.

Sometimes, as we discuss in Chapter 9, doctors cut the dose by half
from one day to the next, while still calling this a "gradual" withdrawal.
Such an abrupt reduction is an imprudent strategy in most cases. Because of ignorance, lack of experience in patient-centered withdrawal, or
even an unacknowledged wish to sabotage your effort, your doctor may
rush ahead and create unnecessary complications. The unfortunate outcome will then be used to prove to you that withdrawal was a bad decision to begin with.

Some of the steps discussed in later chapters of this book, such as
seeking replacement solutions and mastering techniques to cope with
various manifestations of your problem, will help you to show your doctor that you are motivated, responsible, and capable of withdrawing
successfully.

One woman who was prescribed an antidepressant and two tranquilizers for three years said to us: "I told my doctor that if she didn't help
me [to withdraw], I was simply going to do it alone. She didn't misjudge
my determination and turned out to be very cooperative. She looked up
a few references, gave me advice to go slow, and called me once a week.
She later told me that she learned a lot from me."

If attempts to enlist your doctor's cooperation or assistance fail, you
should be neither surprised nor discouraged. Remember that you, and
no one else, will do the actual "work" of coming off drugs. You will feel
the pain, and you will experience the rewards. You will have to deal with
the objections and fears of those around you who resist the idea that at
least some of your current problems are actually drug-induced. You must
therefore try to be in charge of the entire process from the very beginning, from the very first moment you decide for yourself that coming off
drugs is your goal.

The Best and the Worst to Expect from Your Doctor

At best, your doctor will support and even encourage your desire to live
a drug-free life; provide you with factual, medical information on withdrawal effects; recommend a sensible, practical tapering schedule; prescribe, if necessary, another drug that may be less unpleasant to
withdraw from than the one you're currently taking; remain available for

ongoing medical supervision during the withdrawal; refer you to a psychologically minded colleague for counseling during the withdrawal process; and, if you have been taking very high doses of tranquilizers for several years, possibly hospitalize you for detoxification.

At worst, your doctor will dismiss or ridicule your desire to withdraw from drugs, encourage your dependence on drugs, undermine your confidence in yourself, provide you with incorrect information, threaten you with dire consequences, and sabotage your efforts.

If your own doctor refuses to help you, consult another doctor or therapist. Bear in mind, however, that mental health professionals are likely to help you withdraw from drugs only within the context of a sustained relationship and only if they are able to entertain for themselves the idea that nondrug solutions are realistic, desirable options for a range of problems.

Pharmacists are sometimes quite willing to provide patients with withdrawal advice, especially from tranquilizers. As a whole, prodded from within and without, the profession of pharmacy changed over the last two decades, with pharmacists increasing their visibility and competence as counselors and as evaluators of physician-prescribed treatments.[7] Nowadays, because prescribing physicians so often fail to inform their patients appropriately, many people first learn about adverse effects at the drugstore, directly from the pharmacist, or from a printout or pamphlet about the drug received as they filled their prescription.

When pharmacists provide withdrawal advice to patients, they are not contradicting a doctor's medical prescription. When they answer patients' questions about the safest ways to withdraw, they are giving vital information needed by those patients to make intelligent decisions about their future well-being. Indeed, although pharmacists are often pressured to increase patients' compliance in taking drugs, some people find in them a much more sympathetic ear than they do in their doctors. In any case, because of their specific training in pharmacology, chances are that pharmacists are more knowledgeable and sensitive about withdrawal issues than most other health professionals.

Increasingly, mental health professionals without medical training are intimately involved in the prescription situation. Social workers, counselors, and psychologists are today often called upon to inform their clients about medication effects and to monitor these effects when clients are medicated, and to discuss clients' ideas about medications. They serve as educators, counselors, monitors, advocates, and researchers. These professionals sometimes pursue specialized training about psychotropic drugs. As well, many in the profession of psychology are actively lobbying state legislatures to grant psychologists some form of authority to prescribe psychotropic drugs—a move strongly opposed by organized psychiatry. While we are ambivalent about further increases in the number of individuals with the power to prescribe psychiatric drugs, we can also see some potential benefits. Over the past decade many non-medical mental health professionals have gained more specialized knowledge about psychiatric drugs. Hopefully, this may give clients more options about the type of advice they receive when trying to decide whether to take, continue taking, or stop taking medications. But as of now, most professionals exercise the power to prescribe with dangerous abandon.

Set Up a Support Network

More than a doctor or a therapist, your network of friends and trusted acquaintances could become your most valuable resource during the entire withdrawal process. Coming off drugs is an undertaking best done with support from others, especially if you have been taking drugs for several years and have dulled or lost some of your other coping responses.

Although family members and friends can provide invaluable help, we have found that peer counselors or members of a self-help group often offer the best support. Many self-help groups, including Alcoholics Anonymous (AA), help their members to withdraw from psychoactive substances. Although we do not personally know of any "Twelve Steps" support programs designed specifically for users of psychiatric drugs, we believe that such groups might be helpful. However, beware of self-help groups in which the principal objective is to get members to accept the idea that their emotional problem is a disease, that they should consult a medical doctor for it, and that drugs are the best remedy. When these groups discuss medication issues and adverse effects, the aim is to decrease members' resistance to taking drugs.

Less structured self-help groups, such as those found in peer-run mental health centers, are likely to put you in touch with people who have successfully given up psychiatric drugs and who remain available to discuss their experience and give advice. Whether these people have freed themselves wholly or partially from drugs, they may be extremely helpful to you.

People who have been through the process of getting off psychoactive drugs will usually be nonjudgmental and accepting of your plight. They will quickly understand why you want to stop taking drugs. They will not need to be convinced that it's a sensible alternative to your treatment. Possibly, they will have a more positive outlook about your chances than other people will. Even if their motives and experiences were different from yours, talking with them might show you that coming off psychiatric drugs can be accomplished without major drawbacks, while leaving you a stronger person.

How a Friend Can Help

Discussing your wishes, goals, and apprehensions informally with empathic nonjudgmental people—no matter how novice in counseling or lacking in professional credentials they are—can be very beneficial. One way that resource persons can help you is to agree to stay in touch with you during the duration of your withdrawal. But this is not to say that they have to be saddled with the responsibility of "seeing you through" the withdrawal. After all, *you* must take responsibility for your decisions. And in any case, no matter how well-meaning and well-intentioned other people are, they may break their promises. So, rather than becoming disappointed in specific individuals and feeling discouraged, seek out—and make use of—as much social support as you can.

Arrange for your resource persons to talk to you on the telephone on a regular basis—once a day or a few times a week—whether you're feeling fine or not. Perhaps they could also agree to meet you on occasion to offer reassurance and advice, or simply to lend an ear. If they've been through drug withdrawal themselves, they will know that, if you're not feeling well, there is a valid reason. They will know that painful emotions and bodily sensations are to be expected. They will know that people undergoing this potentially difficult experience often lose perspective, despairing over minor drawbacks or exaggerating small victories. They will know that a few reassuring words can do wonders at critical times. They will be able to see if you need additional help, especially if your withdrawal reaction is more serious than you realize. They will also help you avoid making rash or unwise decisions about your life.

Ideally, you should be helped to come off psychiatric drugs within the context of a safe, trusting relationship with an experienced, informed helper. One principle often applied in drug addiction treatment centers is to establish a trusting relationship with an individual who has been through the same process and can provide reassurance, as well as anticipate some of the difficulties involved.

In sum, the process of coming off psychiatric drugs necessitates that you build a social support network. Seeking alliances with like-minded, supportive individuals will strengthen not only your resolve but, quite likely, your abilities in other areas as well. You will feel the beneficial effects of learning to seek support from others beyond the issue of drug withdrawal.

Countless people have been too stigmatized, isolated, scared, or confused to enlist this kind of support. Forced to rely on their own resources, they have nevertheless successfully managed to stop taking psychiatric drugs. However, in the absence of medical supervision, many of these people have incurred increased risks of experiencing unpleasant and even dangerous withdrawal reactions.

Support Networks on the Internet

The degree to which self-help support resources have taken hold in the "online world" attests to their usefulness to many people around the world. No discussion about setting up a support network to handle difficult situations would be complete without reference to the resources available on the Internet.

In his guide to online mental health resources, psychologist and Internet pioneer John Grohol writes: "It is easy to forget that the online world offers not only the ability to 'browse' but also to take part in an interactive, supportive community."[8] Indeed, via the Internet, tens of thousands if not millions of people discuss issues of interest and try to support each other through difficult times.

The Internet has been particularly useful in establishing connections between current and former psychiatric patients. As Grohol points out, online support is indispensable to people who live in remote or rural areas. It is also especially useful to people who have difficulty with face-to-face interpersonal relationships. Still others may find that their emotional problems are less stigmatized in the online world. Above all, the Internet offers an immediate way to "talk" with people throughout the country, and around the world, who are likely to have experienced troubles very similar to your own.

Thousands of self-help discussion groups and forums flourish on the Internet. People discuss their personal difficulties, ranging from alcoholism to weight loss, and offer advice to others. In some groups, people discuss withdrawing from psychiatric drugs.

All that is required for you to begin such a discussion is to enter a forum by getting a password and posting a message. In all likelihood, you will receive several empathic and encouraging replies within a couple of days. If you are lucky, you'll receive some well-informed replies as well. Keep in mind, of course, that most participants will be expressing their personal views and opinions, which are much like those expressed in any other context. In fact, all online comments should be taken cautiously because participants will usually remain anonymous and you will lack the feedback that face-to-face or even telephone conversation provides.

The myriad Web sites devoted to mental health issues and psychiatric drugs require caution. Obviously, the quality of drug-related information on the Web varies greatly. Some of the most commonly used and highly respected sites such as WebMD are sponsored by drug companies. When it comes to the topic of drug withdrawal, we have found the following characteristics to be associated with better-quality information on the Web: (1) the owner or author of the site is clearly identified, (2) the site is easily readable, (3) exact references to the literature are provided, as well as acknowledgments that most knowledge on withdrawal rests on case reports and on first-person accounts, and that most recommendations about specific tapering strategies are the opinions of experts, (4) the site does not sell or endorse "herbal," "nutritional" or other products claimed to hasten withdrawal or to greatly reduce withdrawal effects (without inducing psychotropic effects or creating the potential for future withdrawal difficulties), and (5) the site is not sponsored by drug companies, medical centers, or other groups highly vested in the pharmaceutical and medical industry.

An ongoing dialogue often develops between two or more individuals on the Internet. The following are just a few of the hundreds of messages about antidepressant withdrawal posted during the spring of 1998 on the Health for Life Center message board (www.lexmall.com). They are unedited (except for spelling) and, for the most part, concern withdrawal from the antidepressant Zoloft.

This is what I have been looking for, I feel a lot better now that I have read that other people have the same type of withdrawal that I am having. I can almost cry because like you I was told no problems, just quit . . . yeah, right!! I thought that I had something worse than what this may be. Thanks for having this here. I was on 100 mg of Zoloft for 6 months, and it helped. However I quit 2 weeks ago and this withdrawal is deadly. I have a steady headache, I feel like I am high but the mind is still here, my body tingles, I get twitches, I am exhausted most of the time, I can't stand this anymore. I am dizzy, I have stomach cramps, I am sick. My appetite, well for a few days I was hungry constantly, couldn't stop eating, and now though, I am still hungry but I can't eat. I wonder when it is going to stop, hopefully soon!! [Posted by Tanya on March 26]

Yes . . . me too. However, I think I have taken a safer approach than that recommended by your doctors. I have come down gradually . . . from 200 mgs to 125, to 100, to 75, to 50, to 33.3, to 25, and now to 0. The entire process has taken me about 3 months. When I first used it, I built gradually up to the 200. I experienced TOTAL sexual dysfunction, and knew that I wanted out altogether . . . if I had wanted castration I would've asked! The final part the withdrawal has been the most difficult . . . 25 to 0 . . . and I wonder if I should've gone to 10 or 15 first. But now that I am here, I am going for broke. I have dizziness and mood swings for the last couple days, but they do not seem nearly as severe as those I read about above. I do not believe there is any other way to reduce the withdrawal symptoms. . . . Feel free to "e" me about any of this. Take care and hang in there! [Posted by Ed on April 5]

I really want to stop taking Zoloft, but I'm so scared. Withdrawal has always caused me to experience a deeper depression. I want to stop but don't know how. Anybody got any ideas? [Posted by Kristin on April 12]

I've been withdrawing from 100mg/day Zoloft for three weeks now. The vertigo is worse, not better. I can practically fall down just by turning my head. I'm probably not safe behind the wheel of a car. I have constant headaches, can't think clearly, can't focus my eyes, and a myriad of other symptoms. I'm tired/sleepy, grouchy, emotionally labile. My appetite is history. I get nothing done at work or at home. My temper is so short it's practically nonexistent.

When my doctor and I decided I'd try life without Zoloft again, I asked about withdrawal symptoms and he said, "No problem—just quit taking it." I don't want to take drugs every day. But to avoid feeling like this, I might revise my feelings on the subject! When will this end? Ever? [Posted by Kate on April 13]

I was prescribed Zoloft only 2 months ago (50mg). After the first bottle ran out, I couldn't afford to get another until 2 weeks later. What I experienced in those 2 weeks was horrible! I didn't know what was wrong with me. Now, from reading these e-mails, I know that I was experiencing Zoloft withdrawal. Had I only known! Why didn't the doctor tell me about this? Now I'm afraid I'm going to feel worse trying to kick the drug. In that 2-week period, I started feeling dizzy and sick to my stomach. The dizziness was so bad at one point when I was driving that I had to pull over and park the car for a few minutes. I thought I had the flu. Then my fingers, hands, and part of my arm started to tingle. The dizziness lasted for about 7 days. The last 4 of the 7, I had started taking the Zoloft again. I've been back on the Zoloft now for 6 days. No more dizziness and the tingles are slowly disappearing. They were almost non-existent today. I told the doctor about these symptoms. He told me I probably have a virus. He also told me to keep track of the tingling and other symptoms. He said it could be the early warning signs of a disease. Apparently, doctors are uninformed and my doctor very casually prescribed it to me. How am I ever going to get off this drug? [Posted by Joyce on April 16]

These messages vividly illustrate, in ordinary language, the great variety and potential severity of withdrawal reactions from antidepressant drugs such as Zoloft. They also express the writers' judgments that their doctors were uninformed, prescribed and withdrew drugs too easily, and misinformed them about the withdrawal process. As we have noted and will further discuss, although problems with withdrawal from antidepressants are neither rare nor mild, they have received scant attention until very recently.

Of particular interest, however, are the expressions of relief from some of the writers upon discovering that their discomfort is drug-induced and that they are not alone. Clearly, they received comfort and encouragement from having their experience validated by others, even complete strangers.

Know What Coming Off
Psychiatric Drugs Might Entail

To succeed in your withdrawal, you should have a good idea of the "journey" ahead of you and the events and situations you are likely to encounter. You should anticipate possible problems and understand, in advance, what concrete steps should be taken to reduce these problems.

The good news is that energy, vigor, and memory often return when people stop taking psychiatric drugs. Indeed, you may well discover that you are able to think and focus more clearly, that you are able to feel a wider range of emotions, and that you are more sensitive to cues from your social and physical surroundings.

Anticipate Withdrawal Reactions

You may recall that when you first started taking psychiatric drugs, your body reacted in various ways. For instance, you may have felt more sleepy, sweated more, had bouts of dizziness or nausea, noticed a tremor in your arms or legs, lost your appetite, or experienced various sexual dysfunctions. Possibly one or two of these reactions were somewhat severe, put you out of commission for a few days, and then quickly disappeared as your body became tolerant to the drug or as the dosage was altered.

You may also have reacted emotionally to these changes. Perhaps you felt relieved that the drug was actually having an effect and thus began to feel better about some of the difficulties in your life. Or maybe you were anxious or depressed about having to put up with the physical reactions involved, worried about taking the drug for a long time, or felt apathetic about the prospect of dealing with those people around you who seem to have contributed to your personal difficulties.

Similarly, letting go of a drug is bound to create physical and psychological reactions. Your body will begin to adjust to the absence of the substance. At the same time, the knowledge that you are giving up a drug and the physical changes you are undergoing will stir up various emotions and thoughts. These physical and psychological reactions may be quite subtle or quite obvious, or both. They will often resemble the problems that led to your taking drugs in the first place.

It will help greatly to find out what you can about the withdrawal symptoms associated with the drug you're taking. In Chapter 9, we review this information in detail.

Understand What Influences the Ease of Withdrawal

The severity of your withdrawal reactions will depend on the type of drug you're taking. For example, drugs with a shorter half-life (the amount of time it takes for the body to eliminate half of the drug) tend to produce more intense withdrawal symptoms, even during gradual withdrawal.

Their withdrawal effects are also usually felt sooner after the last dose than those of drugs with longer half-lives. Information on the half-lives of drugs is almost always included in the drugs' official labels published in the *Physicians' Desk Reference*.[9]

The intensity of your withdrawal will also depend on how long you have been taking the drug and how much you were taking on a daily basis. In general, it's more difficult to withdraw from drugs taken at high doses and for several months or years.

The withdrawal process will also be influenced by your general state of health. Advancing age and chronic medical conditions, which render people more vulnerable to adverse drug effects, may also increase the difficulty of withdrawal. Sometimes, however, younger patients report more difficulties than older ones.

In addition, various subjective factors will undoubtedly play a role. Your attitude toward withdrawal is particularly significant. As we discuss below, the psychological fear of withdrawal, unless squarely faced, may represent a powerful obstacle. Your attitude toward physical discomfort is also important. For example, the urge to relieve even minor discomforts with pills may limit your willingness to put up with withdrawal-induced discomforts. Your knowledge of withdrawal reactions will also influence the way in which you deal with these reactions. Knowing in advance that you might experience a temporary withdrawal symptom will help to reassure you that the process is predictable. Finally, the support and encouragement you receive can be decisive. One study has shown that even a single encouraging letter from a doctor may help patients to significantly reduce their drug intake, even in cases involving drugs that have been taken for years and are widely considered addictive.[10]

Look Out for the Return of Your Original Problems

Coming off drugs is often accompanied by the return of some of the original distressing feelings and behaviors that led you to take drugs in the first place. In the psychiatric literature, this phenomenon is usually referred to as a "relapse." Once a drug's effects begin to wear off, your original problems may begin to resurface if their psychological or situational roots have been neglected. Also recall our discussion (in Chapter 1) of how difficult it may be to distinguish between a recurrence of your original problems and an actual withdrawal reaction.

The return of your original problems represents a crucial test of your determination and abilities, as you will be challenged to accept and deal with these emotions and behaviors through constructive means other than drugs.

Anticipate the Possibility of a Long Withdrawal Period

Just as withdrawal symptoms vary, so does the length of time that those symptoms last. Depending on the drug you're taking, and on other factors such as your state of health, your withdrawal process may last several weeks, even months. Renewed energy and vigor, as well as subtle, unpleasant effects, may be experienced over this period. In our clinical experience, withdrawl reactions to many drugs, including the SSRI antidepressants like Paxil and the tranquilizers like Xanax, can be quite protracted, lasting a year or more, sometimes leaving permanent adverse effects.

Unless a medication has been taken for only a few days or weeks, abrupt withdrawal is never advisable. As a general rule, it may require one month of withdrawal for every year of exposure to a drug. For example, a person who has taken antidepressants for two years may require at least a two-month gradual taper. However, there are no strict guidelines and, as emphasized in the next chapter, each individual needs to find a comfortable pace for tapering a drug. The next chapter also examines the withdrawal process in more detail with specific recommendations regarding safety.

Be Prepared to Change Your Routines

If you have been taking drugs for a long time, your lifestyle may become profoundly disrupted as you withdraw. For a few weeks, you might have difficulty sticking to your regular routines. At times, simply knowing that you're trying something different may preoccupy your thoughts to an unusual degree and leave you unable to carry out your regular duties as effectively as before.

Expect Reawakened Feelings

Coming off drugs—especially strong depressants such as tranquilizers, neuroleptics, or lithium—often involves a potentially dramatic reawakening of the senses. This reawakening can lead to feelings of panic in people who do not realize the extent to which their hearing, touch, taste, or sensations of cold and heat can become unexpectedly acute after having been desensitized or anesthetized for long periods.

Handling Disrupted Sleep

Withdrawal from several psychiatric drugs—especially central nervous system (CNS) depressants such as tranquilizers, many antidepressants, lithium, and antipsychotics—often provokes bouts of severe insomnia. And withdrawal from stimulants, and from the more stimulating antidepressants such as Prozac-like drugs, can induce "crashing" with sleepiness and fatigue. Infrequently, the insomnia or excessive sleepiness may last several weeks.

Sleep deprivation can be frightening and emotionally disrupting. A few nights of disrupted sleep may be sufficient to make you lose your resolve. It is important that you manage to sleep between five and eight hours every day, with naps during the day if needed. The mental and physical efforts involved in drug withdrawal require that you rest and renew your energy every day.

If you have a tendency to become high or euphoric ("manic"), the inability to sleep may signal that you are on the verge of a more serious emotional crisis. In this case, you may need to temporarily resume a higher dose of the drug you are taking or to seek a consultation. Also, persistent loss of sleep can make you impatient, irritable, and quick to anger. It can bring out almost any problem that you have had difficulty controlling. In general, however, a temporary period of sleeping difficulties will not be harmful over the long term.

If you find yourself overly sleepy during withdrawal, get lots of rest and try to be cautious in your physical activities. Moderate, safe exercise may be helpful. Don't resort to excessive caffeine or stimulants to stay awake. Your brain needs a break from drugs. The fatigue and somnolence should subside with the gradual elimination of the drug from your body and your brain's return to normal functioning.

Dealing with Strong Reactions from Friends and Family

Those around you may fear that any unusual feelings or withdrawal symptoms are a sign that you are deteriorating or "relapsing" without your medications and need to restart them immediately. They may even pressure each other to "do something" about what's happening to you.

Often, relatives are worried about the harmful effects of drugs on their loved ones. Many of the requests for help and information we receive about drug withdrawal come from concerned family members. However, because they are also bombarded with prodrug propaganda and have so little access to nondrug options, your relatives may believe that they should pressure you to stay on drugs. Anticipate that their choices will sometimes be more restrained than yours.

If you are living with family members, or remain dependent on or closely involved with them, they will naturally have serious concerns about your withdrawal from psychiatric drugs. The problems that led to your taking the drugs may have caused them a great deal of stress and worry, giving them good reason to fear that you will lose control of your emotions or behavior. If you want their encouragement, which depends in part on allaying their fears, you need to be honest about the past consequences of your behavior.

Conflicts embedded within the family itself are often unfairly blamed entirely on the person who has received a psychiatric diagnosis and is taking drugs. Thus, when you decide not to accept your previous role as a "psychiatric patient," others in the family may feel threatened. Perhaps they have become accustomed to focusing on you instead of on their own problems, or on the ways in which they have contributed to their conflicts with you. Anything you do to upset that balance might be strongly resisted by your family. Your relatives may be especially resistant if your withdrawal seems haphazard, careless, or unplanned. In sum, family members can help or hinder your withdrawal, but either way they are bound to be quite concerned.

There is no easy recipe for turning your relatives into allies during this phase. However, sharing your detailed plans about withdrawal, and about life after withdrawal, could help. Making clear your determination to act responsibly will be important to your relatives—and to you. You should also openly acknowledge the difficulties your past behavior may have caused them as well as yourself. Asking for their support in potentially difficult times will be reassuring to them and valuable to you.

Ultimately, your family's fears or apprehensions will be best allayed by seeing you function well without psychiatric drugs.

Don't Overreact to Anger and Guilt

As you withdraw from drugs, you may become angry about the drug treatment that you've received, especially if you were misled or forced to take drugs. The drug effects may have estranged you from some of your most powerful emotions, including your sense of outrage, injustice, and self-preservation. Some of these emotions may resurface when you withdraw. It is very important to keep your anger under control during withdrawal.

Be Flexible About Withdrawal

You and you alone should decide what you can bear while undergoing withdrawal. We believe that there are no hard and fast schedules. You should not withdraw at a faster pace than you desire or feel comfortable about.

Some clinicians may be skeptical about whether tiny doses of a psychiatric medication can actually help to manage or control withdrawal reactions. Despite our own initial skepticism, we have seen patients effectively use tiny doses in the last few weeks and even months of withdrawal. A few individuals have taken as little as one-sixteenth of the smallest available pill over several weeks as a means of controlling their last remaining withdrawal symptoms from tranquilizers, antidepressants, and antipsychotics. For example, tiny doses have managed the nausea associated with Zyprexa withdrawal (see Chapter 9). For some people, a sensitization to drugs[11] toward the last stage of withdrawal appears to explain the impact of minuscule doses. Our experience with these people confirms the importance for each individual to withdraw at his or her own pace.

You and you alone must choose how you will stick to your withdrawal schedule when stressful and anxiety-provoking situations arise. You must decide whether or not to take pills or to increase doses on "hard" or difficult days. You must determine when you are able to use these situations to practice your skills at living without resort to drugs. The important thing is not to push yourself to any extreme in coming off drugs.

For example, when unexpectedly severe reactions are produced by withdrawal, you could reinstitute your previous dose and then proceed with a more gradual taper (see Chapter 8). If this process is well-planned, you are not likely to become overly discouraged. On the contrary, you will be practicing an appropriate, measured response to your body's signals.

Set Up an Action Plan

A detailed action plan increases your chances of success. Here are some suggestions:

1. Plan how you will discuss the topic of withdrawal with your professional helpers, what you think you need from them, and what you intend to do if you cannot gain their cooperation.
2. Plan how you will discuss the topic with your friends or family and how you will deal with any potential resistance.

3. Make sure to stay in touch with trusted friends or relatives who can provide you with feedback on how you're doing throughout the withdrawal process.
4. Write down a detailed withdrawal or taper schedule that specifies daily doses of your drug or drugs, the number of weeks you plan to undergo this process, and the expected end of withdrawal (again, see Chapter 8).
5. Begin your withdrawal in as secure an environment as possible.
6. Improve several of your specific habits related to diet and exercise, so as to strengthen your physical capacity to deal with withdrawal and life after withdrawal.
7. Prepare to accommodate the disruptions of routine that drug withdrawals sometimes provoke, perhaps by temporarily suspending a few stressful activities or preoccupations.
8. Develop alternative solutions to drug use. Before starting the withdrawal process, practice relaxation and stress reduction techniques that will decrease the symptoms of anxiety or agitation that you are bound to experience to some degree or other.[12]

Facing the Fear of Withdrawal

Many individuals continue to take drugs not because they find them genuinely helpful but because they are afraid to stop taking them. Our interviews with patients frequently reveal that drugs do not keep their distress under good control. Many patients actually become insensitive to or hopeless about their continued suffering.

You may become disconcerted if, immediately after you start the tapering process, you feel more anxious and nervous than before. The mere knowledge that you are stopping taking drugs, or have reduced your drug intake, can cause anxiety.[13] You may feel compelled to resume taking drugs even before you experience actual drug-induced withdrawal effects.

The fear of withdrawal often goes beyond the fear of experiencing unpleasant physical sensations. Drug withdrawal presents a potentially frightening challenge to live your life differently without a guarantee that you'll be up to the task. This natural, almost inevitable fear may be worsened by years of being told that you have an incurable disease caused by biochemical imbalances that must be corrected with modern medical panaceas.[14]

Withdrawal also requires that you face the reappearance of familiar, painful emotions from the past—emotions that are best understood as signals for you to deal with the consequences of previous conflicts, abuses, or traumas. The process of withdrawal may confront you with the realization of how much your life has been driven by painful emotions—such as guilt, shame, and anxiety—rather than by well-chosen principles and a love of other people and life.

In sum, deciding to come off psychiatric drugs "forces" you to examine your behavior and lifestyle, your morals and values, your personal history. It compels you to go beyond the veneer of the drug-for-a-disease argument. It requires that you examine the role that drugs have played in suppressing your life and subduing your emotions. These are not the sorts of issues that you might readily reflect upon, but *having* to think about them, and perhaps discussing them with a sympathetic counselor, can become a major unexpected benefit of withdrawal. The self-aware and passionate life is the one most worth living; withdrawing from drugs can empower you to live that richer, more fulfilling life.

— 8 —

How to Stop Taking Psychiatric Drugs

You may feel in a rush to stop taking psychiatric drugs. Perhaps you are experiencing distressing side effects or feel "fed up" with being sluggish and emotionally numb. Beware! It's not a good idea to abruptly stop taking drugs without first making sure that there's no danger involved in doing so. In our opinion, it is almost always better to err in the direction of going too slowly rather than too quickly. Sometimes, the development of a severe adverse reaction may require an immediate withdrawal; but if you are having a serious drug reaction, you should seek help from an experienced clinician.

Once you have begun to withdraw from psychiatric drugs, don't let anyone—not even your doctor—rush you. Especially if there's a chance that you are going too fast, pay careful attention to how you feel physically and emotionally. At the same time, however, you should take into account the warnings of professionals, family members, or friends who believe that withdrawal is causing you more problems than you realize. You may not be the best judge of your emotional condition as you come off drugs, so you should take into consideration the concerns of people you trust.

Gradual Withdrawal Is Its Own Protection

When people take psychiatric drugs, their decision-making faculties may function less effectively. Their feelings are numbed. At these times, if their thinking were expressed in words, it would likely communicate indecision, apathy, or confusion. Or they may experience different feelings in rapid succession, almost as if they were out of control. Because people generally want to think more clearly, to "feel fully" again, and to be more in control of themselves, they are motivated to stop taking psychiatric drugs.

Coming off drugs gradually helps to "contain" the emotional and intellectual roller coaster that sometimes accompanies withdrawal. Indeed, a slow, gradual tapering imposes a discipline upon the withdrawal process. Because of the neglect of the topic of withdrawal, there still are no clearly validated tapering procedures. Almost every clinician writing on the topic today, however, as well as newer recommendations that drug manufacturers are beginning to insert on official drug labels, state that gradual discontinuation is the preferred route. In the absence of a trusted friend or ally to provide feedback on your progress, in the absence of a support network, gradual withdrawal is likely to be the wisest strategy—especially if you are unsure as to how quickly you should proceed. Even if a medical doctor or other health professional is assisting you or monitoring your withdrawal, a gradual taper is usually the safest strategy.

Why Gradual Withdrawal Is Better Than Sudden Withdrawal

The minute a psychiatric drug enters your bloodstream, your brain activates mechanisms to compensate for the drug's impact.[1] These compensatory mechanisms become entrenched after operating continuously in response to the drug. If the drug is rapidly removed, they do not suddenly disappear. On the contrary, they have free rein for some time. Typically, these compensatory mechanisms cause physical, cognitive, and emotional disturbances—which are collectively referred to as the withdrawal syndrome.

The simplest way to reduce the intensity of withdrawal reactions is to taper doses gradually, in small increments. This way, you are giving your brain appropriate "time" and "space" to regain normal functioning. Unless it is clearly established that you are suffering an acute, dangerous drug-induced toxic reaction, you should proceed with a slow, gradual withdrawal. The longer the withdrawal period, the more chances you have to minimize the intensity of the expected withdrawal reactions.

Interestingly, there is some evidence that "gradual discontinuation tends to shorten the course of any withdrawal syndrome."[2] In other words, the actual duration of all expected symptoms from drug withdrawal is likely to be shorter if you withdraw slowly than if you withdraw abruptly. There is also, however, evidence, mostly from personal accounts posted on the Internet by users of antidepressants, that gradual withdrawal sometimes does not lessen the distress of withdrawal reactions. David Taylor, chief pharmacist of Maudsley Hospital in London, described his own SSRI antidepressant withdrawal, stating: "For six weeks or so, I suffered symptoms which were at best disturbing and at worst torturous. This was despite following a cautious, decremental withdrawal schedule."[3] However, slow withdrawal does tend to reduce the risk of severe physical reactions such as seizures or dangerous blood pressure fluctuations. One study surveyed 66 patients who recently discontinued an SSRI antidepressant. One fifth of these people abruptly discontinued the drug, and they experienced exactly twice as many withdrawal symptoms as those who tapered gradually.[4]

In one early study of withdrawal from tricyclic antidepressants, 62 percent of those who withdrew in less than two weeks experienced withdrawal reactions, compared to only 17 percent of those who withdrew over a longer period.[5] Because unpleasant withdrawal reactions are one of the main reasons you might be tempted to abort your withdrawal, a gradual taper increases your chances of succeeding and remaining drug-free.

In addition, it appears that people who gradually reduce their drug intake find a renewed vigor and energy that they now can learn to reinvest. In contrast to a sudden, unplanned cessation, a gradual withdrawal allows them to find constructive ways to use this energy, to appreciate the new confidence in their abilities that they will develop, and to consolidate the new emotional and behavioral patterns that will be learned in the process.

One published account describes the case of a woman who wanted to stop Paxil after taking 20 mg daily for six months. Her doctor abruptly cut this dose in half, to 10 mg daily, and gave her the new dose for one month. Then, during the following two weeks, he gave her 10 mg every other day. On alternate, nondrug days, the woman experienced severe headaches, severe nausea, dizziness and vertigo, dry mouth, and lethargy. The dose was reduced to 5 mg daily but, convinced that this only prolonged her agony, she stopped abruptly. She is reported to have experienced two weeks of various withdrawal symptoms and then to have fully recovered.[6]

A more gradual taper, rather than an abrupt 50 percent reduction at the start, might have reduced the severity of this woman's overall withdrawal reactions. Also, as we discuss ahead, taking a drug every other day during withdrawal should be done only toward the very end of the taper. Granted, many users of psychiatric drugs do cease them suddenly, without experiencing any significant withdrawal pains. Our experience, however, suggests to us that abrupt withdrawal is chosen by people who are not properly informed or supervised, who cannot tolerate their drug-induced dysfunctions any longer, or who act impulsively because they perceive that no one is listening to them or understanding their suffering.

Remove Drugs One at a Time

Many people, perhaps yourself among them, take several psychiatric drugs simultaneously. Today, polypharmacy—the practice of prescribing more than one or two drugs to the same patient at the same time—is quite common and encouraged, especially by physicians presenting in drug company–sponsored symposia. Frequently patients receive an antidepressant and a tranquilizer, a stimulant and a tranquilizer, or an antipsychotic and an anticonvulsant. It is no longer unusual to find children and adults simultaneously prescribed at least one drug from every single major drug class discussed in this book. Such cocktails, if combined with a physician's failure to recognize withdrawal reactions and to monitor patients carefully, leave patients vulnerable to experiencing severe distress. Such cocktails vastly increase the toxicity of each drug and produce dangerous, unpredictable adverse reactions and complicated withdrawal reactions. Patients taking multiple drugs often endure a chronic state of mental confusion, dulled and unstable emotions, and cognitive problems, including memory deficits.

You can withdraw from several drugs simultaneously, but this is a risky strategy. It should be reserved for cases of acute, serious toxicity. In addition, since drugs taken together (such as neuroleptics and antiparkinsonians) often have some similar effects, withdrawing them together can make withdrawal reactions worse. Also, because some drugs suppress or increase blood levels of other drugs, your health care professional should be well informed before making recommendations concerning simultaneous decrements for more than one drug. If you intend to withdraw simultaneously from two or more drugs, you should do so under the active supervision of an experienced physician or pharmacist.

When you take two drugs, your brain tries to compensate not only for the effects of each one separately but also for the effects of their interaction. The physical picture gets even more complicated with each additional drug. The increasing complexity goes far beyond our actual understanding, creating unknown and unpredictable risks during both drug use and withdrawal. In cases of multidrug use, withdrawal is like trying to unravel a thick knot composed of many different strings—without cutting or damaging any of the strings. In this analogous situation, you would have to proceed quite carefully indeed, gradually disentangling one string and continually adjusting the others in response to the ongoing progress.

It is usually best to reduce one drug while continuing to take the others. The process begins anew once you've eliminated the first drug completely and have gotten used to doing without it.

Which Drug Should Be Stopped First?

If you want to get off more than one drug, there are some considerations in deciding which drug to stop first. Let's say you're taking drug "A" to counteract the side effects of drug "B"; in this case, you should probably start withdrawal with drug "B." For example, if you're taking a sleeping pill for insomnia caused by Prozac or Ritalin, you may want to delay withdrawal from the sleeping pill until you have begun to reduce the Prozac or Ritalin. Similarly, if you're taking Cogentin or Artane or some other drug to suppress movement disorders caused by neuroleptics, you should probably first reduce your neuroleptic before you attempt to withdraw from the Cogentin or Artane.

There are no hard and fast rules about which doses to reduce first. In general, however, you should consider initially reducing the dose that's causing the most side effects, such as the afternoon dose that makes you too sleepy or the evening dose that over-stimulates you and causes insomnia. Conversely, you may want to wait until last to reduce or stop the dose that seems to be helping you the most, such as the evening dose of a tranquilizer if you have insomnia. Many people are concerned about difficulty sleeping if they stop the evening dose of a tranquilizer that they are taking several times a day and in that case, they would be wise to begin reducing a dose that is given earlier in the day.

Sometimes there will be other obvious reasons to choose the morning or evening dose as the first one to reduce. When taking tranquilizers such as Xanax or Klonopin, for example, many people find that they awaken in the morning in a state of anxiety or agitation due to withdrawal from the previous dose. Therefore, they may feel more comfortable beginning with a reduction of the evening dose. Others may find that they become excessively sleepy in the afternoon. They might want to begin reducing that dose.

Special Considerations During Withdrawal

Nowadays patients are often treated with multiple drugs at once. In the extreme they may receive one or more from each of the main categories: stimulants, antidepressants, tranquilizers and sleeping pills, mood stabilizers, and antipsychotic agents. If possible, try to address the antipsychotic agents first because they pose severe risks including tardive dyskinesia and potentially lethal neuroleptic malignant syndrome, diabetes, and pancreatitis. However, if the antipsychotic exposure has lasted for several years, it may take many months to withdraw, and therefore it becomes more practical to start with another drug that's easier to stop. But keep in mind that your risk of getting tardive dyskinesia from antipsychotic drugs is high and that the risk increases over time, so it's a good idea to withdraw from these drugs as soon as possible. Also keep in mind that you will probably need a strong support system when withdrawing from antipsychotic drugs.

Because benzodiazepine tranquilizers often provoke unpleasant, lengthy, and potentially dangerous withdrawal reactions, some people choose to withdraw from their use last, after they've experienced withdrawal from other drugs, strengthened their resolve, and gained confidence.

If dangerous drug interactions are present, such as two or more drugs that stimulate serotonin, it may be important to withdraw from one of them at the onset. And of course, if the individual is already suffering from a potentially severe adverse reaction such as abnormal movements caused by an antipsychotic drug or over-stimulation and other mental abnormalities caused by a stimulant or antidepressant, it is necessary to consider as rapid withdrawal as safe and feasible.

In general, withdrawing from multiple psychiatric drugs requires supervision by an especially experienced clinician.

How Fast Should You Withdraw?

How rapidly to stop medication is one of the most critical and difficult questions to address and the process must be tailored to individual needs. In complicated cases, the patient and the health professional should anticipate spending sufficient time to share their views and to outline a general plan. They must also be prepared to re-evaluate the plan on a regular basis. Under no circumstance should the bar be set too high, so that the individual fails and becomes demoralized during the withdrawal.

It is important to withdraw gradually enough to avoid potentially life-threatening physical withdrawal reactions such as seizures and blood pressure spike. If you take one month to gradually withdraw from any psychoactive drug, you will probably avoid the most severe physical withdrawal reactions, such as seizures coming off benzodiazepines or dangerous spikes in blood pressure coming off clonidine (Catapres). In the case of large, prolonged doses of tranquilizers, more than one month should usually be required. By contrast, in the case of Catapres the withdrawal may be limited to a one-week period when withdrawing from routine doses.

In carrying out a one-month taper, the simplest procedure is to reduce the dose by one-quarter (25 percent) every week. However, the plan must not be rigid. At the end of a week, if withdrawal symptoms remain uncomfortable, then the dose can be slightly increased again, or the time on the dose can be extended as needed. A planned one-month taper may end up taking several months.

If an individual has been taking a drug for more than a year, it would not be unusual to plan a month of withdrawal for every year that the drug has been taken. By this method, an individual who has been exposed to antidepressants or tranquilizers for five years could require at least five months to withdraw. If the individual has been taking both kinds of drugs for five years, it may require two separate five-month withdrawals to stop both drugs; but hopefully the process may be shorter.

If a long withdrawal is planned, it may be useful to begin with a reduction nearer to 10 percent for the first dose reduction. It's a matter of testing the waters. If this small reduction turns out to be relatively painless, then a larger dose reduction, such as 25 percent, could be attempted the next time. If, however, even a small reduction is difficult, then don't push any harder. The whole point is to make sure that the taper does not go too fast and remains within the individual's comfort zone.

Unfortunately, there is no way to determine in advance how gradually you need to taper, or how long you need to take, in order to avoid the array of potentially distressing emotional and neurological reactions, such as headaches, irritability, fatigue, and mood swings while withdrawing from SSRI antidepressants; or anxiety, insomnia, emotional instability, and muscles aches while tapering benzodiazepine tranquilizers.

Some people experience only mild reactions throughout their taper and complete it in a few weeks. Others will experience distressing reactions that will force them to proceed much more slowly, in excess of several months, as their body takes time to adjust to each reduction before beginning their next dose reduction.[7] Usually you will know within the first few weeks if the withdrawal is going well at your current pace.

If you have been taking the medications for a long time or if you are worried about withdrawal for any reason, you can test your withdrawal reaction sensitivity by starting with a relatively small and convenient dose reduction. For example, if you're taking four pills a day, break one of them in half. That's a convenient reduction of roughly 12.5 percent. If that feels good after a week or more, then break another pill in half. Now you've reduced the dose by 25 percent. You may want to ask your doctor or pharmacist for the smallest pill size so that you can more conveniently make small reductions.

In regard to the newer antidepressants like Paxil and the tranquilizers like Xanax, some people discover that they must proceed extremely slowly, taking tiny fractions of a pill at the very end of the taper. If the drug comes in a liquid form, such as Paxil, some people end up using a dropper to measure small reductions of the liquid form of the drug toward the end of the taper.[8]

The most important rule is to respect your own feelings and to avoid tapering faster than you find bearable. Stay within your own comfort zone when pacing your withdrawal. Keep in mind that the longer you were taking the drug, and the higher the dose, the more gradual your taper should be. Once again, it's not unusual to require a month of withdrawal for every year of drug exposure.

If you have been taking a drug with recognized abuse potential such as the stimulants or benzodiazepines, in severe cases you may be able to get help from an outpatient or inpatient rehabilitation program.

If at any time the withdrawal symptoms become intolerable, the simplest approach is to return to the previous dose you were taking. Then, if you decide to continue the withdrawal process, you can do so more gradually. Whenever possible, make use of skilled clinical supervision and a strong family and social support network. Overall, most people are able to carefully and safely withdraw from psychiatric drugs.

Again, keep in mind that these withdrawal methods are only guidelines and not absolute rules. Applying them depends on how fast you feel comfortable to proceed and on how much discomfort you experience and can bear between dose reductions.

How to Divide Individual Doses

To follow the above steps, you may have to use smaller doses than those available in individual pills. Drugs usually come in pills of varying doses. As already mentioned, your doctor or pharmacist can provide you with the smallest available pill in order to facilitate your dose adjustments. However, the smallest available pill might not be small enough to ease the discomfort of withdrawal. For example, Lexapro comes in tablets of 5, 10, and 20 mg but some people may require 2.5 mg for their last series of doses.

Most pills have a slit that allows them to be divided in half easily; you can also purchase a small inexpensive device from most pharmacies for cutting pills and tablets. Pills that are slow-release (long-acting) typically cannot be safely divided. Consult your pharmacist or healthcare professional about the safety of dividing the pills you are using.

It is also possible to take most drugs every other day during the withdrawal. However, this should *not* be done early in the withdrawal. Taking psychiatric drugs every other day in routinely prescribed dose sizes can be very stressful on the brain. Taking the drug every other day should be done only toward the very end of the taper when you have reached the smallest available pill. You can then try withdrawing from the smallest pill by taking it every other day, and then every third day, until you feel comfortable stopping. In addition, as already described, some drugs like Paxil come in liquid form and can be dispensed with an eyedropper at the end stages of withdrawal.

To sum up, in withdrawing from many psychiatric drugs, it is not uncommon to have difficulty stopping the smallest available dose. In these cases, it is possible to break the pill into halves or even roughly into quarters. Toward the end of your withdrawal, it is also possible to take the *smallest* available pill every other day and then every third day before stopping completely. In regard to antidepressants and tranquilizers, some people find it very difficult to withdraw from these last little doses and may require weeks or months to finish the process.

*   *   *

This chapter has focused on the mechanics of drug withdrawal. But the most difficult aspects of withdrawal often have to do with fears about giving up drugs, as well as the resurfacing of painful emotions and psychological issues that have been submerged under a drug-induced mental flattening. Before undertaking drug withdrawal, always assess your need for counseling as well as your need for a safe home situation and a supportive social network. When these basic steps are taken before starting drug withdrawal, the vast majority of people can safely taper off their psychiatric drugs.

— 9 —

Withdrawal Reactions from Psychiatric Drugs

In Chapter 4, we discussed adverse reactions that can occur when psychiatric drugs are taken. The present chapter reviews adverse reactions that can develop during withdrawal.

Beware Illicit Use

This book is directed to people who have experienced problems while taking or withdrawing from psychiatric drugs that have been prescribed by doctors according to generally accepted guidelines for their clinical use.

On the other hand, you may be experiencing serious difficulties from using stimulants, sedatives, or painkillers in large amounts, or in combination with each other, or with alcohol. You may have started this use with a routine medical prescription but are now taking much larger quantities and feel you cannot control the cumulative effects. Similarly, if you have been obtaining psychiatric drugs illegally or from multiple doctors, you may have a serious drug dependence problem. If you are snorting, injecting, or inhaling these drugs, you are exposing yourself to extreme dangers.

Under any of these circumstances, you may need immediate professional help that may include a detoxification or drug-rehabilitation unit.

By contrast, this book focuses on problems associated with the ordinary use and withdrawal from psychiatric drugs that have been routinely prescribed by doctors.

Your Doctor May Not Know

All psychiatric drugs can produce unpleasant, disturbing reactions upon withdrawal or discontinuation. For *some* drugs that have been with us for decades, especially the benzodiazepine tranquilizers, withdrawal reactions are well described in the medical literature. Doctors tend to know about them. However, doctors are too often unfamiliar with withdrawal problems associated with many of the other psychiatric drugs they routinely prescribe. Since the first edition of this book appeared, we have observed a definite increase in professional and popular sensitivity about withdrawal reactions of psychiatric drugs, especially antidepressants. However, much more education is needed.

Stimulants such as Ritalin, Adderall, and Dexedrine have been widely used for decades, yet many physicians seem unaware of the marked withdrawal reactions they can cause. The same is true of drugs more recently introduced on the market. All newer antidepressants, such as Lexapro, Cymbalta, Paxil, Prozac, and others, often cause distressing withdrawal, yet many physicians appear to be unaware of this fact. For example, family physicians or primary care practitioners prescribe the bulk of antidepressants. Yet, to our knowledge, the first systematic advice to family physicians concerning the management of antidepressant discontinuation was published in *American Family Physician* only in late 2006.[1]

What we find most disturbing is that, even when doctors do know about the dangers of withdrawal problems from drugs, they often fail to warn their patients.[2] Sometimes they feel too pressed for time to inform their patients about these dangers. Sometimes they simply forget. Sometimes they are concerned that patients will complain about any adverse effect that the doctor mentions or that the patient hears about. At other times, doctors are simply afraid to discourage their patients from taking the medication. However, medical ethics and sound practice require that physicians advise patients about withdrawal problems. There is no legitimate excuse for not doing so.

Once you read this book, you may know much more about withdrawal problems than your physician does. If you are planning to stop or reduce the dose of a psychiatric drug, you may want to share this book with your doctor.

When Am I Having a Withdrawal Reaction?

Withdrawal reactions can be difficult to recognize. For example, consider the case of George who, two nights earlier, stopped taking the Klonopin (clonazepam) that was prescribed for him at bedtime to help him sleep. It's the first time in several months that he has tried to fall asleep without his "sleeping pill." Since stopping the Klonopin, George has been having more trouble falling asleep than ever before. He has been lying awake for hours worrying about what will happen to him if he can't ever fall asleep again without drugs.

George is most likely having a withdrawal reaction from the Klonopin. For several months, his brain has been fighting the effects of the drug, which George has taken on a daily basis. This process has resulted in reactive or compensatory overstimulation of his brain. Now that the drug has been stopped, George's overstimulated brain has taken over and is keeping George awake. Since his insomnia is worse than it was before he started the Klonopin, his withdrawal reaction can be called a "rebound"—a worsening of his original symptoms.

Alternatively, George could be suffering from psychological fear of giving up the drug. If he wasn't so scared about doing without a sleeping pill, he might not be having so much trouble sleeping. Having gotten into the habit of using Klonopin, he may now be afraid to give it up. This withdrawal reaction would be described as psychologically caused, in contrast to the physically caused withdrawal problems we are mostly concerned with. In such circumstances, George would need reassurance from his doctor that he will get used to sleeping without medication.

George could also be suffering from his original insomnia. Indeed, for years, he has tended to worry at night. In the absence of drug-induced sleep, his worrying may have returned. This situation would be described as a "relapse"—a return of the original problems experienced before drug use. Counseling or psychotherapy could be especially helpful in dealing with this aspect of George's insomnia.

Because Klonopin and other sleep-inducing drugs commonly cause withdrawal problems, we are probably correct in specifying drug withdrawal as the most likely diagnosis in George's case. If he gradually resumes more normal sleep in a few days or weeks, this diagnosis would be confirmed. As noted, it is often difficult to distinguish drug withdrawal reactions from other problems, such as a return of the original symptoms.

Usually, however, it's safest to assume that physical withdrawal is playing a role and that a slow, tapered withdrawal will be helpful.

Consider the possibility that you are having a withdrawal reaction if you begin to experience uncomfortable physical or emotional reactions within hours, days, or weeks of reducing or stopping a medication. The same is true if you are experiencing these reactions *between* drug doses. Short-acting drugs are especially likely to cause withdrawal reactions between doses. These culprits include all of the stimulants, the sleeping pills Ambien and Halcion, and the benzodiazepine tranquilizer Xanax.

You may also be experiencing a withdrawal reaction if the reaction is the opposite of the drug effect. For example, if you get very tired and feel that you are "crashing" a few hours after taking a stimulant—or if you get agitated and even "high" a few hours after taking a tranquilizer—you may be going through withdrawal.

Denial of Withdrawal Reactions

For many reasons, our knowledge of drug withdrawal problems is not as advanced as it should be. To begin with, these problems are very complicated. As in George's case, it can be difficult to separate psychological factors from physical ones. Or it can be difficult to determine whether the problems involve physical withdrawal or a return of the individual's original troubles. In addition, different people vary in terms of their withdrawal reactions to the same drug. For example, George may feel nervous and have trouble falling asleep for a few days after withdrawing from Klonopin, whereas Gina may hear a ringing sound in her ears and find that her physical balance is impaired.

As we have mentioned, doctors are often reluctant to admit that withdrawal is a serious problem. Moreover, when they do witness withdrawal reactions, they rarely report them to the appropriate agencies. For example, probable withdrawal reactions from antidepressants such as Paxil and Zoloft are very common, occurring in 30 percent of patients.[3] Yet the number of reports of *all* adverse reactions from antidepressants sent to the FDA varies between 2 and 300 *per 1 million prescriptions.*[4]

Perhaps most important, almost all drug research is paid for and controlled by drug manufacturers, and these profit-driven corporations tend to be very reluctant to identify drug withdrawal problems that might discourage people from using their products. From drug research through medical education and clinical practice, then, many factors interact to inhibit the growth of our knowledge about drug withdrawal. As a result, there is no significant tradition or body of wisdom in psychiatry that focuses on drug withdrawal reactions. All of the emphasis tends to be on how to start and to maintain drugs in patients rather than on how to stop them.

When you talk to your doctor about problems stopping or reducing the dose of your psychiatric drug, *keep in mind that your doctor may not know much about the problem or may even be irrationally denying its existence.* For example, the older antidepressants, commonly called tricyclics, have been in use for more than fifty years, and their withdrawal reactions have been repeatedly documented. Yet some doctors seem completely unaware of the existence of these reactions. A survey in 1997 tested the awareness of psychiatrists and general practitioners concerning antidepressant drug withdrawal. The authors concluded that "a sizeable minority of physicians denied being confidently aware of the existence of antidepressant withdrawal symptoms."[5] The implication is that, in routine clinical practice, at least a "sizeable minority" of doctors make no attempt to diagnose antidepressant withdrawal reactions or to distinguish them from other symptoms. Another recent survey of psychiatrists showed that withdrawal reactions rated near the bottom of the list of factors helping these physicians decide which antidepressant to prescribe to their patients.

Your doctor may also mistakenly attribute your withdrawal reactions to your "mental illness." Especially if you have *unsuccessfully* tried to withdraw from the drug previously, your doctor may try to convince you that you have a "chronic illness" requiring lifetime drug use. The irony is that the longer you stay on the drug, the more likely you are to suffer something beyond a mild reaction when you attempt to withdraw. Your unsuspecting doctor, and even you, might see this as a sign that you "really need" your drug. In reality, what you really need is help in gradually withdrawing.

Defining Physical Dependence

If a drug causes unpleasant effects to some users when they stop taking it, then some of these users will inevitably become physically dependent on it. This conclusion is basic to the definition of physical dependence. According to the World Task Force on sedative-hypnotics, "[p]hysical dependence is defined as the appearance of specific withdrawal symptoms when the medication is abruptly discontinued."[6] Boston University's online Pharmacology Glossary states that dependence "is characterized by the necessity to continue administration of the drug in order to avoid the appearance of uncomfortable or dangerous (withdrawal) symptoms."[7] And a report in the *New England Journal of Medicine* confirms this emphasis: "Use of the term 'physical dependence' implies that an objective withdrawal syndrome will occur after a drug is discontinued."[8]

On the basis of these definitions, we can further conclude that *all psychiatric drugs are drugs of dependence*. This includes drugs, such as lithium, that are not commonly recognized as causing withdrawal symptoms. The occurrence of withdrawal symptoms defines dependence inasmuch as users will experience discomfort when stopping the drug and will experience relief when restarting it. As a result of experiencing discomfort, some will "choose" to remain on the drug only in order to avoid prolonged withdrawal distress. As already described, they may also mistake the withdrawal symptoms for "mental illness" and decide that they "need" the medication. Some authors reject the idea that drugs like antidepressants can make people dependent or addicted because once users stop taking them, they do not engage in "drug-seeking" behavior, that is, they do not try to obtain the drugs by any means or visit different physicians to coax prescriptions from them. But such behavior would be completely unnecessary for drugs that can be so easily and legally obtained from a doctor's prescription.

The existence of unpleasant withdrawal reactions reflects negatively on a drug. For economic and political reasons, drug manufacturers, regulatory agencies, researchers, and individual doctors tend to downplay, ignore, or deny information about a popular drug's withdrawal effects. They will sometimes do so even after convincing evidence has become available for all to see. The resistance and denial have been documented in years past—notably, with respect to the benzodiazepines, the barbiturates, the stimulants, and even the opiates.[9] Yet these very drugs are today considered "classically addictive."

A similar denial of the nature, extent, and implications of withdrawal reactions has occurred with respect to the SSRI antidepressants and others (see next page).[10] Only lately have drug manufacturers and other important players begun to acknowledge that withdrawal reactions are a serious problem. Ironically, these drugs were never tested for their dependence potential and became popular partly because they were offered as replacements for older antidepressants and benzodiazepines—drugs known to cause withdrawal problems.

Withdrawal Reactions Can
Cause "Significant Distress"

Psychiatry's official diagnostic manual, the *Diagnostic and Statistical Manual of Mental Disorders, 4th edition,*[11] or *DSM-IV*, contains a diagnostic category entitled "Substance Withdrawal," described as "the development of a substance-specific maladaptive behavioral change, with physiological and cognitive concomitants, that is due to the cessation of, or reduction in, heavy and prolonged substance use."[12] On the following page, *DSM-IV* emphasizes the discomfort of withdrawal, stating that the "syndrome causes significant distress or impairment in social, occupational, or other important areas of functioning."[13]

This definition appears to be describing withdrawal from illicit or disapproved substances. Yet much prescribed, medically approved psychiatric drug use is also "heavy and prolonged." As we document later in this chapter, withdrawal reactions that can cause severe and long-lasting distress and impairment have been specified for all classes of psychiatric drugs. Two panels of experts have also identified a distinct, complex, and sometimes severe withdrawal syndrome for SSRI antidepressants. However, *DSM-IV* "recognizes" such reactions for only two currently used classes of psychiatric drug: stimulants and tranquilizers.[14]

"Withdrawal" or "Discontinuation"?

For years, writers in the medical literature have interchangeably used the terms *discontinuation, withdrawal,* and *abstinence syndrome.* Increasingly, in discussions of psychiatric drugs, the accepted term is *discontinuation.* In the eyes of some experts, this word is less stigmatizing—to the drugs. We read in an editorial in the *British Medical Journal* that "[t]he common lay belief that antidepressants are addictive probably contributes to the significant undertreatment of depressive illness. It is important not to foster this belief inadvertently—one reason that 'discontinuation reaction' is a better term than 'withdrawal reaction.'"[15]

But this is doublespeak. Rather than provide evidence to address justified fears that antidepressants produce dependence, experts urge that the worrisome phenomena be called by a different name! We, on the other hand, suggest that a sound attempt be made to answer important questions: Do "discontinuation" or "withdrawal" effects drive people to remain on their drugs indefinitely? How frequently are these effects mistaken for relapses? And do these effects mistakenly convince doctors that patients "need" their drugs?

Not long ago, similar rationalizations deluded doctors into believing that long-term tranquilizer treatment was "effective." From the start of benzodiazepine use in 1963, the existence of physical dependence in patients taking clinical doses of benzodiazepines was firmly established.[16] Yet, no fewer than fifteen years later, a prominent expert concluded that "[t]he dependence risk with benzodiazepines is . . . probably less than one case per 50 million months in therapeutic use."[17] As a result of such denial, millions of people became physically dependent on these drugs.

In the remainder of this chapter, we provide a review of medical information about withdrawal reactions to commonly used psychiatric drugs, including the newer ones on the market. We also discuss lesser-known reactions and withdrawal syndromes. We have reviewed the medical literature of the past several decades, looking for published reports concerning discontinuation. Even if your doctor is unsympathetic to our critical stance about medication use, it would be an excellent idea for him or her to read the remainder of this chapter, as it presents what is probably the most comprehensive summary of psychiatric drug withdrawal reactions available anywhere.

Benzodiazepine Withdrawal Reactions

Withdrawal reactions from benzodiazepines—drugs that make up most of the class of minor tranquilizers and ordinarily prescribed sleeping pills—are extremely well documented. For most people who take low doses, the main symptoms of withdrawal consist of increases in tension and anxiety as well as motor and perceptual disturbances. However, the withdrawal reaction can become much more severe and even life-threatening (see below).

Tranquilizers can produce withdrawal reactions after only a few weeks of use. Studies of Xanax, for example, have indicated increased anxiety and panic upon withdrawal after only eight weeks. The longer you take a tranquilizer, the higher the doses, and the more abrupt the withdrawal—the more serious your withdrawal reactions are likely to be. Severe reactions tend to be more frequent with short half-life drugs,[18] Halcion (triazolam, used only as a sleeping pill) and Xanax (alprazolam). Intermediate half-life drugs include Ativan (lorazepam),

Klonopin (clonazepam), Lectopam (bromazepam), Restoril (temazepam), and Serax (oxazepam). Longer half-life drugs include Dalmane (flurazepam), Valium (diazepam), Tranxene (clorazepate), and Librium (chlordiazepoxide). Benzodiazepines can reverse withdrawal reactions from alcohol and barbiturates. Consistent with this fact, they produce a withdrawal syndrome similar to that associated with these substances.[19]

The Discontinuation Syndrome

A task force report of the American Psychiatric Association (1990) divides the benzodiazepine "discontinuance syndrome" into three familiar categories:

1. *Rebound symptoms of anxiety and insomnia—the same as those for which the drug was prescribed, only more severe.* These symptoms usually occur within one to three days of discontinuation. For short half-life drugs such as Halcion, rebound "often means an awakening during the middle of the night, with an inability to return to sleep without a second triazolam dose."[20] For some patients, rebound symptoms last about one week; for others, they abate after two or three weeks. However, many people who experience these reactions do not see them through, since they restart the medication to avoid the distress.[21]

2. *Recurrence symptoms—the return of the original problem.* Indeed, since the drug treatment targets symptoms rather than the cause of the anxiety, you can expect anxiety to return when you stop the drug. And since recurrence and rebound are likely to occur together, your doctor may find it difficult to distinguish one from the other. However, recurrence symptoms tend to last much longer than rebound symptoms.

3. *Withdrawal symptoms—the appearance of discontinuation symptoms that did not exist prior to starting the use of benzodiazepines.* Even relatively moderate withdrawal reactions can include flu-like symptoms such as nausea, vomiting, headaches, muscular pain and stiffness, fatigue, diarrhea, chills, and sweating. Insomnia, anxiety, tension, and an array of unusual sensations inside the head are very common as well. A full-blown withdrawal syndrome can also entail the shakes, blurry vision, extreme

tension and anxiety, acute anxiety attacks, painfully heightened sensitivity to light and sound, severe sleep disturbances,
impaired physical balance and coordination, twitching and
painful muscle cramps, visual and auditory disturbances such
as hallucinations or tinnitus (ringing in the ears), anorexia and
weight loss,[22] and even psychosis, delirium, and seizures.

As just noted, benzodiazepine withdrawal (like alcohol or barbiturate
withdrawal) may involve seizures. Adults and older persons appear to be
equally at risk, but seizures are most likely in cases where high doses
have been used, short half-life drugs have been involved, and withdrawal
is abrupt.[23]

The Doctor's Involvement in Withdrawal

Today, many doctors routinely encourage long-term users of benzodiazepines to withdraw from the drugs. However, many of these patients
are unwilling to do so because they have found the withdrawal symptoms to be intolerable. They remain on the drugs, thanks to doctors who
renew their prescriptions. This is particularly true of older patients,
especially women, who were started on benzodiazepines before doctors
became more aware of their potential for dependence.[24]

The doctor's involvement before, during, and after withdrawal is one
of the most important ingredients for success in difficult withdrawal
processes.[25] Patients who withdraw from benzodiazepines require psychological support. This may range from simple but continued encouragement to more formal anxiety-management techniques such as
breathing exercises, mental exercises, meditation, and group support; it
can also include psychotherapy.

Your doctor can be more effective by using a clear withdrawal protocol
rather than an unstructured, casual taper to "test the waters." It may
help if you are simultaneously provided with written instructions on
each of the steps involved. Although some doctors prescribe Inderal or
Tegretol to minimize benzodiazepine withdrawal reactions, these drugs
have not been shown to be of definite help, except perhaps in urgent
cases when the benzodiazepines must be withdrawn rapidly.[26]

The vast majority of patients are successfully withdrawn as outpatients. In medical textbooks, recommendations for benzodiazepine withdrawal sometimes mention that inpatients might be switched to a

longer-acting drug such as Valium, because withdrawal symptoms are less acute and the relatively larger equivalent dose may be divided more easily. Other doctors believe, to the contrary, that it is best to work with the drug that the patient is accustomed to.

Some medical sources suggest a "10 percent per day" method of tapering benzodiazepines, but we believe that this poses an undue risk to patients. In cases where doctors feel they must taper relatively rapidly without hospitalizing the patient, a "10 percent per week" schedule is more reasonable. This is also the conclusion reached in a systematic review of withdrawal trials of benzodiazepines: "Progressive withdrawal (over 10 weeks) appeared preferable if compared to abrupt since the number of drop-outs was less important and the procedure judged more favourable by the participants."[27] Clinical experience with benzodiazepines also suggests that extension of the withdrawal period is not harmful, especially after the initial dose has been decreased by 50 percent. In ordinary circumstances, however, patients should be allowed to share in controlling the process, especially in regard to slowing it down.

Antidepressant Withdrawal Reactions

In Chapter 4, we divided antidepressants into four classes: tricyclics, monoamine oxidase inhibitors (MAOIs), Prozac-like drugs that stimulate serotonin, and atypicals. Predictable symptoms of withdrawal from most of these drugs are now well documented, although many psychiatrists and even more general practitioners remain unaware of them.

Tricyclic Antidepressant Withdrawal Reactions

Stopping the use of tricyclic antidepressants produces a "bewildering assortment"[28] of withdrawal symptoms, affecting between 20 and 100 percent of users and lasting up to three months. You are at highest risk of experiencing withdrawal reactions from tricyclics if you have been treated with high doses for many years and are rapidly withdrawn.[29]

So many different physical symptoms can result from withdrawing from tricyclic antidepressants that it is helpful to divide them into categories. The following withdrawal symptoms may occur alone or in combination, and to varying degrees.

1. Gastrointestinal upset with abdominal pain, vomiting, dry mouth, drooling, and loss of appetite. Nausea is a common and very disturbing symptom of withdrawal from these drugs.

2. General feelings of physical and mental distress or discomfort that are difficult to define or describe but resemble exhaustion or the flu. "Weird sensations inside the head" are occasionally reported by individuals.

3. Emotional manifestations including tension, jitteriness, irritability, anxiety, panic, depersonalization, apathy, depression, "mood swings," and even psychotic mania. Within a few days after withdrawal, some people develop full-blown manic episodes with racing thoughts, hostility, very poor judgment, and reckless and dangerous behavior. These psychoses may persist long after the drugs have been discontinued and may not respond to treatment with other drugs.[30]

4. Mental dysfunction, commonly including memory difficulties and, in more extreme cases, disorientation and delirium (extreme confusion).

5. Sleep disturbances, including insomnia, excessively vivid dreams, nightmares, and breathing difficulties during sleep.

6. Abnormal movements, including uncontrollable movements of almost any muscle of the body (dyskinesias), muscle spasms (dystonias), parkinsonism (slowed, rigid movement), and akathisia (inner agitation that compels a person to move). The muscle spasms can be very painful, and the akathisia can feel like being tortured.

7. Cardiac arrhythmias that can be dangerous.[31]

We have seen cases in which people, after many years on these drugs, have been withdrawn without ever fully recovering from withdrawal symptoms. Some, for example, continue to suffer indefinitely from nausea and memory problems.

As noted earlier in the book, most of these symptoms—including mania and other mental disturbances—can also occur during treatment from direct antidepressant toxicity.

Children, too, suffer from tricyclic antidepressant withdrawal.[32] In one case involving an eight-year-old boy, the abrupt withdrawal of a tricyclic provoked such severe nausea, vomiting, and abdominal cramps that the boy had to be hospitalized because of dehydration.[33] "Mental irritability" and heart irregularities have also occurred in infants born to mothers taking tricyclic antidepressants during pregnancy.[34]

MAOI Withdrawal Reactions

Problems related to discontinuation from monoamine oxidase inhibitors (drugs such as Nardil, Parnate, Eldepryl, and, in Canada, Manerix) are less documented than for other classes of antidepressants, probably because these drugs are less frequently used. The proportion of patients who experience withdrawal reactions is unknown because we lack systematic studies.[35] What we do know, however, is that if you stop an MAOI, withdrawal reactions can last from "days to weeks."[36]

Some clinicians believe that ". . . MAOI withdrawal is usually not a serious problem,"[37] whereas others maintain that it "produces syndromes of much greater severity than those precipitated by the withdrawal of [tricyclics]."[38] One review mentions "serious cognitive impairment and catatonia that may lead to hospitalization, which can appear when [MAOIs] are discontinued."[39]

Other withdrawal reactions include anxiety, agitation, paranoia, pressured speech, headaches, lowered blood pressure upon standing, muscle weakness, shivering, and tingling, burning sensations under the skin.[40] Mania can also occur.

Here are two accounts of grave withdrawal reactions from MAOIs.

A thirty-four-year-old woman was started on a gradual taper from Nardil. She felt burning sensations, and abruptly quit the drug. She became "hostile, loud, aggressive, disoriented in time and place . . ." She "lunged at imaginary objects. . . . She was delirious for 3 days after receiving the last dose of phenelzine. . . . Though hospitalized for only 72 hours, she did not fully recover for 6 weeks."[41]

In a case involving a twenty-one-year-old woman treated for bulimia, Nardil was abruptly removed because the woman experienced severe dizziness upon standing. As a result, "[s]he was sleepy, spent most of her time in bed, and was confused for 3 days and disoriented for 4 days following the last dose. . . . She did not recognize her mother or her room. She entered a state of catatonic stupor and was hospitalised."[42]

Withdrawal Reactions from
Antidepressants that Stimulate Serotonin

This group of drugs includes the selective serotonin reuptake inhibitors (SSRIs) such as Prozac, Zoloft, Celexa, Paxil, and Luvox. Effexor, Wellbutrin, Remeron, and Cymbalta can cause similar withdrawal reactions to these drugs.

In 1996, and again in 2004, a panel of psychiatric experts sponsored by antidepressant drug manufacturers met to discuss the withdrawal syndrome from SSRIs. The first panel observed that many of the reactions reported "are similar to those of tricyclic withdrawal, but a variety of novel symptoms are also associated with the stoppage of SRI therapy."[43] The new symptoms included "problems with balance, sensory abnormalities, and possibly aggressive and impulsive behavior."[44]

That first panel found that the SSRI discontinuation syndrome encompasses the following frequently reported clusters of physical symptoms:

> (1) disequilibrium (e.g., dizziness, vertigo, ataxia), (2) gastrointestinal symptoms (e.g., nausea, vomiting), (3) flu-like symptoms (e.g., fatigue, lethargy, myalgia, chills), (4) sensory disturbances (e.g., paresthesias [tingling, burning sensations], sensations of electric shock), and (5) sleep disturbances (e.g., insomnia, vivid dreams).[45]

The panel also noted two "core psychological symptoms" of SSRI withdrawal—anxiety/agitation, and "dramatic" crying spells and irritability—as well as overactivity, depersonalization, decreased concentration/slowed thinking, lowered mood, confusion, memory problems, and abnormal movements.

The 2004 panel confirmed all of the first panel's observations, as well as ours, and recognized both the astonishing variety of reported symptoms (over fifty) and the uniqueness of most cases. The new panel observed that the SSRI withdrawal syndrome "usually" appeared within one to seven days after discontinuation, even if the drug was taken for only one month. It estimated that the syndrome "usually" could last up to three weeks. The new panel reorganized the array of withdrawal symptoms into six clusters: (1) neurosensory (including vertigo, tingling and burning sensations, shock-like reactions, and various intense nerve and muscular pains), (2) neuromotor (tremor, spasms, loss of muscular control, and visual changes), (3) gastrointestinal (nausea, vomiting, diarrhea, loss of appetite and weight loss), (4) neuropsychiatric (anxiety, depressed mood, suicidal ideation, irritability, impulsiveness), (5) vasomotor (heavy sweating, flushing), and other neurologic symptoms (insomnia, vivid dreaming, fatigue, chills). The panel observed that these groups of symptoms tend to occur together, with most patients experiencing symptoms from each group. It also confirmed previous observations that a full withdrawal syndrome could emerge from missed doses and drug holidays.[46]

Based on our own clinical experience, on the information reviewed by this panel of psychiatric experts, as well as on other recent studies and reviews,[47] we have found, as with tricyclic withdrawal, a vast assortment of symptoms associated with the SSRI discontinuation syndrome. Here are a few examples.

A thirty-two-year-old man who discontinued Prozac after six months of use awoke with "painful extensor muscle spasms" and "protruding tongue movements."[48] A thirty-year-old woman tried to stop taking Luvox when she became pregnant but "was overwhelmed by strong feelings of aggression (she felt that she 'could murder someone')." This occurred on two distinct withdrawal occasions, and the woman was unable to stop the Luvox.[49]

One of us has reported a case of "crashing" from SSRI withdrawal. A woman spontaneously decided to reduce her Zoloft from 100 mg to 50 mg per day. Within a couple of days, she lapsed into "exhaustion and fatigue, profound depression, and a compulsive, alien-feeling desire to kill herself."[50] All of these symptoms disappeared soon after the woman resumed the 100 mg dose. In another publication, we describe a young woman who became suicidal when discontinuing Prozac.[51]

In two cases involving middle-aged men, neither with a history of major psychiatric problems, Paxil withdrawal led to severe symptoms. For twelve days after abrupt withdrawal, one man experienced marked hypomania. The second man developed various physical symptoms, then began to express "intense" homicidal thoughts—a condition that lasted for five weeks.[52]

One woman on Lexapro reduced her 10 mg per day dose to 5 mg a day, and three weeks later stopped altogether. One week later, she began to experience "electric shock–like sensations or visual flashes lasting for about 1 second each. This was followed by a phase of spatial disorientation that lasted for about 30 seconds and was experienced as highly unpleasant and frightening." This occurred about three times a day over two weeks.[53]

One report describes three consecutive female patients who experienced "severe physical symptoms of withdrawal" when stopping Effexor. Effexor is not an SSRI, but like the SSRIs it stimulates serotonin. The women could not stop the drug, even after repeated attempts at tapering. These patients were finally able to discontinue the Effexor only by switching indefinitely to Prozac.[54]

After three months of taking Prozac, a young woman tried unsuccessfully to withdraw from the drug on three different occasions. Each time, she experienced extreme dizziness and instability. She was examined by specialists who ordered many tests, including magnetic resonance imaging (MRI) of the brain. The tests were negative. The symptoms were relieved each time by the readministration of Prozac, but none of her doctors suspected a withdrawal reaction. She was eventually tapered successfully over twelve weeks.[55]

A thirty-two-year old woman took 300 mg of Effexor daily for eight months. She tried to withdraw abruptly on three occasions but failed due to unbearable headaches, gastrointestinal distress, fatigue, and other symptoms. "She remains on a regimen of venlafaxine [Effexor], 100 mg t.i.d."[56] A man withdrawn from Effexor experienced "severe akathisia" (compulsion to move). This condition abated "within hours" of restarting the drug, which was later gradually tapered and withdrawn.[57]

In a lengthy paper on antidepressant withdrawal difficulties, and in a Web site chronicling his relentless querying of public officials in Britain about the safety of medicines, journalist Charles Medawar summarizes numerous reports of SSRI withdrawal reactions and the underreporting of these reactions by doctors, as well as the stonewalling by government agencies and drug manufacturers about their examination of SSRI withdrawal risks.[58] Included among these reports, which were dated from 1988 to 2003 and numbered more than one hundred and twenty-five, were a dozen that noted distinct withdrawal symptoms observed in newborn infants whose mothers took either SSRIs or other antidepressants during pregnancy. Much like the older antidepressants, the SSRIs can on occasion cause withdrawal mania.[59]

Withdrawal reactions affect between 20 and 80 percent of persons who stop SSRIs abruptly. Based on a conservative estimate that 50 percent of individuals suffer from withdrawal reactions, we would have to conclude that hundreds of thousands of people are affected every year in the United States alone. Most of these reactions are mild or moderate, yet can be distressing enough that patients would wish to avoid them. Few valid estimates of severe reactions exist: Rates of 20–30 percent were reported in a symposium.[60]

Withdrawal reactions from SSRIs typically occur after one to four days of discontinuation, although they may begin weeks later in the case of long half-life drugs such as Prozac. There seems to be a consensus in the published literature reporting on clinical studies and surveys of consumers that short half-life drugs, especially Paxil, seem most often implicated. On average, withdrawal reactions persist for seven to twenty-five days (from one day to thirteen weeks). One study of Cymbalta did find that patients taking the highest dose reported significantly more withdrawal symptoms than those on the lowest doses.[61] As yet, however, the number of studies remains too small to draw valid conclusions about the relationship between dose and length of drug use, on the one hand, and the risk of withdrawal reactions, on the other.

SSRI withdrawal reactions involve many different physical, emotional, and mental symptoms, the full range of which has probably not been charted.[62] They occur with both abrupt and more gradual withdrawal but seem to be attenuated by a *truly* gradual withdrawal that lasts three months or more. In our estimation, however, abrupt withdrawal is too frequent, regardless of whether medical supervision is provided.

Withdrawal reactions appear to be more frequent—or at least more acute—in the case of SSRIs with shorter half-lives, such as Paxil, Luvox, and Zoloft. Withdrawal reactions from longer-acting drugs like Prozac seem to appear much later. They can begin up to twenty-five days after the drug is stopped. Because they are so delayed, they are not visible in short-term studies; moreover, patients tend not to attribute these delayed withdrawal reactions to stopping the drug.[63]

GlaxoSmithKline, the manufacturer of Paxil, was recently required by the FDA to modify its label to add emphasis to the danger of withdrawal reactions. This label change occurred at the time that Peter Breggin was acting as a medical expert in a California lawsuit aimed at requiring similar modifications. Under "Precautions," the new Paxil label lists the following reported withdrawal symptoms: "Dysphoric mood, irritability, agitation, dizziness, sensory disturbances (e.g., paresthesias such as electric shock sensations and tinnitus), anxiety, confusion, headache, lethargy, emotional lability, insomnia, and hypomania."[64] The section refers to the occurrence of "serious discontinuation symptoms" and "intolerable symptoms."

We have found that a small number of patients cannot tolerate the anguish associated with withdrawing from Paxil and similar antidepressants, and instead reluctantly decide to remain on the drugs indefinitely. In such cases, we would advise consulting with more than one health provider about approaches to withdrawal. Further attempts to withdraw at a later date should not be ruled out since the intensity of withdrawal reactions may vary at different times.

As M. Lejoyeux and J. Adès (1997) point out, "Patients who are classified as having a relapse while they are discontinuing therapy may, in fact, be suffering from unrecognized discontinuation symptoms."[65] As previously noted, the 1996 expert panel found that "dramatic" crying spells are a "core psychological symptom" of SSRI withdrawal. No wonder it's tempting to mistake this reaction for a relapse of depression. It is anybody's guess as to how many patients are resumed on antidepressants because they are suffering from withdrawal reactions that are mistakenly diagnosed as depressive relapses, but the number is undoubtedly large.

Atypical Antidepressant Withdrawal Reactions

Withdrawal reactions to the atypical antidepressants are generally less well documented than for other types of antidepressants. There exists scarcely any information on the effects of withdrawing from Ludiomil (maprotiline). Withdrawal reactions from Wellbutrin or Zyban (buproprion), Serzone (nefazodone), and Remeron (mirtazapine) are likewise barely documented in the medical literature. One report describes a withdrawal syndrome from abrupt cessation of Serzone, consisting of "dizziness, nausea, vomiting, sweating, anxiety, insomnia, and restlessness," which lasted three days.[66] Another report describes a similar reaction (which also included burning sensations under the skin) following the sudden withdrawal of the antidepressant Remeron.[67]

Withdrawal reactions to Effexor (venlafaxine) have been discussed in the previous section, as this drug has many effects in common with Prozac-like drugs that stimulate serotonin. One researcher found that serious withdrawal effects within mere hours of stopping Effexor or reducing the dose can affect physical and motor coordination to such a degree that patients should be explicitly advised not to drive a car.[68] Asendin (amoxapine), a combination of a neuroleptic and a tricyclic antidepressant, will share important withdrawal effects with antipsychotics and tricyclics (such as flu-like symptoms, agitation, and movement disorders), and readers should consult the appropriate sections in this chapter.

Several withdrawal effects have been documented with Desyrel (trazodone), including mania and hypomania, nausea and recurrent vomiting, and visual hallucinations.[69] Within 36 hours of trazodone withdrawal, one patient developed a "syndrome of overwhelming anxiety, depersonalization, insomnia, and nightmares" which took five days to subside.[70]

As discussed in previous chapters, the absence or rarity of reports of withdrawal effects from specific psychiatric drugs in no way indicates that a drug is free of such effects. The reader withdrawing from atypical antidepressants should proceed slowly and expect almost any kind of effect associated with other antidepressants.

Stimulant Withdrawal Reactions

Stimulants are frequently used to control the behavior of children. The amphetamines Adderall, Desoxyn, Dexedrine, and Gradumet, as well as the amphetamine-like Ritalin, are the most commonly prescribed. Stimulant drugs are also given to adults to treat "attention deficit-hyperactivity disorder," narcolepsy, depression, and obesity. Other stimulant-like drugs have been used for diet control, including phentermin (Fastin, Adipex) and mazindole (Sanorex). Another diet control drug, fenfluramine, was recently taken off the market in Canada and the United States because it harms human heart valves. Caffeine, of course, is a mild stimulant that is commonly used.

Ritalin and the amphetamines are very similar to cocaine in terms of how they affect brain chemistry and function. Although the impact of stimulants on dopamine neurotransmission is usually viewed as the main cause for the euphoria or "pleasure" that encourages people to keep using these drugs, recent research has also focused on another neurotransmitter, serotonin. Cocaine and other stimulants block the removal of serotonin from the synapses between brain cells.[71] Since the SSRI antidepressants have similar effects, it is not surprising that withdrawal from stimulant drugs and from Prozac-like SSRI antidepressants share many features.

Described in many case reports for nearly three decades, "stimulant withdrawal was largely overlooked [by doctors] for years."[72] Clinicians have tended to dismiss the severity of stimulant withdrawal or to characterize it as "merely psychological." Because stimulant withdrawal typically lacks some of the more visible *physical* manifestations of withdrawal from drugs classically used to excess, such as alcohol and the opiates,[73] it is easier to overlook.

"Crashing" is the best-known effect of withdrawing from stimulants. During this state, you are likely to feel emotionally upset, and to lack energy and motivation. This depressive, fatigued state is the result of your brain's attempt to overcome the previous state of artificial stimulation. Similarly, if stimulants cause you to be less hungry, a marked increase in appetite and weight gain may accompany withdrawal.

The deep depression and apathy usually last no more than three to ten days. However, as confirmed in a psychopharmacology manual, they may "reach serious clinical proportions" and "persist for weeks" in "unstable individuals."[74] Thoughts of despair and suicide may accompany this "crashing." A longer phase of general physical and mental slowing follows it. Paradoxically, you may also suffer from insomnia, anxiety, and irritation.

DSM-IV specifies certain criteria for a withdrawal syndrome associated with the group of stimulant drugs that includes Ritalin and cocaine. The symptoms it lists are fatigue; vivid, unpleasant dreams; insomnia or excessive sleep; increased appetite; and psychomotor retardation or agitation.[75]

Rebound reactions are also common. In the case of amphetamines and Ritalin, rebound phenomena show up when children are taken off the drug abruptly or miss a dose. Typically, they experience an increase in agitation, restlessness, excitability, and distraction.[76] Rebound reactions are, by definition, more intense than the same symptoms experienced before taking the drug. They may occur within hours of the last dose of a stimulant and can persist for days.

In a double-blind controlled study, parents and teachers of "normal" boys given a *single* dose of amphetamine observed marked rebound phenomena five hours after the drug was administered.[77] There is no doubt that parents, teachers, and doctors repeatedly mistake these rebound reactions for signs that the child's "attention deficit-hyperactivity disorder" is worsening and that the child "clearly needs" the drug.

There are case reports of delirium, psychosis, and severe confusional states upon amphetamine withdrawal.[78] Similarly, researchers have documented psychosis and deep depressive symptoms with suicidal thoughts upon withdrawal of Ritalin in children.[79] There is a case report of stuttering priapism (intermittent, long-lasting painful erections) in an adolescent withdrawn from Concerta.[80] As we discussed at the beginning of this chapter with regard to adverse reaction reports sent to the FDA, the relative paucity of reports of withdrawal-induced distress is not a good indicator of their true frequency.

Most of our knowledge about withdrawal reactions after stimulant use comes from studies of adult cocaine users. Amphetamine withdrawal has been studied less; and methylphenidate (Ritalin) withdrawal, even less still.[81] Millions of children take stimulants daily. It is truly remarkable that researchers are not systematically investigating this hazardous phenomenon.

Should withdrawal from stimulants be abrupt or gradual? The specialized literature contains recommendations to withdraw stimulants *abruptly*, on the grounds that no dangerous physical symptoms will occur. One psychopharmacology textbook is quite explicit: "When a patient who is dependent on stimulants is hospitalized, stimulant administration should be stopped abruptly. No tapered withdrawal is necessary."[82] The writers of that passage nonetheless confirm that withdrawal from large doses will "often" produce "a withdrawal syndrome consisting of depression, fatigue, hyperphagia [excessive eating], and hypersomnia."[83] Yet, rather than recommend a gradual withdrawal to attenuate incapacitating reactions, the authors speculate on the value of treating them with antidepressants!

We see no reason to endorse abrupt withdrawal from stimulants, unless they have been used for a short time or sporadically, with few or no ill effects between episodes of use. Two doctors who described an arduous withdrawal of Ritalin from two older men emphasized that "a drug free state may not easily be achieved by following the widely accepted recommendation to stop daily stimulant doses abruptly."[84]

Lithium and Anticonvulsant Withdrawal Reactions

Lithium withdrawal raises the serious issue of confusing withdrawal difficulties with relapse. In fact, lithium withdrawal reactions exactly mimic the manic symptoms that lead to the start of lithium treatment. Doctors prescribe lithium primarily to treat mania; often, mania rapidly follows lithium withdrawal. How is the doctor or patient to know whether this condition is withdrawal mania or a return of the original psychiatric problem?

Some doctors refuse to see a specific syndrome of withdrawal from lithium. Others suggest that a true lithium withdrawal syndrome cannot merely resemble mania but that "tremor, dizziness, and sometimes epileptic seizures" should also be observed.[85] We believe, however, that the latter opinions are further instances in which doctors have thoughtlessly attributed disturbed reactions after drug withdrawal to the patient's "underlying illness" rather than to the drug treatment itself.

The rapid recurrence of mania can happen even among patients who have been taking the drug for years, are seemingly "well-stabilized," and are withdrawn from it for only four or five days.[86] In one study, researchers abruptly switched twenty-one previously manic patients to placebos. They had taken lithium continuously for an average of four years. The authors write: "Within 14 days on placebo, 11 patients relapsed into severe psychotic states with paranoid, manic and depressive syndromes. . . . Most of the other patients not relapsing into psychotic states reported anxiety, nervousness, increased irritability and alertness, [and] sleep disturbances."[87]

One review systematically examined fourteen published studies of lithium withdrawal involving 257 "manic-depressive" patients with an average of thirty months of stable lithium treatment. Of the new manic episodes that occurred, more than 50 percent were experienced within three months of withdrawal. Also observed was a staggering 28-fold increase in the risk of new manic episodes for patients just withdrawn from lithium.[88] Another review of published and unpublished studies on lithium withdrawal yielded similar conclusions.[89] This evidence led one doctor to state candidly: "[F]rank manic symptoms are the defining feature of significant withdrawal effects and appear to be of a comparable severity to those seen in manic illness generally, often requiring hospital admission."[90]

Withdrawal from lithium increases the likelihood of rebound depression as well as mania. A study of 14 patients and 28 controls showed that lithium withdrawal led to "a high immediate relapse rate." However, once these patients recovered from the rebound withdrawal reaction, their overall outcome over the next seven years was "not worsened by discontinuation." This is good news for patients who are considering withdrawal from lithium. According to this study, once they have recovered from the withdrawal reaction, their prognosis is as good as for patients who remain on lithium.[91]

Increases in energy and alertness, heightened emotional response, increased concentration, and decreased thirst are sometimes reported even in patients who do *not* experience mania during withdrawal.[92]

An editorial in the *British Journal of Psychiatry* openly states that when patients take lithium for less than two years, they risk undergoing frequent recurrences of manic episodes shortly after withdrawal. The author, a psychiatrist, believes that these are genuine withdrawal effects and recommends informing patients of the danger before they decide to undertake lithium treatment.[93] Nonetheless, the same psychiatrist maintains that taking lithium for more than ten years does not carry this withdrawal risk. This conclusion contradicts well-accepted clinical experience indicating that the longer a drug is taken, the greater is the risk of withdrawal reactions.

Psychiatrists are belatedly beginning to realize that the rapid recurrence of mania after lithium withdrawal is a real withdrawal effect. However, many practicing doctors undoubtedly continue to attribute withdrawal-induced mania to their patients' "chronic disease." These doctors then persist in exposing their patients to lithium despite its many long-term adverse effects.

Over the past decade, the use of lithium to treat mania or bipolar disorder has been mostly replaced by a crop of drugs originally developed to treat epilepsy. Most of these anti-seizure or anticonvulsant drugs, which include older drugs such as Tegretol and Depakene, and newer drugs such as Topamax and Neurontin, have not been approved by the FDA to treat mania or bipolar disorder. However, Lamictal and Depakote are now approved for treating manic disorders.

Several previous reports described anticonvulsant withdrawal reactions, focusing on the risk of seizures in patients having received these drugs to treat epilepsy or other seizure disorders. Now that hundreds of thousands of people who do not suffer from seizures are prescribed anti-seizure drugs, withdrawal reactions are likely to be more varied. Nonetheless, as has occurred previously with every wave of "newer" drugs, there is still a dearth of published reports of withdrawal reactions.

Tegretol (carbamazepine) is an anticonvulsant drug widely used as a treatment for many problems, including mania. Upon withdrawal, Tegretol can provoke serious emotional flare-ups—including paranoia, hostility, and agitation—in previously disturbed people.[94] These withdrawal reactions can also occur in mentally stable individuals, as in one documented case involving a patient treated for a physical disorder.[95] Although probably less frequently than withdrawal from lithium, withdrawal from Tegretol can also cause rebound mania.[96] Other anticonvulsants or anti-epileptic drugs such as Depakene (valproic acid), Depakote (divalproex sodium), and Dilantin (phenytoin), are also widely prescribed in psychiatry. The risk of seizures needs to be considered when any anticonvulsant drug is withdrawn, whether or not a seizure disorder was previously present. Other symptoms of anticonvulsant withdrawal may commonly include anxiety, muscle twitching, tremors, weakness, nausea, and vomiting. A case of withdrawal reaction in an eighty-one-year-old man maintained for five years on Neurontin (gabapentin) and then tapered over one week described "severe mental status changes, severe somatic chest pains, and hypertension" appearing ten days after the last dose. Upon reintroduction of the drug, the symptoms subsided within 24 hours. The authors propose that "a gabapentin taper should follow a course similar to that of a benzodiazepine taper— slowly and over a period of weeks to months."[97]

Antipsychotic or Neuroleptic Withdrawal Reactions

Antipsychotic or neuroleptic drugs include Clozaril, Haldol, Mellaril, Navane, Prolixin, Risperdal, Zyprexa, and others listed in Chapter 4. They produce many physical and psychological withdrawal reactions, including weight gain, abnormal movements, and psychosis. These reactions vary from merely unpleasant to life-threatening, from transient to irreversible. Antipsychotics have been widely used for fifty-five years, and distinct withdrawal syndromes were documented in the first decade of their use. Yet, as with most psychiatric drugs, these syndromes have not been sufficiently studied.[98]

Interest in antipsychotic withdrawal syndromes has been renewed, however. As we discuss in this section, researchers now realize that abrupt withdrawal—an exceedingly common practice—escalates rates of "schizophrenic relapse." Furthermore, after withdrawal from atypical antipsychotics such as Clozaril, a violent reaction characterized by delirium with psychosis may occur. Interest in withdrawal has also been sparked by the nursing home reform initiated by the Omnibus Budget Reconciliation Act of 1987 (OBRA). The act mandated nursing homes and other institutions receiving federal funds to implement dose reductions and withdrawals of neuroleptic and sedative drugs.

Three Types of Antipsychotic Withdrawal Reactions

A common type of antipsychotic withdrawal reaction resembles withdrawal from tricyclic antidepressants. It involves rebound of the brain's cholinergic neurotransmitter system. Because neuroleptics such as

Mellaril, Navane, Thorazine, and Stelazine suppress this system, it rebounds, or "goes into overdrive," when the drugs are removed.[99] Other neuroleptics, such as Haldol and Compazine, have strong antinausea effects; when they are withdrawn, nausea is a likely reaction.

Cholinergic rebound produces unpleasant symptoms similar to a bad attack of flu, such as nausea, vomiting, diarrhea, headaches, chills, sweating, and a runny nose. Emotional upset frequently occurs as well. These symptoms usually last about one to four weeks, depending on how long the drug has been used. However, we are aware of some patients who have suffered lasting effects. Especially in cases where the vomiting becomes severe or breathing becomes difficult, medical attention may be required. In children, "the reaction is often more severe, and it may on occasion occur after missing a single dose."[100] Clinicians have noted that "[f]igures of up to 50 percent of subjects affected by [cholinergic rebound] withdrawal seem standard."[101]

A second group of withdrawal reactions involves abnormalities of movement. Because antipsychotics suppress the dopaminergic neurotransmitter system, which controls voluntary movements, removal of the drug can result in involuntary spasms, twitches, tics, tremors, and other muscular movements. Withdrawal reactions may include a "Tourette-like syndrome" characterized by motor tics and vocalizations.[102] Many of these movements involve the face and neck, but any muscle function may be affected, including talking, swallowing, and breathing. These withdrawal reactions can be painful, disfiguring, and disabling. They are more fully described in Chapter 4 in connection with tardive dyskinesia.

In some cases, the movements gradually cease after a few weeks; this phenomenon is known as withdrawal emergent dyskinesia. (Other names for it are withdrawal parkinsonism, withdrawal dystonia, and withdrawal akathisia). If the movements persist for four weeks or longer, they are diagnosed as tardive dyskinesia or one of its variants. In about one third of cases, these movements lessen substantially or, in very few cases, disappear gradually over a period of months. Most cases persist indefinitely. Accompanying these movement disorders are unpleasant mental states such as depression and indifference in cases of parkinsonism, and anxiety, despair, and anger in cases of akathisia.[103]

Not everyone views these abnormal movements as *true* withdrawal reactions, for the simple reason that they are ordinarily first observed *during* drug use (Chapter 4). In many cases, however, abnormal movements become apparent or worsen only when the patient is reducing or stopping the drug.[104] Astonishingly, one review of antipsychotic withdrawal reactions does not mention abnormal movements.[105]

A third group of withdrawal reactions involves a wide range of psychological and behavioral symptoms, including insomnia, anxiety, agitation, irritability, and organic psychosis. Psychotic withdrawal symptoms are variously called tardive psychosis, supersensitivity psychosis, or withdrawal psychosis.[106] Frequently accompanied by abnormal movements, they include hallucinations, delusions, confusion, and disorientation.

Tardive psychosis is considered controversial by some investigators, and researchers have reported widely different rates. However, we believe that clinical and scientific evidence confirms its existence.[107] After years of suppression of the dopamine system by these drugs, the brain compensates for their effects. When the drugs are discontinued, the hyper-aroused dopamine system takes over. Psychotic reactions upon abrupt withdrawal have been observed in individuals with no history of psychotic symptoms, such as patients taking antipsychotics for tic disorders.[108]

Among developmentally disabled individuals who have been treated with neuroleptics, withdrawal frequently leads to profound emotional disturbances. This worsening of behavior, called "withdrawal-induced behavioral deterioration,"[109] usually lasts for several months[110] and can become permanent. However, a substantial number of people may improve if kept off the drugs. One author notes that "it is not generally appreciated that severe behavioral symptoms which emerge during neuroleptic dosage reduction can be transient." As a result, "[i]f symptoms do appear during drug taper, the usual clinical practice is to reintroduce the drug, often at doses higher than the original."[111]

Cases of neuroleptic malignant syndrome (see Chapter 4) have also been documented upon neuroleptic withdrawal. NMS involves impaired consciousness, abnormal movements, fever, and other symptoms, sometimes ending in the patient's death.[112]

Withdrawal from Atypical Antipsychotics

Withdrawal reactions from Clozaril (clozapine) involve not only cholinergic and dopaminergic supersensitivity but also rebound. Several case reports describe a quickly occurring withdrawal syndrome "with rapid onset of agitation, abnormal movements, and psychotic symptoms." According to one author, "These appear to be much more rapid than syndromes seen after stopping conventional [neuroleptics]."[113] Others have found that the "severe agitation and psychotic symptoms . . . resolved rapidly and completely upon resumption of low doses of clozapine."[114]

Two cases of sudden emergence of brand-new obsessive-compulsive symptoms, one of which also involved "Tourette's syndrome-like tics," have been described after clozapine withdrawal. In both cases, clinicians observed a "complete disappearance" of symptoms upon resumption of clozapine.[115] Another person treated for two years developed "severe insomnia, restlessness, and chills" after clozapine was withdrawn. These symptoms disappeared when clozapine was reinitiated, appeared three months later when doctors again withdrew it, and disappeared once more upon readministration of the drug.[116] In another study, twenty-eight patients were evaluated seven days after abrupt clozapine discontinuation; of these, 61 percent developed withdrawal reactions. Most of the reactions were rated "mild" with agitation, headache, or nausea; but four patients experienced more uncomfortable withdrawal involving nausea, vomiting, or diarrhea. Another experienced "a rapid-onset psychotic episode requiring hospitalization."[117] The study does not specify how many patients with "mild" agitation during the first seven days after withdrawal went on to develop more severe episodes of agitated behavior. According to a recent report describing four serious cases of Clozaril withdrawal, two patients were unable to walk, another had a lurching gate, and two gagged while eating or drinking.[118]

One article entitled "Clozapine as a Drug of Dependence" confirms the existence of a "clear somatic withdrawal sign" in laboratory animals after treatment with clozapine.[119] The drug was seen as the prototype for atypical neuroleptics when first introduced in the United States in 1990. Over time, so-called atypical neuroleptics or antipsychotics such as Risperdal, Seroquel, Zyprexa, Geodon, Abilify, and Invega—enthusiastically promoted as safer drugs than the older neuroleptics—seem to increasingly resemble the conventional drugs they were meant to replace.

Like the SSRI antidepressants, Seroquel has actions on the serotonin system, and it's not surprising that some withdrawal reactions from it might resemble those of SSRI drugs. One case report described a thirty-six-year-old woman on 100 mg a day of Seroquel who, upset over her large weight gain on the drug, decided to stop the drug and was advised by her doctor to reduce the dose by half. "After one day, she reported nausea, dizziness, headache and anxiety severe enough to preclude her normal activities." Her symptoms continued despite returning to a higher dose. A more gradual reduction of 12.5 mg every five days, aided by an anti-nausea drug, also failed. She was successful on a third attempt when her doctors added an older antipsychotic drug to her regimen, although her nausea persisted for two more days after her last dose.[120]

"Relapse" or "Withdrawal"?

In cases where patients are withdrawn from extended antipsychotic use, much of what gets called "schizophrenic" or "psychotic" relapse may actually be unrecognized withdrawal reactions. Withdrawal symptoms such as agitation, restlessness, and insomnia are also likely to be mistakenly attributed to the patients' mental condition. By now, this situation may be depressingly familiar to the reader. It reflects the same confusion that we noted in regard to withdrawal from antidepressants, minor tranquilizers, lithium, and stimulants.

Indeed, because of the resemblance between many withdrawal symptoms and patients' prior emotional problems, clinicians not only blame the reaction on the "underlying disorder" but also recommend continued treatment with the offending agent. These clinical errors persist despite telltale signs such as rapid onset of the symptoms after the drug is discontinued and rapid relief after it is reinstated. They persist even despite observations that "[r]eal psychotic relapse rarely occurs during the first weeks of withdrawal."[121]

The controversy over the value of antipsychotic treatment will likely increase as clinicians continue to observe differing relapse rates between abruptly and gradually withdrawn patients; as it turns out, many patients who are gradually withdrawn do not need any further medication. According to one study,[122] "There is a nearly twofold difference in relapse risk between abrupt and gradual withdrawal of [antipsychotic] agents,"[123] whereas an earlier comprehensive analysis concluded that the relapse rate among patients withdrawn from antipsychotics is three times greater than that among patients kept on the drugs.[124] However, when other researchers reanalyzed these data to distinguish between patients quickly withdrawn and those more gradually tapered, the latter had one-third the relapse rate of the former![125] In terms of relapse rates, then, prolonged drug treatment appears to be no better than a gradual tapering.[126]

Of course, prolonged treatment is much more dangerous. Indeed, researchers are beginning to suggest that brain changes resulting from long-term drug treatment may create "pharmacologic stress factors" or "iatrogenic-pharmacologic stress effects" that, combined with abrupt withdrawal, increase the vulnerability to relapse.[127] Taking drugs and then abruptly stopping them might weaken patients' capacity to respond to stress in the future.

When to Withdraw from Antipsychotics?

The circumstances in which antipsychotics withdrawal should be strongly considered or attempted are so numerous that full coverage is not possible. We can, however, provide a few guidelines that reflect generally recognized medical knowledge and practice:

1. Antipsychotics must be withdrawn any time there are signs of potentially life-threatening drug-induced disorders, such as neuroleptic malignant syndrome or bone marrow suppression with compromise of the immune system. Fatalities can result from failure to adhere to this guideline.
2. Antipsychotics should be withdrawn, if at all possible, at the first sign of tardive dyskinesia. Most of the very severe, disabling cases of tardive dyskinesia result in part from failure to follow this guideline.
3. Antipsychotics should be withdrawn as quickly as possible from patients who have reached forty years of age, since rates for tardive dyskinesia further escalate with age.
4. Antipsychotic withdrawal should be attempted, if at all possible, in cases where patients who have been taking the drugs for months or years no longer show severe or disabling psychotic symptoms.

Given the high probability of irreversible effects of antipsychotics, any doctor following patients who are undergoing long-term treatment must seriously consider lowering the dose to the absolute minimum. In many such patients, the minimal dose will actually be zero. In general, patients should be given neuroleptics for the shortest possible time in the smallest possible doses. We believe that a more rational practice of psychiatry would eliminate the use of such dangerous medications.

Research on OBRA-87, the congressional legislation regulating the use of psychotropics and physical restraints in nursing homes, shows that it had the intended impact, especially in terms of reducing the use of neuroleptics.[128] The use of benzodiazepines, also targeted by the legislation, has likewise decreased. We still need better documentation of how these changes are improving the residents' quality of life. Meanwhile, however, it is clear from several studies that *up to half of institutionalized elderly patients can be successfully withdrawn from neuroleptics.* Tapered withdrawals are usually successful, residents infrequently display increased levels of agitation, and most are able to remain off the drugs for extended periods.[129] Overall, these drugs are so dangerous to the elderly that they should not be prescribed to them.

How Long Should Antipsychotic Drug Withdrawal Take?

Antipsychotic drugs should be completely stopped at the first sign of any abnormal movements. Too often doctors try to guess whether or not a particular abnormal movement, like eye blinking or grimacing, is related to tardive dyskinesia. Any abnormal movement should be considered a probable manifestation of tardive dyskinesia when the patient is taking antipsychotic drugs, including the newer ones; and the drug should be stopped as quickly as possible.

Some physicians believe that the newer antipsychotic drugs are less likely to cause tardive dyskinesia. At present, the data is insufficient to make this claim and the FDA requires the same tardive dyskinesia warning for all antipsychotic drugs. Nearly all of the antipsychotic drugs, including Risperdal and Zyprexa, suppress function of the dopamine nerves and therefore can cause tardive dyskinesia.

An occasional unscrupulous report claims that the newer antipsychotics can "improve" tardive dyskinesia because they tend to suppress the symptoms. In reality, any drug that suppresses tardive dyskinesia is likely to cause it as well. This phenomenon is called masking. Giving the newer antipsychotics to control tardive dyskinesia is likely to worsen the disorder in the long run.

In non-emergency situations where tardive dyskinesia is not suspected, antipsychotic drugs should be withdrawn slowly, keeping in mind that it is not unusual to take at least one month to withdraw for every year of exposure, so that a patient who has taken neuroleptics for two years is likely to require at least two months to withdraw (see Chapter 8). Also keep in mind the risk of withdrawal psychosis. A temporary worsening of the patient's condition is likely toward the end of withdrawal or shortly after the drug is stopped. This should not in itself prevent eventual, if gradual, withdrawal from antipsychotic drugs.

Primate research confirms that withdrawal should proceed very slowly because drug-induced changes may last for several months after the last dose. In a laboratory study, thirty-eight healthy monkeys were observed daily for 108 weeks. For the first 25 weeks, "baseline" information was gathered. From week 25 to week 72, the monkeys received long-lasting injections of fluphenazine (Prolixin). The main findings during this period were "highly significant decreases in self- and environment-directed behaviors and affiliation," meaning that the animals paid much less attention to themselves, their companions, and their surroundings. As of week 73, drug injections were ceased, and "[a]ggression showed some increase during early drug discontinuation, accentuated by stress." (This outcome resembles the withdrawal agitation observed in humans.) Importantly, the investigators state that "[r]ecovery of normal (baseline) behavioral scores began by week 7 after the last treatment." In other words, it was not until two months after the last dose that the animals began to display normal behavior. Ultimately, "tardive dyskinesias persisted in 30 percent of the animals for a prolonged time."[130]

Based on clinical experience bolstered by research, we suggest that if you are withdrawing from neuroleptics, you should avoid making major changes in your life during and shortly after withdrawal. Allow for a "coasting" period of at least several weeks to shake off drug effects, with emphasis on improved nutrition, exercise, and general well-being. In particular, strengthen your social relationships and avoid new, unpredictable sources of stress and tension.

Rebuilding your life without resort to drugs after years of antipsychotics can be especially difficult. You may have acquiesced to taking drugs that you actually experienced as toxic and mind-numbing, and this submissiveness, compounded by drug effects, may have weakened your ability to make independent decisions. You will benefit from careful planning and preparation, building a support network, and practicing nondrug options to deal with stress and anxiety.

Antiparkinsonian Withdrawal Reactions

Antiparkinsonian drugs such as Cogentin, Kemadrin, Artane, and Symmetrel are frequently prescribed to suppress the movement disorders, such as parkinsonism, commonly caused by neuroleptics. About half of the patients who receive older antipsychotics also receive antiparkinsonian drugs.

Antiparkinsonian drugs are also described as "anticholinergic" because of their chemical action in suppressing cholinergic activity in the brain.[131] Rebound cholinergic hypersensitivity causes a large proportion of the withdrawal effects of antiparkinsonian drugs, which resemble those of tricyclics and neuroleptics and can be equally complex and varied. Several studies have demonstrated the typical flu-like symptoms of nausea, vomiting, chills, weakness, and headache, as well as the insomnia and restlessness that occur upon withdrawal from these drugs.[132]

In a rare double-blind, placebo-controlled withdrawal study, the authors found "a recognizable withdrawal syndrome"—namely, an increase in anxiety manifested by "irritability, tension, palpitations and headache," various physical complaints (relating especially to the gastrointestinal tract), dizziness upon standing, and irregular heartbeats. In addition, psychotic symptoms flared up within days of withdrawal and lasted up to three weeks.[133] Eight of the eleven withdrawn patients (73 percent) displayed these "obvious withdrawal-related symptoms."

Other studies, too, have observed psychotic flare-ups, which are usually accompanied by a resurgence of abnormal movements. Indeed, investigators directly relate these psychotic symptoms—including delusions, hallucinations, suicide attempts, and isolation—to physical symptoms of rigidity, restlessness, akathisia, and parkinsonism.[134]

In one such study, the authors state plainly that "the anticholinergic withdrawal syndrome resembles the negative schizophrenic syndrome in many important respects. Its occurrence in schizophrenic patients may be mistaken for psychotic decompensation and result in inappropriate treatment."[135] A case report also describes a severe catatonia (immobility) upon abrupt withdrawal of Symmetrel.[136]

Furthermore, one case of a severe reaction resembling neuroleptic malignant syndrome was reported upon withdrawal of antiparkinsonians, even though the patient had never received neuroleptics.[137]

Since antiparkinsonian drugs worsen tardive dyskinesia and impair memory, withdrawal can provide extra benefits. In particular, withdrawal can improve the symptoms of tardive dyskinesia[138] and can cause a "dramatic increase in memory scores on the Wechsler Memory Scale."[139]

As with all psychiatric drugs, withdrawal from antiparkinsonians should be gradual and tapered, thereby decreasing the recurrence of abnormal movements originally suppressed by the drugs. Gradual withdrawal is also less likely to lead to a reinstitution of the drugs.[140]

How Gradual Is "Gradual Withdrawal"?

As we saw in Chapter 7, the so-called gradual or tapered antidepressant withdrawals mentioned in the published literature are often too rapid. In one report, for example, "gradual" refers to a seven-to-ten-day withdrawal period;[141] in another, it refers to withdrawal over four days;[142] in a third, it refers to a 50 percent reduction for five weeks, then no drug each alternate day for one week, then abrupt cessation.[143] In two additional reports, "gradual" means a 50 percent reduction in dose for one week, then abrupt cessation.[144] In a review of forty-six case reports of SSRI withdrawal reactions, twenty-three involved abrupt withdrawal, twelve involved tapering over two weeks or less, and only six involved tapering over more than two weeks.[145] None of the last eighteen tapers used something like the gradual, patient-centered methods described in Chapter 8. Finally, in a review of nearly sixty studies involving patients with diagnoses of schizophrenia or other psychoses who were withdrawn from neuroleptic drugs, the authors report that in most studies specifying the speed of withdrawal, the process was completed in less than a week, usually in *one day*.[146]

Rarely do investigators suggest that the taper period needs to be extended for several weeks; in fact, twelve weeks and fourteen weeks are the longest periods cited in the above-mentioned reviews. In one case of severe dizziness occurring upon successive, failed trials of Zoloft withdrawal in a twenty-nine-year-old man, the doctors contacted the drug manufacturer for help. They were advised to proceed with "extremely slow dosage titration."[147] Specifically, a reduced dosage was prescribed every other day for three weeks, then every third day for the next six weeks, then every fourth day for two more days, at which time the Zoloft was finally discontinued. Overall, the withdrawal lasted eleven weeks.

No such recommendation to proceed with "extremely slow" withdrawal appears in the official product monographs for Zoloft or any other antidepressant. As noted, as a result of FDA requirements, makers of SSRI and other antidepressants have begun to include warnings about discontinuation symptoms and recommendations of "gradual reduction in the dose rather than abrupt cessation . . . whenever possible" (as cited in the Cymbalta label, in the 2007 *Physicians' Desk Reference*), but no guidelines are given, in contrast with guidelines for initiating drug taking. Thus, both doctors and patients should be actively encouraged to proceed more slowly and carefully when psychiatric drugs are withdrawn. The gradual methods described in Chapter 8 constitute a sensible guideline in this regard.

Overview of Psychiatric Drug Withdrawal Reactions

In an authoritative 500-page book focusing solely on adverse effects of psychiatric drugs, fewer than five pages are devoted to withdrawal effects associated with all categories of drugs.[148] This finding reflects the inadequate level of psychiatric interest and knowledge in such reactions.

Psychiatric drugs may induce a wide range of adverse effects when they are taken, and they may induce a wide range of adverse effects when they are withdrawn. Recognized withdrawal syndromes are a regular, common feature of the use of all psychiatric drugs. But as we have seen, doctors who prescribe these drugs too often fail to warn the patients who take them.

Because they produce unpleasant withdrawal reactions, psychiatric drugs must be considered drugs of dependence. In other words, at least some users will restart the drugs due to withdrawal-induced discomfort. These individuals will continue their drug use simply in order to avoid withdrawal reactions. The countless first-person reports posted on the Internet by users of SSRI antidepressants, for example, provide unusually vivid evidence that this phenomenon occurs all too frequently. Unfortunately, when withdrawal reactions lead to prolonged drug use, users risk experiencing more severe withdrawal reactions later.

As noted, the relatively small quantity of *published* case reports describing withdrawal reactions cannot be taken as a valid indicator of the actual frequency of their occurrence. As a rule, withdrawal reactions from most psychiatric drugs have been ignored or simply not recognized as such. However, studies specifically designed to look for such reactions have found them in 60–80 percent of patients. A full 20 percent may undergo "severe" reactions.

Doctors often focus on the *physical* consequences of withdrawal, such as nausea, tremors, or seizures, while failing to identify the *emotional* withdrawal symptoms that so often contribute to the resumption of drugs. Emotional withdrawal reactions such as anxiety, depression, insomnia, confusion, and irritability can actually have a greater impact on patients than purely physical symptoms.

The three main categories of emotional and behavioral withdrawal reactions are anxiety, depression, and psychosis. Anxiety reactions appear to be common upon withdrawal of central nervous system (CNS) depressants such as benzodiazepines and other tranquilizers, most of the antidepressants, antipsychotics, lithium and anticonvulsants used as mood stabilizers, and antiparkinsonians. Depressive reactions appear to be common upon withdrawal of stimulants and SSRIs. And psychotic reactions appear to be common upon withdrawal from neuroleptics, lithium, and antiparkinsonians. Still, evidence from case reports and studies suggests that any psychiatric drug may produce any of these withdrawal reactions.

In addition, over a dozen studies so far have implicated expectant mothers' use of antidepressants during pregnancy with the appearance of a peculiar "neonatal abstinence syndrome." In one well-controlled study, a full 30 percent of 60 infants whose mothers took antidepressants for prolonged periods, including during the third trimester, developed the syndrome, which lasted up to four days; 13 percent of the infants had severe reactions. The most common symptoms were tremor, gastrointestinal problems, an abnormal increase in muscle tone (hypertonicity), sleep disturbances and high-pitched cries. None of the 60 infants without exposure to SSRIs developed the syndrome.[149] There is some debate whether this represents an actual withdrawal reaction or a sign of direct drug toxicity in the serotonin system.

Furthermore, clinicians and researchers do not always correctly describe the symptoms that occur upon withdrawal. In many cases, pro-drug bias and habitual resistance to acknowledging withdrawal effects lead them to use relatively neutral, ambiguous terms (such as *agitation, restlessness, anxiety,* and *psychomotor retardation*) in place of terms like *psychosis*.

Undoubtedly, many withdrawal reactions from all categories of drugs are mistakenly treated as "relapses" by prescribing physicians, thus moving the focus away from possible drug involvement and toward the patient's "underlying disorder." Many researchers also approach the problem timidly, often failing to describe or emphasize withdrawal reactions. As a consequence, patients suffer, and the public is kept uninformed.

So that patients can provide truly informed consent for the drugs they are taking, doctors must fully describe withdrawal or discontinuation in terms of adverse drug reactions with a "frequent" probability of occurrence. It is the doctors' duty to make sure that patients actually grasp and then remember the nature and likelihood of all important adverse reactions, including withdrawal reactions. Similarly, in their official drug monographs, drug manufacturers need to provide accurate summaries of reports of withdrawal reactions, as well as detailed guidelines for tapering their products, just as they provide guidelines for how to initiate treatment.

The best way to minimize the risk of severe withdrawal reactions is not to take psychiatric drugs in the first place. The second best approach is to plan a slow, gradual withdrawal involving close monitoring and a systematic, ongoing program of information, counseling, and reassurance. Unfortunately, however, abrupt withdrawal remains too common in clinical practice. Abrupt withdrawal is imprudent and may result in additional distress and disability. Except in emergencies, patients who are stopping their use of psychiatric drugs and the professionals who are assisting them should proceed gradually and maintain this gradual pace until complete cessation is accomplished, even if the early stages of withdrawal present no difficulties.

— 10 —

Withdrawing Your Child from Psychiatric Drugs

Chapters 7, 8, and 9 of this book were largely directed to adults who want to withdraw from drugs. However, as nearly all of the principles outlined in those chapters are relevant to children, they *must* be read prior to this one.

The most general of these principles include gradual withdrawal, the involvement of family members and a support system, and guidance from an experienced professional. We also emphasized the importance of paying attention to your own feelings, and of personally planning and managing your own withdrawal experience. Obviously, children—especially young children— cannot plan or control their own medical care: They need parents and other adults to do it for them. But they can and should play a major role in every step of the planning, and, as with adults, their feelings should be given special attention throughout the process. Precisely because children have immature or even impaired competence, their caregivers are obligated to try hard to seek and be responsive to children's views and feelings.

Since children who receive stimulants are by far the largest group of minors on psychiatric drugs, we will focus on stimulant withdrawal among children diagnosed with "attention deficit hyperactivity disorder." However, most of the observations that follow apply equally well to children being withdrawn from any psychoactive drug. It is now increasingly common for children to receive atypical antipsychotics and anticonvulsants.

The emphasis in this chapter is on younger children—preadolescents who are too young to participate effectively in treatment decisions and who cannot easily describe in words their responses to the drugs they are taking. Older children who are better able to communicate and make decisions can become actively involved in a manner more similar to that of adults. Indeed, depending on their maturity, older children can help to monitor the rate of their withdrawal from drugs in much the same way as adults do.

Special Precautions

Children are often given drugs for sedation that pose special problems if stopped abruptly. Regardless of whether they have epilepsy, youngsters taking sedatives and drugs used for the treatment of seizures can experience seizures during withdrawal. These drugs include all the minor tranquilizers such as Klonopin and Xanax, as well as anticonvulsants such as Depakote, Tegretol, Dilantin, Lamictal, and Topamax. Even among children who have never been manic, lithium can cause mania during withdrawal. And even among children who have never been hypertensive, abrupt clonidine (Catapres) withdrawal can trigger a hypertensive crisis. Withdrawal from stimulants such as Ritalin and Adderall, and antidepressants such as Paxil, Celexa, Effexor, Prozac, and Zoloft, can cause "crashing" accompanied by depressed and even suicidal feelings.

To learn about adverse effects and withdrawal effects associated with any drug your child is taking, be sure to review the information in earlier chapters of this book as well as in other resources.

Your Child's Previous Experience with Withdrawal

Children, like adults, vary greatly in terms of the intensity of their withdrawal response when taken off stimulant drugs. Some children experience little more than rebound hyperactivity or tension for a few hours. Others, especially after months or years of exposure to drugs, may undergo an extensive and uncomfortable withdrawal. The manifestations of withdrawal also vary. Some children may exhibit increased rebelliousness, hyperactivity, and insomnia; others may display apathy and a greater need to sleep.

Many children are routinely taken off stimulant drugs every weekend. If this is the case with your child, acute symptoms of withdrawal are probably not going to be a problem after the child's drug use has permanently ceased. Nonetheless, previous problems may resurface after a few weeks or even months as you, your child, and the school deal with this new drug-free experience.

Have you ever gone on vacation and forgotten to bring your child's drugs along, or stopped the drugs for some other reason? Such experiences should give you a sense of what your child's response will be during the acute phase of the upcoming planned withdrawal. However, keep in mind that withdrawal reactions can vary from one time to the next even in the same child.

Rebound and Withdrawal Effects

Some doctors tell parents that children and adults "react differently" to stimulants. This is untrue. Any withdrawal reaction can occur in both children and adults.

As previously described, children commonly experience withdrawal symptoms from stimulants within a few hours after taking the last dose. If they take Ritalin at 3 P.M., for example, they are likely to be more nervous, anxious, and "hyper" by evening. This stage of drug withdrawal is called *rebound*.

Some doctors tell parents that rebound cannot start after a delay of several hours following the last dose and that it cannot persist for a prolonged period of time. In fact, rebound routinely starts as long as five to ten hours after the last dose. And if no more stimulant is administered, the rebound can become a long-term withdrawal reaction that lasts days or weeks. In some cases, it may take a month or more for children to calm down after stopping stimulants during the summer vacation. These withdrawal effects would manifest themselves even longer if the children were subjected to the more demanding and stressful regimen of a typical school.

Identifying the Source of Potential Problems

When planning your child's withdrawal, you must take into account how and why your child was put on drugs in the first place. If your child was medicated because of "school problems" in the absence of "home problems," then you may have fewer or less severe parenting issues to deal with during withdrawal. Nonetheless, *new* parent-child conflicts are likely to develop during this process.

On the other hand, if you agreed to medicate your child because of his or her behavior around you, then you will almost certainly need to work very hard on parenting issues as your child comes off the drugs. This work will require a serious self-examination of your own behavior, along with openness to constructive criticism from your spouse or other family members and careful attention to any opinion your child is able to voice. In addition, you will have to work closely with anyone who shares caregiving responsibilities with you, since consistency is an important part of successful childrearing.

Useful parenting books can be found at bookstores and libraries. Look at a variety of such books and then select one or two for careful reading and reference. You may also want to attend parent training classes and seek consultations with an expert in parenting.[1]

If it turns out that your own confusion or inconsistency in parenting is a main cause of your child's difficulties, you should greet this as good news—indeed, the best possible news! It means that being a parent matters, that there's nothing wrong with your child that can't be fixed through your efforts and those of your family. Although it may initially seem easier to think that someone or something else is the cause of your child's problems, such thinking ultimately wrests the power out of your hands. In making the decision to stop medicating your child, you should reaffirm yourself as a parent and retake responsibility for your child.

Focusing on Problems in the Family

Suppressed Maturation

When children have been on psychiatric drugs for years, their psychological and social development may be suppressed. Instead of struggling through the normal developmental stages, these children are pushed through their growing-up period in a drug-induced state of conformity. They may not learn to know and to express themselves, to handle emotional pain, to work out conflicts with others, and to take charge of their own behavior. Their sense of autonomy and personal responsibility is almost always impaired. All these issues may surface acutely during withdrawal and require special parental attention.

Learning New Parenting Skills

None of us are born good parents: We have to learn this complex, subtle array of skills "on the job." In effect, we go through the same developmental stages as our children, but from our own perspective and with our own specific learning processes. However, when our children are medicated, we don't have the opportunity to learn the skills involved in raising a drug-free child. We become accustomed to turning to medication as the answer. At the same time, we might cease examining ourselves and our own parenting skills. Parents *and* children have to learn new skills during and after drug withdrawal.

Doctors, teachers, school psychologists, and other child welfare workers often recommend medication to parents when they should instead recommend or offer a consultation or seminar on parenting skills. Even parents who have successfully raised several children may have trouble finding the right approach to another of their offspring. Every child is a new challenge. In fact, your child's special assets, such as high energy and an independent nature, may be testing your parenting skills. And every new challenge in a family's life presents new stresses and opportunities for you and your children. Consultations with a family-oriented therapist who is skilled at identifying your *vulnerabilities* as a parent at this particular time in your life, and with this particular child, can be the critical factor in helping your child withdraw from drugs.

Many parents keep their children on drugs because they feel too guilty or ashamed to face the mistakes they have made. They feel so humiliated by criticism of their parenting that they cannot face the need to learn new approaches. By contrast, the most successful parents are those who freely admit that they routinely make mistakes and need to make constant readjustments in the ways that they relate to their children. Give up any pretense you may have about being a "perfect" parent, and assume that you've got a lot to learn. It's a matter of accepting the axiom that we're all human.

Other parents keep their children on medication because they have been told that their child suffers from a "severe neurobehavioral disorder" that will worsen unless treatment is instituted with drugs. Virtually every childhood distress, delayed achievement, or misbehavior has been labeled a disorder. Ask your doctor what medical tests or evidence, besides the child's behavior, necessitates a medical-sounding diagnosis.

Preadolescent children are incredibly responsive to any improvement in parental behavior. Sometimes just a few good consultations with a parenting expert can help you significantly change your child's life for the better. Especially in regard to managing difficult behaviors, such as anger and resentment, new parental approaches can transform a young child's responses overnight.

Learning to Give More Attention

Most parents suffer from "parent attention deficit disorder." They rarely find enough time to give their children all the attention they need and deserve. In effect, their children get leftover time.

In modern society, with its increasing economic pressures on families and its many single-parent homes, drugs have become a kind of babysitter; children make fewer demands on parents while on drugs. If you are going to take your child off psychiatric drugs, be prepared to spend additional time with him or her. This can be the single most important and potentially satisfying decision of your life—to spend more time with your child on a routine basis throughout the period of your child's dependency on you.

The Father's Special Role

Many if not most children routinely seen for medication have fathers who are not sufficiently involved in their children's lives. Especially in cases involving boys who are disobedient and resent authority, the father is often the main source of the difficulty—and thus the main source of potential improvement. Such boys need a stronger father-son bond through which to learn disciplined and respectful behavior. However, in cases where dad is spending time with the child but a corresponding behavioral improvement is not taking place, he may be acting too much like a pal and not enough like a parent. When a father is lax as a disciplinarian, the child is encouraged to take advantage of his mother or other caregivers, imposing an impossible burden upon them.

Paying Attention to Your Child's Feelings and Wishes

In addition to the principles of slow and cautious withdrawal that we emphasize, it is important that you pay special attention to your child's feelings. Every single day during the withdrawal period, talk and play with your child, and fine-tune your sense of how your child feels.

Bedtime presents a good opportunity for visiting with your child, especially if he or she is having trouble falling asleep during drug withdrawal. But be sure to check in before and after school as well. If you're at work during the day, call in *every day* when your child gets home from school. Like our other suggestions, this one can become a deeply satisfying habit that lasts throughout childhood and contributes to the love and trust that you share with your child.

Make clear to your child that withdrawal from drugs can be difficult and that you want to hear about any unusual or uncomfortable feelings or thoughts. Reassure your child that you will pay attention, respond, and perhaps alter the medication schedule if necessary.

Playing games can help a young child express potentially delicate feelings and thus help you communicate with the child. For instance, you can have two stuffed animals chat with each other. Start by making up any subject matter you can imagine, especially if it's cute and funny. Then ask your child to have the animals talk with each other. At an opportune time, introduce the topic of "feelings" into the conversation between the animals. Eventually, you can ask them how they feel now that they are taking fewer pills. You may be astonished to hear your previously reticent child begin to reveal information in the form of a dialogue between the two stuffed animals.

Another playful approach involves storytelling. Ask your child—with lots of prompting, if necessary—to make up a story about a little girl or boy. After the story begins, you can suggest that the child in the story is having trouble getting along at home or in school. Then direct the story to what happens if the little girl or boy starts and then stops taking medications. You may find that your child tells you about herself in her story.

Another way to enlist your child's cooperation is to inform him about the potential difficulties he may experience during withdrawal. Children often become more responsible when responsibility is entrusted to them. And the prospect of coming off their drugs often motivates children to improve their conduct.

Don't worry about giving your child too much opportunity to voice his or her feelings and wishes; you can still remain in charge as the parent. If anything, your increased interest in your child's feelings will encourage your child to be more responsive to yours.

Focusing on Problems at School

Children are most often put on stimulants because of pressure from school. Many schools encourage parents to seek medical consultations in order to medicate the children and control their classroom behavior.

In the past, hyperactivity and other forms of disruptive actions were the major target behaviors. More recently, schools have begun advocating drugs on the assumption that they also contribute to improved learning and academic performance. However, there is no body of scientific evidence to support this hope. Most reviews and panels have concluded that stimulants have not been shown to improve learning or academic performance.[2] Like other psychoactive agents, they are far more likely to impair mental function.

If Your Child Is Inattentive

If your child's main problems at school are daydreaming, forgetting things, and otherwise acting "inattentively," you should be able to stop the stimulant drugs with relative ease. Simply explain to the teacher that you'd rather have a child who daydreams than a child who can't daydream. You might also point out that there are no scientific data confirming the usefulness of stimulants for treating inattention.[3]

Ask the teacher's support in increasing your child's attention in school, perhaps through more individualized instruction aimed at stimulating your child and addressing specific educational needs. In addition, spend time outside of school cultivating your child's academic interests in a fun manner. Take your child to the library and to museums, movies, concerts, and other educational activities. But do not resort to drugs to "improve" your child's attention. Drugs only blunt imagination and fantasy life without making any genuine improvement in the child's actual ability to focus.

If Your Child Is Underachieving

Some teachers give better grades to children on drugs because the drugs make them more conforming. But better grades are not worth the price of drug-induced conformity. And, as already noted, drugs do not improve actual academic achievement or learning.

Many well-meaning parents have chosen to medicate their children to improve their grades. If you are among them, we urge you to reconsider your priorities. Your personal relationship to your child should be a much higher priority than grades. Indeed, your child will benefit much more from feeling loved and appreciated by you than from getting good grades. Stop struggling with your child about homework and focus on enjoying parenthood. Let the teacher, a tutor, or a relative or friend help with homework if doing so relieves some of the tension between you and your child. A month or two of relief from conflict over studies may enable you to improve not only your relationship but also your perspective on what's important in the long run for your child. In our opinion, nothing is more important than the quality of your personal relationship with your child.

We also urge you to place a higher priority on the integrity of your child's brain than on good grades. As your child grows up, he or she will have multiple opportunities to develop an interest in school and in education. For that matter, some people don't settle down to studying until they are adults, and others, of course, do very well in life despite doing very poorly in school. So, whereas future opportunities for school abound, your child will *never* be able to get a new brain unaffected by drugs.

If your child is in danger of flunking a grade, you may feel a particular urgency about correcting the situation. This concern is understandable, but do not let it override two of the most important aspects of your child's life—the relationship between the two of you, and his or her ownership of a brain unimpaired by drugs.

Maintaining patience with children who underachieve is a far more positive action than medicating them. And, in any case, there are many other ways to help children perform better in school. The best one is to spend time with your child—playing interesting games, going to museums, and, in general, engaging in activities that make learning a part of your family life. Tutoring, especially in reading, is often the most effective educational intervention available. Reading with your child is not only academically beneficial but it can improve your relationship.

If the School Insists

As noted, many schools pressure parents to put their children on medication, especially if they are disruptive in class or require more attention than the teacher is willing or able to give. Private schools may threaten to expel the children. Public schools use other forms of psychological pressure that can be equally threatening.

If you are a parent who is determined not to drug your children, you can put your energy into considering the many better alternatives that exist. First, work closely with the school on improving your child's disruptive behavior. Spend time in class observing your child's behavior, or have a friend or relative do so. Your visits will have the added advantage of making clear to your child—and to the teacher—that you take these difficulties seriously. Do everything you can to ensure that the school meets your child's needs.

Resistance from schools is to be expected. Dealing with teachers and school officials who understandably resist changing their habits in order to accommodate your child's needs requires time, effort, patience, and ingenuity. But, as an alternative to medicating your child, it has the clear advantage of squarely framing the difficulty in *educational* terms, and of encouraging adults around your child to come up with solutions.

We sometimes advise parents to tell the school authorities something along these lines: "I know that Ritalin has a good chance of making my child more compliant in class, but that's just not the kind of 'improvement' I want for my child. I do not beat my child if he suffers a setback in class, and I refuse to drug my child for the same purpose." You may also express your concern about exposing your child to drugs that cause agitation, growth stunting, and heart problems that the FDA has explicitly warned about.

Second, discuss your child's problems at school with an independent counselor, psychologist, or educational consultant. If the professional is unwilling to visit the school, you may want to find another resource.

Third, remember that many wonderful children who become creative adults were not meant to spend day after day in large groups learning rote material. Consider other schools as well as the wide variety of home-schooling programs that are available.

Withdrawing from Multiple Drugs or Multiple Daily Doses

In Chapter 8 we discussed the principles involved in choosing which drug or which dose to start reducing. Recall that if a second drug has been given for a side effect caused by the original drug, the second drug should not be withdrawn until after the dose of the original one has been reduced. Thus, for example, if your child was given Klonopin to overcome Ritalin-induced insomnia, cutting back on the Ritalin should be your initial step.

Alternatively, if a specific drug dose is causing adverse effects, you might begin by reducing that dose. For example, if the afternoon dose of clonidine is making your child too sleepy—or the afternoon dose of Ritalin is making your child too wide awake at bedtime—start reducing it.

Sometimes one or another dose may be the more practical one to reduce. If your child's behavior at home is relatively easy to manage compared to his or her school behavior, then start by reducing the dose that you give after school.

When to Start Withdrawal

Your child should be withdrawn from psychiatric drugs of any kind as soon as possible. They are detrimental to your child's growing brain and overall development. Even if you and your child's doctor believe that the psychiatric drugs have been helpful, they should be stopped as soon as feasible. In cases where drugs are being used to treat children or adults, the smallest possible dose for the shortest possible time is always the best practice. In children with growing, vulnerable brains, the need to avoid toxic exposures is especially critical.

Remember, your child's behavior may temporarily worsen during withdrawal. A positive, loving, patient, engaging environment is very important at this time. If your child is going off to summer camp or some other activity away from home, withdrawal ideally should be *complete* at least a few weeks beforehand.

If your child has been on drugs for a year or longer, and if school behavior is a major problem, you may want to wait until summer vacation to begin to withdraw the drugs. Or you may want to begin a slow, cautious withdrawal during the school year. If the school reports that the child is "getting out of control," you might have to hold off until summer.

As parents ourselves, we would rather take our children out of school than to drug them for the purpose of staying in school. We would prefer any viable alternative to giving psychoactive drugs to our children, including major changes in our own lifestyle in order to provide better for our children's needs.

We recommend reading Peter Breggin's *Talking Back to Ritalin*[4] as a part of any decision to start or stop stimulant drugs for the behavioral control of children. His book discusses many subjects covered in the present chapter, in considerably greater detail—including how to deal with schools and how to develop your parenting skills.

Understanding Your Therapist's Fears About Nonuse of Drugs

Many people reading this book are seeing physicians or psychotherapists who are urging them to start or to stay on psychiatric drugs. If you are being pressured to use drugs, you may find it helpful to understand your doctor or therapist as a human being with his or her own concerns, fears, and conflicts about your desire to be drug-free.

When Your Therapist Says You Need Drugs

You may not have intended to take psychiatric drugs when you first sought help. After a few therapy sessions, your therapist may have raised the issue. Or perhaps, when therapy wasn't progressing as well as you hoped, you wondered about trying drugs. One way or another, your therapist made a referral to a psychiatrist and, after a fifteen- to thirty-minute visit with the doctor, you were started on drugs.

You may have had mixed feelings about starting on drugs. If your therapist suggested it, you may have concluded, "I must be worse off than I thought. Even my therapist can't help me. Maybe I do have a biochemical imbalance. Maybe it is genetic."

Even if it was your own idea to seek medication, you may have had reservations or questions. Was it all your fault that therapy wasn't progressing so well? Maybe your therapist was on the wrong track. Maybe you could benefit more from a different therapist or another kind of therapy. Possibly you wondered about changing therapists, using herbs and other alternative healing methods, going to a holistic healing center, or trying to make it on your own without professional help. Maybe you wished your therapist had said, "Don't give up on yourself and don't give up on your therapy. We can do it without drugs!"

Therapists Are People, Too

Your suspicion may have been correct: If you were not doing as well as you hoped in therapy, it may not have been your fault. Therapy is a relationship, and there are innumerable reasons why relationships fail to fulfill their promise. There may be a lack of congeniality between the participants, a clash of personalities or values, conflicting viewpoints, a lack of mutual understanding. Maybe the relationship got off on the wrong foot and never recovered. Perhaps neither of you feels comfortable with the other. Your therapist may remind you too much of your father or mother, or your child; or you may remind your therapist too much of his mother or father, or child. Maybe your therapist has problems similar to yours and never solved them. Maybe your therapist is going through a difficult time in his or her own life, or simply doesn't know how to do therapy well. In short, the sources of difficulty in therapy are as numerous as the causes of difficulty in any relationship.

Finding the right therapist is comparable in difficulty to finding and cultivating a best friend. Both friendship and a good therapeutic relationship require persistence, luck, patience, hard work, and perhaps a blessing.

Unfortunately, some therapists automatically blame the client for any lack of success in therapy. They may justify themselves by saying, "I did not recommend medication until it was obvious that therapy by itself wasn't working." But this assertion—"therapy . . . wasn't working"—holds many unexamined assumptions. Therapy isn't a thing, like a dentist's drilling machine, that works or doesn't work. It isn't something that comes in fixed doses with specific effects, such as 250 mg of penicillin. Rather, therapy is a relationship. And the failure of the relationship can as readily be caused by the therapist as by the client. Commonly, both contribute to this outcome.

So Many Kinds of Therapy

Each client possesses unique ideas about the aims of therapy. One client wants relief from anxiety or depression, another wants to get at the roots of personal problems from childhood, still another is focused on finding a more liberated approach to living. Some clients have no stated aims; others have many.

Parents often seek help in regard to their children from very divergent perspectives. Some parents see themselves as part of the problem; they want guidance in resolving conflicts with their offspring. Other parents see the difficulty as residing in their children; they expect the children to be diagnosed and treated. Therapists also have specific ideas about the aims of therapy. They identify themselves by numerous different "schools" with descriptive phrases such as cognitive therapy, behavioral therapy, existential therapy, phenomenological therapy, insight therapy, relationship therapy, supportive therapy, rational-emotive therapy, psychoanalytic therapy, psychodynamic therapy, experiential therapy, biofeedback, noetic therapy, psychospiritual therapy, psychoeducational therapy, client-centered counseling, neurolinguistic programming, and more. When children are involved, the number of approaches expands to include play therapy and a variety of parent training approaches.

Some therapists are eclectic, tailoring several different techniques to their clients; others have one particular approach that they use for everyone. Many therapists work with anyone who comes to their office; others specialize. Some therapists work one-to-one; others work with families or groups. Similarly, therapists can vary in their goals for therapy. One therapist, for example, may recommend relief from anxiety or depression through drugs along with psychotherapy, another may offer a behavioral or cognitive program for learning new ways of acting and thinking, still another may try to liberate the individual from early trauma or misguided lessons learned in childhood. Some therapists have very clear-cut aims for their patients even before they enter the office, others try to tailor the therapy to the unique goals of the client as they unfold.

Some therapists take a warm and caring approach, and share some of their own feelings and experiences; other therapists are more distant and reserved, sharing almost nothing of themselves. Some try to build a relationship of equality and mutual respect, whereas others are authoritarian and controlling.

Some address their patients by their first name but expect to be called "doctor." Some rarely call their clients by any name. The method of addressing clients, and of being addressed by them, often reflects basic attitudes regarding authority and control.

Many therapists explore clients' problems without any formal approach at all; others have definite routines and programs. Some set no time limit at all on therapy; others offer a specific number of sessions. Some therapists work in medical surroundings similar to a surgeon's consulting room; others work in home offices that express their unique personalities and family life.

A therapy that meets one person's needs may seem futile, frightening, or even ludicrous to another person. For that matter, even a single individual's response to one or another kind of therapy may vary over time. Some people take to therapy with ease and gusto; others find it painful and even alien.

Given the broad spectrum of attitudes and approaches among clients and therapists, as well as the infinite differences in personality, it is absurd to think that anyone should be put on drugs because one or another therapy "didn't work."

What to Do When the Therapy Is Failing

If you aren't doing well in therapy, it's not because there is something wrong with you. Rather, it's because the *relationship* isn't achieving the desired aims of one or both of the participants. And when desired aims aren't being achieved, it certainly isn't going to help if one of the participants starts drugging the other.

Given the infinite number of therapeutic relationships that might potentially be formed, searching for the right therapy makes a lot more sense than turning to drugs after the failure of one, two, or even three of these relationships. Consider experiencing a number of different therapies and therapists if you don't find a perfect match on the first try.

On the other hand, you might feel too insecure or shaky to stop therapy before finding an alternative. Remember, it's your right to keep working with one therapist while you check out another. Optimally, you should be able to tell your therapist that you're seeking additional or alternative help; but if you feel uncomfortable doing so, you don't have to inform your therapist that you are considering a change.

What Do We Have Faith In?

Choosing between drug therapy and psychotherapy, or deciding on a combination of the two, often has more to do with faith than with science or reason. In modern times, many sophisticated people feel uncomfortable with their need for faith. They deny it and end up having distorted, unspoken, or covert faith in material things. People used to have faith in their employers, but that is rarely the case today. They may instead try to have faith in their own intelligence and, especially, in their training, education, and experience in the workplace. They may also turn to money, earning lots of it as a form of security. They have faith in money.

When we grow up, we do not stop being children—we simply disguise that fact. We continue to have all the same basic needs for security, love, and faith.

Children begin by having faith in their parents. Later they may develop faith in other people around them, as well as in people they have never met, from movie stars to sports heroes. As they mature, adults tend to evolve and find new kinds of faith, including their own particular ethics, values, and religion. In order to develop healthy adult relationships, they must learn to have faith in individual people. In short, they must learn to trust.

A person's ultimate faith can be defined in terms of where he or she turns when feeling frightened, self-doubting, desperately depressed or anxious, hopeless, or shaken to the core. Nowadays many people turn to mental health professionals as their ultimate source of security and hope. They have faith that these professionals can make them psychologically or spiritually well. Without realizing it, they are placing themselves in the hands of healthcare specialists who may have little psychological or spiritual awareness—people who have put their faith in medical diagnoses, biological explanations, and drugs.

But isn't psychiatry science? Isn't faith in psychiatry based on facts? On research? Can't we "trust in research"?

The sad truth is that, in the field of psychiatry, it is impossible to "trust in research."[1] Nearly all of the research in this field is paid for by drug companies and conducted by people who will "deliver" in the best way possible for those companies. Even if the particular research project isn't drug company–sponsored, the researcher is bound to have strong ties with drug companies that control the research field, finance most of the conferences and meetings involved, and provide other perks such as consulting jobs. In addition, the drug companies and the drug researchers share a common belief in drugs. They also share a set of values about the kinds of statistical manipulations that can be tolerated, about the kinds of data that can be accepted or rejected, and about the standards for success. Almost always, if any kind of statistically significant numbers can be wrung out of the data—regardless of their real meaning—the clinical trial will be touted as "proof" of the safety and efficacy of the drug in question. Indeed, it is almost impossible to collect data in such experiments without coming up with "significant" correlations and "positive" results.

Sadly, even well-informed people too often put their faith in psychiatry and psychiatric research. It is the same as putting their faith in a drug company.

Therapists Are Losing Faith in Themselves

Many psychiatrists nowadays have no faith in psychotherapy; others simply don't know how to do it. They are medically trained and rely on medical methods, and they believe that aberrant genes and biochemicals are the most significant causes of psychological suffering. Still other psychiatrists may continue to believe in talking therapy but feel pressured to give medication by colleagues as well as by patients and their families.

Even many nonmedical psychotherapists—mental health professionals who specialize in talking therapies—feel coerced into going along with the latest fads in psychiatric diagnoses and medication. HMOs, PPOs, and other insurers often pressure therapists and clients alike to seek treatment with drugs. And psychotherapists, including clinical psychologists, counselors, and social workers, are being trained to believe that medication must be used in any situation that seems difficult. The end result: Therapists have begun to lose confidence in themselves.

If your therapy isn't progressing well or if you appear to be in a crisis, your therapist may feel "out on limb" and insist on your taking a drug. Therapists have emotional vulnerabilities exactly like anyone else. Your emotional crisis can turn into an emotional crisis for your therapist.

Even caring, experienced, ethical therapists may find that their personal concerns get in the way of encouraging you to work with them without drugs. They may worry about how you will do without the drugs, but they may also fear what will happen to them if you "get worse" without drugs. Instead of being focused on what you want and need, your therapist may become more worried about his or her professional image, about criticism from colleagues for not giving drugs, even about a lawsuit from your family if you do poorly without drugs.

The Exaggerated Fear of Lawsuits

Organized psychiatry has fueled the fears of therapists by making threats and, in one well-publicized instance, by asserting that a private psychiatric hospital "lost a malpractice suit" because it didn't prescribe drugs for a patient. In fact, the hospital settled the lawsuit out of court in a rather cowardly manner. Furthermore, this particular suit was a rarity.

Psychiatrists who prescribe drugs and electroshock are the ones who are most regularly sued in the mental health field. And innumerable malpractice suits are threatened or brought each year against medical doctors, including psychiatrists, as a result of damage done by their prescription of psychiatric drugs and electroshock. Meanwhile, very few psychotherapists are sued by patients or their families for any reason. Many psychiatrists have multiple lawsuits brought against them; few psychotherapists have any. As proof of this point, the malpractice insurance premiums paid by psychiatrists are much higher than those paid by psychotherapists.

More specifically, there have been very few malpractice suits brought against therapists for failing to recommend medication. But therapists' fear of being sued is exaggerated by biological psychiatry as yet one more method of intimidation. Although such lawsuits are possible, they are not likely, especially among therapists who take the time to explain their views and to contrast them with the prevailing opinions expressed by psychiatrists.

Faith in Ourselves Versus Faith in Medication

If we do not hold drugs in reserve as a last resort, then we are faced with relying on ourselves—our own personal resources—including our capacity to be empathic, to understand, to help in the creation of new and better solutions. This is true whether we are trying to help ourselves, friends, family members, or patients without encouraging the use of drugs.

When you and your therapist reject medication as an alternative, you in effect declare, "Working together, we have the personal resources to lick this problem." Many professionals are afraid to take such a stand. They lack confidence. They hope for a greater power to rely on beyond themselves, their clients, and other mere mortals. Nowadays the ultimate Higher Power is medication. It is especially frightening to reject this "power" because drug companies and biological psychiatry have convinced a large segment of the population that drugs are the answer, perhaps even the *only* answer.

When we decide not to turn to medical interventions to ease our distress or to solve our crises or suffering, we define ourselves, and other human beings, as the ultimate resource. We communicate to ourselves or to a client or friend, "You and I together, and with the help of other people, possess the necessary resources to solve or transform your suffering and this crisis for the better."

Understanding Your Therapist's Fears

Consistent with the principle that therapists are people, too, they may respond with many fears if you reject the suggestion of drugs or show an interest in discontinuing them. Therapists, like the general public, have been bombarded with prodrug propaganda. During their training as psychologists, counselors, or social workers, they may have been required to attend prodrug lectures by biological psychiatrists. Many mental health professionals feel dependent on psychiatrists for referrals or for jobs, and tend to accept what they advocate. They may fear criticism from their colleagues or from psychiatrists if they don't "go along with the program"—and nowadays drugs are the program.

If you are depressed, your therapist may become concerned about your potential to hurt yourself or to commit suicide. Therapists have been led to believe that antidepressant drugs can help to prevent suicide. Few of them realize that there is no convincing evidence that any psychiatric drug can reduce the suicide rate, but that there *is* evidence that many drugs, including antidepressants, increase the suicide rate.[2] As reviewed in Peter Breggin's introduction, the FDA now warns doctors and users of the capacity of antidepressants to increase suicidal thinking and behavior.

If you can honestly do so, you should allay your therapist's fears by making an agreement that you won't harm yourself and that you will instead talk about any self-destructive tendencies you might have. Also consider making contingency plans in advance—agreeing, for example, to always phone or wait until the next session rather than doing anything drastic. Your therapist will feel much more comfortable about supporting your nonuse of drugs if you make clear your willingness to work together and to take responsibility for not harming yourself or anyone else.

Some individuals take the position that "it's my own business if I hurt myself." But when a person attempts or commits suicide, a tidal wave of suffering results. Therapists are not immune to this. Faced with a client's suicide, they feel not only guilt and remorse, as well as loss; they feel that they have failed. They may also fear for their reputations or worry about their legal vulnerability to a lawsuit brought by the family or by you, if you survive.

Nowadays, therapists often fear being sued. They do not know that mental health professionals are rarely sued for not giving drugs. By contrast, it is *common* for psychiatrists and other physicians to be sued by their patients because of adverse drug reactions.

Above all, therapists need to understand that the best guarantee against getting sued is to have good relationships with their clients. It is very rare for patients to sue doctors or therapists when they feel that they have been treated in a thoughtful, considerate, informed, and caring manner. Patients and clients, as well as their families, can almost always accept honest mistakes. What they resent is indifference, manipulation, and callous disregard for their well-being.

Let your therapist know that you appreciate his or her concerns about your desire not to take psychiatric medication, and promise not to hold your therapist responsible for any risks that you choose to take in regard to rejecting or withdrawing from medication. You might even suggest signing a form in which you acknowledge that nonuse of drugs is your decision and that you are following through on it after having been fully warned about the potentially negative consequences.

Your therapist has probably been taught that psychiatric medications have positive long-term effects and that many patients should stay on them for a lifetime. Thus, if you have been taking drugs for years, your therapist may feel that you are assuming too big a risk by trying to "do without them." He or she probably has no idea that few, if any, psychiatric drugs have been proven to bring about long-term beneficial effects, even by the standards of researchers who favor drugs.[3]

There are no lifetime studies of drug efficacy. As described in Chapter 2, most studies of psychiatric drugs last four to six weeks and often have to be statistically juggled to make them look positive. Even when researched over the longer term, these drugs tend to be associated with increasingly adverse effects and no evidence of efficacy. It may be useful for your therapist to read this book and others[4] in order to learn that there is little scientific basis to most claims for the efficacy of psychiatric drugs even over the short term, and almost no evidence for their value over the long term. There is simply no justification whatsoever for the commonly made claim that some people need to take psychiatric drugs for the rest of their lives.

In fact, most of the difficulties involved in "doing without drugs" are the result of drug withdrawal. Patients most often have trouble stopping drugs not because they are useful but because they create dependency.

Personalities and Power

Biological Psychiatrists

Both of the authors of this book have been active in several professional arenas, giving us the opportunity to compare the characteristics and personal styles typical of the various professions. Psychiatrists as a group are much more controlling, authoritarian, and emotionally distant than other nonmedical mental health professionals. Now that the profession is dominated by its biological wing, it attracts doctors who feel more comfortable writing prescriptions than relating to people. These tendencies, in turn, are reinforced by their training in clinics and mental hospitals, where they are taught to exert power and authority over patients and other professionals and where they learned to lock up people against their will, to administer electroshock, to write orders for solitary confinement and restraint, to control every aspect of the patients' daily routine, to prescribe toxic drugs while denying their devastating adverse effects, and to generally maintain an authoritarian and distant relationship with their patients.

As a result, psychiatrists tend to seek power not only on the hospital ward and in the office but in administration and politics as well. They frequently become powerful leaders in the health field. In politics, they are extraordinarily effective. The mental health lobby, funded by drug companies and led by organized psychiatry, is one of the most powerful in the nation's history.

Biological psychiatrists—who comprise the majority of today's psychiatrists—tend to react in a very suppressive manner to those who oppose them, including dissidents in their field. They ostracize their critics and have been known to drive them from their positions in schools or other institutions. This behavior is consistent with the authoritarian and controlling approaches they are taught during their training.

Psychotherapists

In our experience, nonmedical psychotherapists tend to be less authoritarian, less controlling, and less remote than medical doctors and especially psychiatrists. Doing psychotherapy day-in and day-out tends to promote acceptance of the inevitable autonomy of clients or patients. Therapists tend to learn to respect their own limits and to focus on strengthening the people they are trying to help. When doing their jobs correctly, they exert their influence through empathy, understanding, and wisdom—not manipulation and control.

Psychotherapists, by nature, are not very political or bureaucratic. They tend to be private souls, feeling most comfortable in the settings in which they have chosen to work—intimate, secluded, well-protected spaces. Focused on understanding and helping individuals, they often lack concern or insight into the economic and political forces that drive the mental health profession and society. Rarely do they participate actively in the major controversies within the mental health field.

Unlike biological psychiatrists, "talking doctors" have no source of funding or power in large industries, private foundations, or the government. They have no massive lobbying group in Washington. Even psychiatrists who practice psychotherapy have little or no influence at the National Institute of Mental Health (NIMH) or the American Psychiatric Association, both of which are dominated by their biologically oriented colleagues.

Not only do psychotherapists lack a broader economic power base, but their personal incomes tend to lag far behind those of psychiatrists who prescribe drugs, perform shock treatment, and confine people in hospitals. Organizations that represent psychotherapists, such as the American Academy of Psychotherapists, are also economically and politically weak. By contrast, organized psychiatry, as exemplified by the American Psychiatric Association, has gained enormous wealth, and hence influence, through its funding by the drug industry.

Organized psychiatry—with its natural tendencies toward accumulation of power and its funding from drug companies—now dominates the field of mental health, whereas psychotherapeutically oriented practitioners can rarely achieve positions of professional influence. Many hold precariously onto whatever positions they can get on journals and in clinics, professional schools, and national organizations. It is no exaggeration to say that they live in fear. To gain the enmity of a biological psychiatrist in a professional institution—such as an association, university, hospital, clinic, professional journal, or government agency—is to risk one's job and career.

You and your therapist may find it encouraging to learn that there is an organization of professionals that speaks truth to power in the field of psychiatry. The International Center for the Study of Psychiatry and Psychology (ICSPP), in Bethesda, Maryland, was founded in the early

1970s in part to resist the growing power of biological psychiatry (see Appendix C). It provides a network of mutual support and shared information for professionals and concerned laypersons. It also sponsors a peer-reviewed journal, *Ethical Human Sciences and Services*, that is devoted to scientific research and analysis unsullied by professional and economic interests. Each year the ICSPP holds an international conference devoted to the principle of helping people in psychological distress without resort to drugs.

If you are a client or patient who wishes to stop or to reject psychiatric medication, it is extremely important that you understand your therapist's or doctor's fears and concerns, and are able to offer rational reassurance that you will take responsibility for your decision and personal conduct.

The next chapter offers suggestions for therapists who wish to favor psychotherapy over psychiatric medication as a treatment for their patients or clients. If you are in therapy, you may find it useful to share these suggestions with your therapist.

— *12* —

Guidelines for Therapists Who Do Not Advocate the Use of Psychiatric Drugs

In the previous chapter we described the atmosphere of intimidation within the mental health field that makes many psychotherapists fearful about treating their clients without resort to drugs. We also noted that many therapists have become unrealistically afraid that they will be sued for failing to recommend drugs.

In reality, many successful malpractice suits are brought against psychiatrists for damaging their patients with drugs, whereas a relatively small number are brought against psychotherapists for treatment failures.[1] Moreover, there are few if any cases in which psychotherapists have been successfully sued for failing to recommend or to refer for medication. A recent review of causes for malpractice suits against psychiatrists does not even mention the failure to prescribe medication, although it does list many risk factors associated with the prescription of drugs.[2]

There are no certain protections against malpractice suits or other recriminations from patients or colleagues; individual professionals must handle these legitimate concerns according to their own values and concerns. However, if you are a therapist or psychiatrist who does not advocate the use of medication, there are ethical principles and guidelines that can be helpful to both you and your clients. If you are a client whose therapist or psychiatrist is fearful about not stopping or not starting you on medication, you may want to ask him or her to read this chapter.

Suggested Guidelines

The following guidelines are presented in concise form for purposes of clarity; they should not be interpreted as hard and fast rules or as legal standards of care. In short, they are suggestions intended to stimulate your thinking and to point you in useful directions.

1. *Inform your clients about the prevailing biopsychiatric viewpoint.* When the issue of medication comes up, make clear that most psychiatrists nowadays prescribe drugs for almost every patient they see, including those with relatively mild cases of anxiety and depression. In this way, you can ensure that your clients understand the current biopsychiatric emphasis on medication and are aware of the ready availability of drugs if they want to obtain them elsewhere.

2. *Clarify the reasons for which you do not professionally agree with or encourage the use of medication.* In a way that is consistent with your particular beliefs, explain your professional opinion and experience in regard to medications. For instance, we often point out our beliefs that the drugs are highly overrated, that their adverse effects are commonly underrated, that they often do more harm than good, and that they impair the very mental faculties needed for maximizing psychotherapy.

3. *Recommend consultations and readings from both viewpoints.* Explain that you support your clients' right to seek other opinions at any time during therapy, but note that many or even most psychiatrists will hold an opposing opinion to yours. You can also suggest reading materials from both viewpoints; but bear in mind that most clients will already have been inundated with examples of the biopsychiatric viewpoint in advertising, in the media, and in books.

4. *Do not pressure your clients to go along with your particular philosophy of therapy.* Remember that your job is to empower your clients to make decisions—not to make decisions for your clients. For example, rather than trying to talk your client out of taking drugs, simply state your own wish not to participate in encouraging drugs and give your reasons why. Do not become personally invested in stopping your clients from taking drugs; it's their decision.

In addition, reassure your clients that you will gladly continue therapy even if they decide to obtain medication from someone else at the same time. But warn them in advance that they are likely to be pressured to take drugs by psychiatrists and other medical doctors, so that they can be prepared to deal with it.

5. *Avoid making referrals for psychiatric drugs if you believe they will not be helpful.* Therapists, in our opinion, are not ethically obligated to make referrals for a service that they do not favor and that is readily available through other sources. Instead, explain to your clients that, *on their own,* they can easily find psychiatrists and other physicians who prescribe drugs. You can point them to potential sources of doctors, such as the phone book, the nearest medical school or mental hospital, and the local or national office of the American Medical Association or the American Psychiatric Association. But you do not have to participate in finding a practitioner whose approach you do not advocate.

6. *Unless they have been taking drugs for a very short time, always warn clients about the dangers of abruptly stopping any psychiatric medication.* Except when a patient is suffering from a potentially serious adverse drug reaction, it is better to err on the side of caution and advocate slow withdrawal. You do not have to be a medical doctor to develop expertise in drug withdrawal problems. Familiarize yourself with the information in this book and other sources about the hazards of drug withdrawal.

7. *If you have knowledge about adverse drug effects, share it with your clients.* You are not "interfering" if you discuss the adverse effects of psychiatric drugs that another professional is prescribing for your client or patient. Nor can you assume that a prescribing physician has given your client a sufficiently complete picture of these adverse effects. For example, the written handouts that doctors provide to their patients are often inadequate.

If you are comfortable doing so, use a recent edition of the *Physicians' Desk Reference,* bolstered by other sources, to review with your clients the adverse effects of any drug that has been prescribed for them. Make clear that every drug has so many potential side effects that you cannot describe them all.

Be sure not to claim more expertise than you actually have. Encourage your clients to get as much information as possible on their own and from other doctors.

8. *If you are a nonmedical therapist with clients who want to withdraw from drugs, consider referring them to a physician.* Nonmedical therapists can and do develop the competence to help their clients withdraw from medication, but it is generally a good idea to enlist the aid of a physician to supervise the withdrawal process. This individual could be a family practitioner, internist, or neurologist, rather than a psychiatrist. Physicians who consider themselves "holistic" are likely sources of this kind of

help. You may, of course, have to educate the physician in proper withdrawal methods; toward that end, the present book would be useful.

Some competent, ethical nonmedical therapists do successfully help their patients withdraw from drugs with little or no help from physicians. In the current medical climate, dominated by biopsychiatry, nonmedical therapists may have to step in to provide information and expertise.

9. *If your clients are favorably inclined, consider involving their families, friends, and other resources.* Withdrawing from psychiatric drugs can be a very difficult and painful task, occasionally requiring hospitalization for detoxification. Individuals faced with such circumstances often benefit from the support of family members and friends. In joint consultation with the client and therapist, family and friends can be alerted to signs of drug withdrawal that the client may not be able to perceive or recognize during the withdrawal period. They can be reassured that troubling emotional and personality changes are often short-lived and limited to the withdrawal process. And they can help by discussing with the client what should be done during times of upset. If a therapist does involve family and friends, this arrangement must be made with the whole-hearted agreement of the client—ideally, in the client's presence and with his or her active participation. It must also be respectful of the client's ultimate autonomy and right to confidentiality.

10. *If the therapy is not going well, and cannot be fixed, refer the client to another therapist rather than encouraging the use of psychiatric drugs.* We have urged clients to view therapy as a relationship, and to decide against being drugged when the relationship is failing. Similarly, therapists should avoid recommending drugs simply because they feel unable to help a particular client without them. Instead, if the therapy cannot be improved, the therapist should openly discuss the therapy problems with the client, keeping in mind the potential goal of making a referral for a consultation or a new attempt at therapy.

There is, of course, the danger that a client will feel rejected or abandoned when their therapist suggests consulting with or seeking another therapist. However, the suggestion can be made tactfully, with emphasis on the therapist's own limits and the client's stated dissatisfactions. And the referral can be made as a consultation with an additional professional to see if a new approach might be helpful or if new insights can be generated. Meanwhile, the therapist can emphasize that the lack of progress by no means indicates any inadequacy on the client's part. Keep in mind that, even if the suggestion to seek additional or alternative help raises issues of rejection, that outcome is preferable to raising false and demoralizing questions for the client such as "What's the matter with my brain?" or "Can't I manage my life without drugs?"

During the transition, the therapist should express a preference for continuing the sessions until the client makes up his or her mind about a change. If the client seems fearful or unstable, the therapist—with the client's consent—may decide to participate actively in the transition process.

11. *Make notes in your therapy record to indicate that you have had conversations with your clients about drugs.* Note that you have discussed with your clients the alternative of seeking drug treatment from someone else. If relevant, also note your discussion of any warnings not to stop drugs abruptly and without supervision. If your clients have read your written views or heard you speak in public about them, confirm that they have been informed about the controversy and your own professional stand. In the future, this written record can help you and your clients to recall your discussions. It may also be useful if your clients or their families ever make a mistaken claim against you for not fully informing them. However, this eventuality is remote if you have been thoughtful and respectful in dealing with your clients.

Stand Up and Be Counted

If you are a therapist, we hope you will join the increasing number of our colleagues who are taking a stand in favor of psychological, social, and spiritual approaches to helping people. Many are openly criticizing the biopsychiatric viewpoint. Our colleagues are doing so not only for their own professional satisfaction and identity but for the sake of the truth and of the well-being of their patients and clients. Many of them have also become acquainted with or joined the International Center for the Study of Psychiatry and Psychology (www.icspp.org; see Appendix C), or The Alliance for Human Research Protection (www.ahrp.org; see Appendix D).

If you are a client, expect the best of your therapist. Encourage him or her to trust you, and to work toward the goal of empowering you to live a responsible, loving, and creative life without resort to mind-altering medications. We hope you may also be inspired to join the International Center for the Study of Psychiatry and Psychology or The Alliance for Human Research Protection.

The final chapter of this book describes some of the essential psychological principles involved in dealing with emotional crises and extreme suffering without resort to drugs. These principles should be useful to therapists and clients alike, and to any individuals who want to improve their capacity for self-help or for helping others.

— *13* —

Psychological Principles for Helping Yourself and Others Without Resort to Psychiatric Medications

There are several basic psychological principles for dealing with emotional crises and extreme emotional suffering in ourselves and in others without resort to psychiatric drugs.[1] These principles will be helpful to you whether or not you are in therapy. They may also be useful to your therapist, since many "talking doctors" now need encouragement and inspiration to deal with difficult situations without resorting to drugs.

How can the same principles be useful to you and to your therapist? There is nothing magical about therapy. It is a professional relationship based on psychological and ethical principles for empowering you and improving your life. Therapy is unique in part because it establishes limits and ethical protections for the client;[2] but the same psychological principles that work in therapy can also work for you without therapy. Moreover, they can enable you to better help a friend or loved one during emotional upsets.

1. *Identify and overcome your self-defeating feelings of helplessness.* At the root of almost all disabling emotional reactions lies a feeling of childlike helplessness. By the time you are desperate enough to seek help or to consider taking psychiatric drugs, this feeling has manifested as a loss of faith in yourself and other people. You have begun to feel personally overwhelmed and alienated, and incapable of getting adequate support from anyone else. In this state, you may try to get others to confirm how

bad your situation has become. You may even want them to feel sorry for you and to cater to your feelings of helplessness. All of these outcomes are understandable, but they are also very self-defeating.

Whether or not you are in psychotherapy, one of your first goals should be to identify and overcome your feelings of helplessness, alienation, and distrust. You need to focus on regaining faith in yourself and in anyone else you want to help you. The basis of any successful helping relationship is the other person's caring attitude toward you, which in turn encourages you to care about yourself.

Try not to drag your therapist, or anyone else, into your helpless, fearful state of mind. As we describe in the previous chapter, therapists are people, too, and your feelings of helplessness can stimulate similar feelings in them. It can be very useful to openly discuss your feelings of helplessness and fear without acting as if they have overcome you. It can also help to relate these feelings to your experiences as a child when you really were helpless.

2. *Focus on your unique emotional reactions to a crisis or stress.* If something dreadful is happening in your life, it's easy to focus on the details that seem to be making you feel helpless and overwhelmed. You may be telling yourself, "Who wouldn't fall apart" when faced with cancer, divorce, the death of a loved one, or the loss of a job.

People vary enormously in terms of their responses to even the most devastating threats and losses. Even when a threat is very real, it's the individual's subjective response to it that remains key to the outcome. Some people are demoralized when they learn, for example, that they have cancer; others mobilize to maximize their chances and make the most of their lives. In cases of divorce or separation, one person may be devastated while another ultimately feels liberated and renewed.

It can inspire you to realize that human beings are capable of persevering and even growing in the face of seemingly overwhelming adversity. You may become able to respond to your crisis as you would to a challenge, even a gift.

Expect your counselor to be less focused on helping with the specific details of what you're going through than on guiding you to see how you can improve your personal reactions to them. You are far better able to handle crises when you focus on understanding your unique, subjective emotional responses rather than the facts of the crisis itself. Your goal should be to grow in the face of the crisis—to transform it into a creative experience.

3. *Be glad you're alive, and find someone else who is glad the both of you are alive.* Like many others, when you undergo a crisis you may resent being alive. But resentment inhibits your willingness to use all of your resources to overcome your problems. Look for a counselor or therapist who will greet you with gladness that you're alive. If you do not feel welcomed with zest and joy, something is missing in the relationship. Over time, it may end up causing more harm than good by lowering your sense of self-worth and your expectations for a robust life.

By contrast, when greeted by another person who is glad you are alive, you will discover that your emotional crisis is not as overwhelming as you previously thought. You are not alone; you are even worth something to another person. It's the beginning of recovery.

4. *Avoid getting into "emergency mode," and reject desperate interventions or extreme solutions.* When faced with feelings of hopelessness and doom, you (and anyone helping you) may be tempted to gear up for emergency mode. But it's important that you don't try to get your psychotherapist to go along with your desperate feelings. Drugs, unnecessary hospitalization, even electroshock treatment could result.

To avoid overreacting to clients' fear and hopelessness, therapists need to understand their own vulnerabilities. If they are terrified of cancer or AIDS, then they must remain especially alert not to encourage their clients' terror in the face of these health crises. Similarly, if they are uncomfortable with their own aggressive impulses, they must make the effort to avoid pushing their clients into greater fear of their own anger.

Some emergencies may call for quick action, but these instances are relatively rare. Almost always, if your therapist can maintain his or her own sense of calm and connectedness, you, too, will begin to feel more safe and secure, more rational, and more capable of finding positive new approaches.

Focus on finding a *rational, loving,* and *confident* center in yourself that can rise above your emotional crisis or suffering. Try not to get caught up in the "emergency." Expect your therapist to have a healthy perspective that communicates a confidence that the problem can be dealt with. The term *healing presence*[3] describes the helper's capacity to be empathic regardless of the fear and helplessness, anguish and alienation, that are experienced by clients during an apparent emergency.

5. *Resist the impulse to have something done to or for you, and instead seek help in strengthening yourself.* Consistent with overcoming your

feelings of helplessness and with avoiding "emergency mode," don't ask your therapist to do anything *for you*. Although it may be tempting to try to involve your therapist in your life—for example, by asking him or her to talk to your family or employer on your behalf—it is generally better to find the strength to follow through yourself. Similarly, don't ask your therapist to do anything *to you* in terms of giving you drugs or urging you to check into a hospital. Seek to empower yourself, and look for a therapist who wants to aid in that process.

6. *Don't drug your painful feelings.* During periods of emotional pain and turmoil, give your mind a chance to function without drug-induced impairments. That is the only way to transform these seemingly negative experiences into opportunities for growth. At such times, you need unimpaired mental faculties and a full range of emotions. You need to welcome your painful feelings as signs of life and as signals that point the way to self-understanding and change. Indeed, by welcoming your most painful feelings, you will be enabled to view these emotions in a far more positive light, one that transforms helpless suffering into positive energy.

The idea of "welcoming" painful emotions may seem beyond the capacity of many people when they are severely distressed. By the time they are upset enough to consider turning to therapy or to drugs, they usually want to get rid of their emotions. It is unfortunate and potentially tragic that many therapists and doctors go along with this wish for the self-destruction of strong feelings. To be genuinely helpful, they should instead remind their patients that strong emotions of any kind are necessary and potentially liberating signals or reflections of their psychological or spiritual state.

Therapy is often helpful precisely because it can support your attempts to feel your "worst" feelings. Ultimately, all people need other people—professional or not—to help in successfully understanding and triumphing over painful emotions. All people need others to deal with life's inevitable emotional challenges and upheavals.

Medications not only suppress and confuse feelings, they can stimulate dangerous ones. As discussed in Chapters 3 and 4, antidepressants and minor tranquilizers can cause agitation and mania as well as disinhibition with loss of impulse control. If an individual is already teetering on the verge of losing control, the drugs can become even more dangerous.

7. *Bear in mind that most emotional crises and suffering build on a chain of earlier stresses and trauma.* Although a current crisis may seem to be

the cause of your distress, it is more likely the proverbial straw that broke the camel's back. But when you are feeling overwhelmed, it can be very difficult to see beyond the immediate events. For this reason, you may want to seek help in understanding prior events in order to gain a better perspective on your present crisis.

8. *Avoid inviting other people to take over for you.* When you are feeling helpless and despairing, you may be tempted to give signals that invite others to take over your life. But unless you really want someone to intervene, don't act as if you cannot take care of yourself. Don't say things that may mislead others into thinking that you might hurt yourself or someone else. If you are feeling that desperate, then it is better to take responsibility for yourself—for example, by asking for more help or by finding a safe place to stay where other people can give you around-the-clock support.

We hope that therapists reading this book will also realize that the use of emotional threats or even direct force, such as involuntary commitment to a mental hospital, is rarely if ever the best way to handle a crisis. In fact, we believe that involuntary treatment is wrong in principle and contrary to genuinely therapuetic approaches. Such interventions may stave off an immediate suicide, for example; but in the long run, by disempowering and humiliating the individual, they commonly do more harm than good. At times, a therapist may find it necessary to point out to a client that there are voluntary alternatives, such as crisis centers and psychiatric hospitals; but bringing up these alternatives can indicate to the client that the therapist is afraid the situation cannot be handled through their mutual personal resources. However, clients also need to realize that any contact with psychiatric institutions, especially in times of crisis, can lead to involuntary treatment.

There are no studies confirming the usefulness of emotional bullying or more formal measures such as involuntary psychiatric treatment. They also offend basic human rights. And, in any case, intuition and self-reflection are likely to convince us that people don't benefit from being forced into conformity with a therapist's expectations. Clearly, the development of an empathic relationship requires mutual respect rather than coercion.

9. *Be kind to anyone who is trying to help you, including your therapist.* Too often, individuals end up emotionally attacking the very people they have asked for help. They mount these assaults for many different reasons: because they feel vulnerable about asking for help, or embarrassed

about "having problems" or "being a patient," or fearful of rejection, intimacy, or authority. A host of issues from childhood and from current circumstances may surface at various times in the therapy relationship.

Sometimes the attack is a preemptive strike aimed at putting other people off balance before they can mount their own attack. But, ironically, the more they attack their therapist—or anyone else—the more fearful they will become of counterattacks.

Whatever the cause, any persistent tendency to attack usually reflects an enduring pattern of self-defeating behavior that can be traced back to things they learned to do to survive in childhood.

Therapists, remember, are ordinary people themselves. They are best able to offer their care and understanding when they feel safe and valued. Conversely, they will find it more difficult to be caring toward you if you make them feel defensive, humiliated, or rejected. Your therapist's professional job is to create a good relationship with you; but he or she cannot do it alone. Help out by doing your best to build trust.

Therapy should be a place of safety and security in which you can express your deepest hurts and most tender feelings, a place where you can examine your most important dreams and ideals. It should be a place where you can express anything that you feel—and inevitably you will sometimes want to express anger at the person who is trying to help you. But if you persistently communicate in ways that threaten, frighten, or humiliate this person, you will end up repeating self-destructive patterns that need changing. You will also make it harder for your therapist to help you. You might even mistakenly encourage your therapist to recommend drugs or other drastic solutions—out of sheer fear or frustration.

Nothing stated above should undermine any rational complaints you may have about your therapist. As we have emphasized throughout, therapists are people, and good ones are as hard to find as lifelong friends. You may have to "shop around" to find the right one. But you'll never get the best that any of them have to offer if you attack them.

10. *Know that empathy and caring lie at the heart of any helping relationship.* When people look for help, they usually feel so badly about themselves that they don't expect anyone to care about them in a personal way that says, "I understand and sympathize with your feelings and your situation. I don't feel superior to you. Given what you've been through, I'm not sure I could have handled it any better than you."

Expect your therapist to work hard at caring about you and understanding you. You should also work hard at understanding and caring about yourself. Finding someone who can show empathy for you is perhaps the single most important aspect of your healing.

Probably no personal work is more important for therapists than opening our hearts to those we are trying to help.[4] But why does empathy so often feel like "work," even for experienced therapists? There are many reasons. As therapists, we may be frightened by the degree of another's distress. Out of fear for the patient, we may be overly focused on quickly resolving the crisis or emergency. We may become concerned about what others will think of us if things go wrong. We may feel that we lack the experience needed to help the person.

Most likely, perhaps, we find it hard to empathize with the suffering of another because it evokes our own personal suffering. In our effort to control our own feelings, we shut off the source of the stimulation—the other person's suffering.

11. *Remember that we need each other!* By the time people end up seeking help or turning to psychiatric drugs, they may have begun to think, "I have to do it on my own." Many individuals come to this false conclusion after feeling so let down and betrayed by others that they believe they have no choice other than to withdraw into themselves.

When people go to a doctor, they are likely to be reinforced in their belief that the problem is strictly their own to solve. The process of receiving a diagnosis, such as major depression or panic disorder, and of taking a drug, emphasizes how alone they are in their struggle. In reality, however, most problems grow out of relationships—going all the way back to childhood. Psychological or spiritual well-being requires new and improved relationships.

Popular psychology too often emphasizes people's responsibility for themselves to the exclusion of the importance of other people in their lives. They are told, for example, "You can't be loved until you love yourself" or "No one can make anyone else happy." They are encouraged not to "need others too much." But while there may be some truth to these admonitions, they miss the central point of life—that people are all enormously dependent upon one another for almost everything good in life. From infancy on, they are molded by their relationships with others. In adulthood, they are as strong as their relationships with others. No one ever became truly successful by relying on the principle that "I can do it on my own."

At those times when you are emotionally upset, your judgment—especially with regard to choosing friends or helpers—may be clouded. You may turn to the wrong person. There is no easy solution to this problem;

it should be a major concern when you seek help because you could end up choosing the wrong therapist as well. But don't "give up on people"; people are what life is all about.

If you are in therapy, you may want to think about involving a loved one in the process. Any improvement in communication and caring between you and a loved one is likely to go a long way toward strengthening your ability to overcome your suffering and to build a better life.[5]

12. *Realize that emotional crises and suffering are opportunities for accelerated personal growth.* Crises and extreme suffering provide a window into your greatest vulnerabilities. They allow you the opportunity to explore your worst fears. They bring out and confront you with the raw material of your human existence. The self-understanding gained from this realization can be applied throughout your life, enabling you to develop a deeper psychological awareness of yourself and others. You gain not only a new understanding of your own vulnerabilities but genuine insight into and respect for the human condition.

When you face and understand your worst fears, and then overcome them, you will feel greatly empowered. No longer held back by self-defeating emotional reactions, you will gain faith in yourself. You will discover that you can triumph over seemingly impossible threats to reach new heights of psychological and spiritual transformation.

Indeed, emotional crises and suffering offer potential for escalating growth as you learn to handle your greatest vulnerabilities and most painful emotions. As your confidence is regained, any crises you experience will become opportunities for even more exceptional growth. You will discover that even your worst fears can be handled, overcome, and turned into opportunities. Once your confidence is restored, improved approaches, even solutions, can almost always be found. You will end up feeling stronger than you did before the crisis began.

We introduced this book with a discussion of the human need for faith. We talked about the many different ways in which people seek guidance or help in dealing with life's inevitable suffering. Now we want to reemphasize that the choice is not between psychiatric drugs and other forms of "therapy," including the psychological or therapeutic guidelines suggested in this book. Rather, the choice is between psychiatric drugs and all of life with its many rich resources.

Psychotherapy is but one of many psychological, social, educational, political, and spiritual approaches that people can take when attempting to deal with emotional pain and suffering. Our approach to therapy, too, is but one among many. Once people become free of the biopsychiatric viewpoint and drugs, life presents an infinite spectrum of alternatives for dealing with emotional suffering and for living a more fulfilling existence. Above all else, we believe that all people need a set of ethics, principles, and ideals with which to guide their lives, including reliance on a brain unimpaired by toxic agents.

However, when people become focused on medical experts and psychiatric drugs as the "solution," life becomes compulsively narrow. Their options become even more limited as the drugs inevitably begin to impair their awareness, rendering them less able to understand or to redirect their lives. Eventually they feel they have no alternative other than perpetual reliance on one or another psychiatric drug.

In this book we present the limitations of psychiatric drugs. We point out why and how to stop relying on them. Our goal is not to present a complete philosophy of life but to help you approach life in your own unique way—unimpaired in your journey by toxic substances.

Appendix A:
Psychiatric Medications
in Common Use

I: *Antidepressants* [1]

Selective Serotonin Reuptake Inhibitors (SSRIs)
   Celexa (citalopram)
   Lexapro (escitalopram)
   Luvox (fluvoxamine)[2]
   Prozac and Sarafem (fluoxetine)
   Paxil (paroxetine)
   Zoloft (sertraline)

Other Newer Antidepressants
   Cymbalta (duloxetine)
   Effexor (venlafaxine)
   Remeron (mirtazapine)
   Symbyax (Prozac + Zyprexa, a newer antipsychotic)
   Wellbutrin and Zyban (bupropion)

Older Antidepressants (partial list)[3]
   Anafranil (clomipramine)
   Elavil (amitriptyline)
   Parnate (tranylcypromine)
   Tofranil (imipramine)
   Vivactil (protriptyline)
   Surmontil (trimipramine)

---

[1] The new FDA "black box" warnings apply to all antidepressants but in fact were developed based on the SSRIs and newer antidepressants and not on the older ones.

[2] The brand name Luvox has been withdrawn from the market but the drug is still available in the generic form.

[3] All the older antidepressants can cause psychiatric adverse drug reactions including mania and psychosis but they much less commonly come up in our clinical and legal experience. A more complete list can be found in various textbooks, especially *Drug Facts and Comparisons* (2007), a readily available annual publication.

II: Stimulants

Classic Stimulants[4]

Adderall, Adderall XR (amphetamine mixture)
Desoxyn (methamphetamine)[5]
Dexedrine (dextroamphetamine)
Focalin, Focalin XR (dexamethylphenidate)
Ritalin, Concerta, Daytrana (methylphenidate)
Vyvanse (lisdextroamphetamine)

Others

Cylert (pemoline) [no longer available]
Strattera (atomoxetine)

---

[4] All are Drug Enforcement Administration (DEA) Schedule II "narcotics," indicating the highest risk of tolerance and dependence (addiction).

[5] Few people realize that doctors can prescribe methamphetamine, the deadly drug of addiction, to children for ADHD.

III: Tranquilizers and Sleeping Pills[6]

Benzo Tranquilizers

Ativan (lorazepam)
Klonopin (clonazepam)
Librium (chlordiazepoxide)
Serax (oxazepam)
Tranxene (chlorazepate)
Xanax (alprazolam)
Valium (diazepam)

Benzo Sleeping Pills

Dalmane (flurazepam)
Doral (quazepam)
Halcion (triazolam)
ProSom (estazolam)
Restoril (temazepam)

Non-Benzo Sleeping Pills

Ambien (zolpidem)
Lunesta (eszopiclone)
Sonata (zaleplon)

---

[6] All are DEA Schedule IV narcotics, indicating a risk of tolerance and dependence (addiction).

IV: Antipsychotic Drugs (Neuroleptics)

Newer (second- or third-generation or atypical) Antipsychotics[7]

Abilify (aripiprazole)
Geodon (ziprasidone)
Invega (palipcridone)
Risperdal (risperidone)
Seroquel (quetiapine)
Symbyax (olanzapine + Prozac, an SSRI antidepressant)
Zyprexa (olanzapine)

Older Antipsychotic Drugs

Clozaril (clozapine)
Etrafon (antidepressant plus Trilafon)
Haldol (haloperidol)
Loxitane (loxapine)
Mellaril (thioridazine)
Moban (molindone)
Navane (thiothixene)
Prolixin (fluphenazine)
Serentil (mesoridazine)
Stelazine (trifluoperazine)
Taractan (chlorprothixene)
Thorazine (chlorpromazine)
Tindal (acetophenazine)
Trilafon (perphenazine)
Vesprin (triflupromazine).

Antipsychotics Used for Other Medical Purposes

Compazine (prochlorperazine)
Inapsine (droperidol)
Orap (pimozide)
Phenergan (promethazine)[8]
Reglan (metoclopramide)

---

[7] Sertindole is another atypical neuroleptic currently going through the FDA approval process.

[8] Usually classified as an antihistamine but has neuroleptic qualities and can cause tardive dyskinesia. All drugs in Table IV are neuroleptics and can cause tardive dyskinesia.

V. Lithium and Other Drugs Used as "Mood Stabilizers"

Depakote (divalproex sodium) [anti-epileptic drug]
Equetro (extended-release carbamazepine) [anti-epileptic drug]
Lamictal (lamotrigine) [anti-epileptic drug]
Lithobid, Lithotabs, Eskalith (lithium)

Off-Label or Unapproved Mood Stabilizers

Catapres (clonidine) [antihypertensive drug]
Gabitril (tiagabine)
Neurontin (gabapentin) [anti-epileptic drug]
Tegretol (carbamazapine) [anti-epileptic drug]
Tenex (guanfacine) [antihypertensive drug]
Topamax (topiramate) [anti-epileptic drug]
Trileptal (oxcarbazepine)

Appendix B:
About the Authors

Peter R. Breggin, M.D.

Peter R. Breggin, M.D. has been called "the conscience of psychiatry" for his efforts to reform the mental health field, including his promotion of caring psychotherapeutic approaches and his opposition to the escalating overuse of psychiatric medications, the oppressive diagnosing and drugging of children, electroshock, lobotomy, involuntary treatment, and false biological theories.

Dr. Breggin has been in the private practice of psychiatry since 1968, first in the Washington, D.C., area and now in Ithaca, New York. In his therapy practice, he sees individuals, couples and children with their families. As a clinical psychopharmacologist, he provides consultations and is active as a medical expert in criminal, malpractice, and product liability lawsuits, often involving the harmful effects of psychiatric drugs. He has been an expert in landmark cases involving the rights of patients.

Since 1964 Dr. Breggin has written dozens of scientific articles and approximately twenty books. Some of his many books include *Toxic Psychiatry*, *The Heart of Being Helpful*, *Talking Back to Ritalin*, the *Antidepressant Fact Book*, and with co-author Ginger Breggin, *Talking Back to Prozac* and *The War Against Children of Color*. His forthcoming book, *Medication Madness: 55 True Stories of Mayhem, Murder, and Suicide Caused by Psychiatric Drugs*, will be published in early 2008.

At various stages of his career he has been decades ahead of his time in warning about the dangers of lobotomy, electroshock, and more recently, antidepressant-induced suicide and violence, as well as many other recently acknowledged risks associated with psychiatric drugs. From the *New York Times* and *Wall Street Journal* to *Time* and *Newsweek*, and from *Larry King Live* and *Oprah* to *60 Minutes* and *20/20*, his work has been covered in major media throughout the world.

In 1972 Dr. Breggin founded the International Center for the Study of Psychiatry and Psychology (www.ICSPP.org). Originally organized to support his successful campaign to stop the resurgence of lobotomy, ICSPP has become a source of support and inspiration for reform-minded professionals and laypersons who wish to raise ethical and scientific standards in the field of mental health. In 1999 he and his wife Ginger founded ICSPP's peer-reviewed scientific journal, *Ethical Human Psychology and Psychiatry*. In 2002 they selected younger professionals to take over the center and the journal, although Dr. Breggin continues to participate in ICSPP activities.

Dr. Breggin's background includes Harvard College, Case Western Reserve Medical School, a teaching fellowship at Harvard Medical School, three years of residency training in psychiatry, a two-year staff assignment at the National Institute of Mental Health (NIMH), and several teaching appointments including the George Mason University Institute for Conflict Analysis and Resolution and the Johns Hopkins University Department of Counseling.

Dr. Breggin's website is www.breggin.com.

David Cohen, Ph.D., L.C.S.W.

David Cohen is Professor of Social Work at Florida International University in Miami. As a licensed clinical social worker, Dr. Cohen works with adults and children and consults on legal cases. He is often consulted by individuals and families who wish to wean themselves off psychiatric drugs.

Dr. Cohen holds degrees in psychology and social welfare from McGill University, Carleton University, and the University of California–Berkeley. He was previously a professor at University of Montreal and has been a visiting professor at Institut national de la santé et de la recherche scientifique (INSERM) in France.

Dr. Cohen has authored or coauthored more than 100 publications, and received the Elliot Freidson Award for Outstanding Publication in Medical Sociology from the American Sociological Association in 2003. His edited books include *Challenging the Therapeutic State* (1990) and *Tardive Dyskinesia and Cognitive Dysfunction* (1993). His French-language books include *Médicalisation et contrôle social* (1994) and *Guide critique des médicaments de l'âme* (1995). He recently edited with Gwynedd Lloyd and Joan Stead *Critical New Perspectives on ADHD* (2006, winner of the NASEN/Times Educational Supplement Prize for best academic book).

Dr. Cohen's research has included large-scale surveys of psychotropic prescription practices, clinical investigations of drug-induced movement disorders, and in-depth qualitative inquiries of consumers' perceptions of psychotropic drug effects. His research is grounded in critical perspectives on individual, professional, and social uses of prescribed psychotropic drugs. Dr. Cohen is presently designing and evaluating a publicly-funded, evidence-based curriculum based on critical thinking about psychotropic drugs for non-medical mental health professionals.

More about Dr. Cohen and his work can be found at: www.davidcohenphd.com.

Appendix C:
The International Center
for the Study of
Psychiatry and Psychology

The International Center for the Study of Psychiatry and Psychology (ICSPP) is a nonprofit international center for professionals and non-professionals who want to raise ethical and scientific standards in psychology and psychiatry. The board of directors, advisory council, and membership include hundreds of professionals in many fields spanning psychology, counseling, social work, nursing, psychiatry and other medical specialties, neuroscience, education, religion, and law, as well as concerned laypersons.

Founded in 1971 by psychiatrist Peter R. Breggin, M.D., ICSPP began its successful reform efforts with opposition to the international resurgence of psychosurgery. ICSPP has also opposed the use of electroshock treatment, the rampant escalation in the use of psychiatric drugs, and coercive psychiatry in general. In the mid-1990s ICSPP organized a campaign that caused the U.S. government to withdraw its proposed "violence initiative," a government-wide program that called for intrusive biomedical experiments on inner-city children in the hope of demonstrating biological and genetic causes of violence. Some of ICSPP's most recent reform efforts are directed at the growing trend to psychiatrically diagnose and medicate children. Because of its many successful efforts on behalf of truthfulness and justice in the psychosocial and biomedical sciences, ICSPP has been called "the conscience of psychiatry."

ICSPP has divisions in North America, Europe, and Australia. The center offers a general membership. It publishes a newsletter and maintains an active Web site that features commentaries about contemporary problems in the human sciences. Each year ICSPP hosts a national conference that is open to the public.

ICSPP sponsors a peer-reviewed journal, *Ethical Human Psychology and Psychiatry*, published by Springer Publishing Company. The journal features scientific papers, reviews and commentaries that raise the level of ethical awareness concerning research, theory, and practice. The journal examines issues in contemporary human services with critical analyses that span the psychosocial and biomedical sciences.

In 2002 Dr. Breggin and his wife Ginger Breggin passed leadership of ICSPP to younger professionals and Dominick Riccio, Ph.D., a New York City psychologist, is currently the international director. Meanwhile, Dr. Breggin continues to make presentations at the ICSPP national conferences and to contribute to the journal. None of the leaders of ICSPP are paid. Everyone is a devoted volunteer.

Information about ICSPP membership, the journal, national meetings, and other activities can be obtained on the center's website, www.icspp.org. An annual subscription to the journal is included in the membership. Membership currently costs only $100 per year, including the journal. By supporting ICSPP, you support the reform movement in psychiatry; by joining ICSPP you can meet and communicate with concerned professionals and laypersons who share your desire to raise the level of ethical conduct, critical awareness, and genuine science within psychiatry and psychology.

Appendix D:
The Alliance for Human
Research Protection

Founded in 2001, the Alliance for Human Research Protection (AHRP) is a national network of laypeople and professionals dedicated to advancing responsible and ethical medical research practices, to minimizing the risks associated with such endeavors, and to ensuring that the human rights, dignity, and welfare of human subjects are protected.

Much of what passes as knowledge on the effects of psychiatric drugs has been obtained in clinical trials and other studies involving human subjects. AHRP has been in the forefront of efforts documenting how the design, conduct, and findings of such studies are tainted by conflicts of interest resulting from the drug industry's funding and control of clinical trials.

By means of daily infomails, public testimonies and conferences, education, media exposure, and appeals to conscience and social justice, AHRP stands up and speaks out for the human rights of research subjects — especially those who are vulnerable or susceptible to coercion and exploitation, such as disadvantaged children, older persons with impaired reasoning capacity, disadvantaged populations living in underdeveloped countries, as well as prisoners and members of the armed forces.

AHRP's daily infomails serve as catalysts for public debate. They contain exceedingly useful information for patients and their families, journalists, academics, lawyers and advocates, and other concerned observers.

Nearly all of the AHRP's work is performed by unpaid volunteers, who donate both time and other resources to the organization. Thus, AHRP offers a unique point of view, untarnished by conflicts of interest. Its Web site offers an extensive archive of searchable materials, news reports, and other documents.

AHRP is a nonprofit, tax-exempt educational organization under Section 501C–3 of the Internal Revenue Code.

To sign up to receive infomails, join or make a donation to AHRP, or search the AHRP databases, visit www.ahrp.org or http://ahrp.blogspot.com.

Notes

New Introduction by Peter Breggin

1. For some Breggin publications since the first edition of this book, see Breggin (1998, 1999a-c, 2000, 2001a&b, 2002a&b, 2003, 2006a-e). The articles can be obtained from www.breggin.com.

2. The FDA failed to mention that the three positive studies were drug-company sponsored and conducted by drug company drones.

3. Food and Drug Administration (2004b).

4. Food and Drug Administration (2004a). Emphasis added.

5. Food and Drug Administration (2005a).

6. Food and Drug Administration (2005b).

7. GlaxoSmithKline (2006).

8. Officially called the Psychopharmacologic Drugs Advisory Committee (PDAC).

9. Pp. 165 ff.

10. My product liability report against GlaxoSmithKline can be found on www.breggin.com. I published portions of it with introductory explanations in *Ethical Human Psychology and Psychiatry,* the journal sponsored by the International Center for the Study of Psychiatry and Psychology (Breggin, 2006 b-d).

11. See Moncrief (2006) for similar observations.

12. *Physicians' Desk Reference* (2006, p. 1504, first column). It's buried amid a mountain of other data.

13. Kirsch et al. (2002). Also see Kirsch and Sapirstein (1998).

14. Food and Drug Administration (2005d, 2006).

15. Gelperin and Phelan (2006). Quotes in this section are from pp. 3–4 of the FDA in-house memorandum.

16. Food and Drug Administration (2005c).

17. In addition to emphasizing this data in a verbal exchange with another expert who was denied the risk of stimulant-induced psychosis, I presented my

breakdown of data from the FDA's spontaneous reporting system in my published report to the Consensus Development Conference (Breggin, 1999b).

18. The data is described and tabulated in greatest detail in *Talking Back to Ritalin, Revised* (2001, pp. 43–44).

19. Cherland and Fitzpatrick (1999).

20. Breggin (2006e). The technical term for medication spellbinding is *intoxication anosognosia*.

New Introduction by David Cohen

21. Lieberman et al. (2005).

22. Cohen (2002).

23. Trivedi et al. (2006).

24. Rush et al. (2006).

25. Perlis et al. (2006).

26. Lieberman (2006).

27. Cooper et al. (2006).

28. Blader and Carlson (2007).

Chapter 1

1. The short duration of studies involving psychiatric drugs, and the scarcity of long-term studies of adverse effects, are discussed in Breggin (1991, 1997a, 1998a) and Breggin and Breggin (1994).

2. Vitiello (1998).

3. Cases of violence and suicide related to psychiatric drug effects are described in Breggin and Breggin (1994) and Breggin (1997a). Moreover, Peter Breggin has testified in a number of legal cases involving harmful or dangerous behavioral reactions associated with drugs such as Prozac, Zoloft, Xanax, Klonopin, and Ritalin. Examples of legal cases are listed on www.breggin.com.

4. For more thoroughly documented critiques of biological psychiatry and psychiatric drugs, see the following: Breggin (1991, 1997a, 1998a); Breggin and Breggin (1994); Cohen (1990, 1994, 1997); Fisher and Greenberg (1989, 1997); Jacobs (1995); Mender (1994); and Mosher and Burti (1994).

Chapter 2

1. PRNewswire, 1998. The group referenced in the bibliography is the Global Alliance of Mental Illness Advocacy Networks (GAMIAN).

2. Olfson et al. (2006).

3. This marketing strategy is described by Tanouye (1997) and by psychiatrists Vitiello and Jensen (1997). It is also reviewed in Breggin (1998a, ch. 15).

4. Lacasse and Leo (2005).

5. American Psychiatric Association. (2005).

6. Breggin (1998a). See also Chapter 3 for a discussion of Ritalin.

7. Documented in Breggin (1983a, 1997a) and Cohen (1997a).

8. This concept—that psychiatric drugs always impair brain function—is explained in detailed medical terms in Breggin (1997a, ch. 1).

9. Confirmation that all psychiatric drugs disrupt biochemical processes in the brain can be found in summary form for most drugs in almost any psychiatric or psychopharmacological textbook. Euphemisms such as *enhancing* or *activating* may be used in such books, but the reader should be able to ascertain that in each case a measurable change in the brain's normal function is involved.

10. Selemon et al. (1999).

11. Cohen and Jacobs (2007).

12. Within the privacy of professional writings, various experts in the field agree that no biochemical abnormalities have been demonstrated in psychiatric disorders. Textbooks are filled with speculations, often specifying several potential biochemical mechanisms, but in no case can they claim that such speculations have been proven. Indeed, the textbook chapters usually conclude with an admission that nothing has been proven but that "breakthroughs" are anticipated.

13. Cohen (1997b) describes the first use of Thorazine as a surgical anesthetic in France in the early 1950s.

14. Barnhart et al. (2004); Garland and Baerg (2005); Hoehn-Saric et al. (1990); Obproek et al. (2002).

15. Breggin (1991, 1997a).

16. In addition, Jacobs and Cohen (1999) show how clinical trials of psychiatric drugs deliberately ignore various wide-ranging or persistent impairments in patients' sensitivity and self-awareness, by focusing exclusively on "improvements" in a few target symptoms from a behavior checklist.

17. See Fisher and Greenberg (1997, 1989) and, more recently, Antonuccio et al. (1999). The lack of effectiveness of psychiatric drugs is also discussed in Breggin (1997a, 1998a) and Breggin and Breggin (1994).

18. This point is further discussed below and in Chapter 3.

19. Horgan (1999).

20. For a discussion of placebo effects in clinical trials involving antidepressants, as well as the ability of investigators to break the double-blind by figuring out who is taking active medication, see Breggin (1991, 1997a), Fisher and Greenberg (1989, 1997), and Kirsch and Sapirstein (1998).

21. Cohen and Jacobs (2007).

22. Evidence that antianxiety drugs actually worsen the condition of patients can be found in Breggin (1991), Jacobs (1995), and Marks et al. (1989).

23. See Breggin (1998a) for a detailed review of the literature on Ritalin. See also Swanson (1993) for similar conclusions from within the establishment concerning Ritalin's limited effectiveness.

24. Breggin (1997a) describes the kinds of studies used for drug approval. More specific information concerning Prozac as a model drug can be found in Breggin and Breggin (1994).

25. Breggin and Breggin (1994) discuss clinical trial length in detail. In regard to Prozac, only a small number of patients managed to complete the brief four-to-six-week trials. See also Breggin (1997a) and Cohen and Jacobs (2007) for a discussion of how FDA drug trials are conducted.

26. The effects of neuroleptics are described and documented with citations to the literature in Breggin (1991, ch. 3) and Breggin (1997a, ch. 2), as well as in Cohen (1997a).

27. Breggin (1997b).

28. For critiques of the efficacy of psychiatric drug therapy, see Antonuccio et al. (1989, 1994, 1995); Beck, Rush, Shaw, and Emery (1979); Bleuler, 1978; Breggin (1991, 1997a, 1998a); Breggin and Breggin (1994, 1998); Breggin and Stern (1996); Fisher and Greenberg (1989, 1997); Greenberg et al. (1992); Karon and VandenBos (1981); Kirsch and Sapirstein (1998); Moore (1998); Mosher and Burti (1994); and Wexler and Cicchetti (1992). The many books and articles by Carl Rogers (1961, 1994), often based on research studies, also address the efficacy of therapy. Rogers (1994) ultimately links the success of therapy to empathy on the part of the therapist.

29. Reported by Peter R. Breggin, M.D.

30. The Harvard-Radcliffe Mental Hospital Volunteer Program is described in the first chapter of Breggin (1991). The original book about this program, including a description of the case aide project, can be found in Umbarger et al. (1962). The program was so successful that it received praise as a prototype in the final report of the Joint Commission on Mental Illness and Health of the U.S. Congress (1961). The shift in political power to biological psychiatry a decade or two later effectively terminated this program and others like it.

31. Contrary to psychiatric mythology, the advent of neuroleptic drugs, such as Thorazine, did not "empty the hospitals." These drugs take effect within minutes; the emptying process did not begin for a decade or more. What really led to the mass discharge of patients from the hospitals (often to the streets or to wretched nursing homes and board and care facilities) were administrative changes, about which many books have been written (reviewed in Breggin, 1991).

32. Soteria House, originated by Loren Mosher (1996; Mosher and Burti, 1994), provided this successful model. Its efficacy was demonstrated by controlled studies, but its fate was sealed when psychiatry became dominated by its biological wing.

33. See de Girolamo (1996).

34. For detailed descriptions of the economic forces that push drugs and perpetrate the myths of "biochemical imbalances" and drug efficacy, see Breggin (1991, 1997a, 1998a), Breggin and Breggin (1994, 1998), and Cohen (1990, 1994).

Chapter 3

1. Reported by Peter R. Breggin, M.D., who presented this grand rounds at Suburban Hospital in Bethesda, Maryland, circa 1993–1994. Prozac-induced violence is documented in detail in Breggin and Breggin (1994) and updated in Breggin (1997a).

2. On a number of occasions, Peter Breggin has consulted on cases in which patients have attempted suicide or committed homicide for the first time after starting a psychiatric drug. This outcome should be a red flag indicating that the drug may have caused or contributed to the destructive behavior. Yet in many of these cases, doctors continued or even increased the dose of the offending drug after the suicide attempt or murder.

3. Cohen and Jacobs (1998) have proposed a "Model Consent Form" for psychiatric drug treatment.

4. See the related discussion and notes in Chapter 2.

5. These warnings can be found in any recent edition of the *Physicians' Desk Reference*.

6. These well-established drug-induced disorders are discussed in most psychiatric and pharmacological textbooks, including those listed in Appendix A. More details are provided in Chapter 4.

7. Trifiro et al. (2006).

8. Documented in detail in Breggin (1998a).

9. The official FDA-approved labels for the benzodiazepine minor tranquilizers—such as Xanax, Ativan, and Valium—now recognize that these drugs are intended for short-term use only (see the individual drug labels as reproduced in any recent edition of the *Physicians' Desk Reference*). The label for Xanax, for instance, makes clear that the drug may not only worsen anxiety but also cause addiction. Xanax, as an example of these drugs, is discussed in detail in Breggin (1991), Jacobs (1995), and Marks et al. (1989).

10. Breggin (1997a) discusses the events leading to the inclusion of neuroleptic malignant syndrome in drug labels, as well as the overall FDA process.

11. See American Psychiatric Association (1994, p. 273) for a brief discussion of some of the different meanings of *psychosis*.

12. American Psychiatric Association (1994), p. 123.

13. Discussed in detail in Breggin (1997a). Breggin (1994) testified about these secret documents in the Wesbecker case.

14. In this connection, see Chapter 4 as well as *Medical Letter* (1998) and Bender (1998a).

15. In the trials used for the approval of Xanax for panic disorder, most patients had more anxiety after a few weeks on the drug than before they first took it. For a discussion of the worsening anxiety condition of patients treated with Xanax, see Marks et al. (1989) and Breggin (1991, 1998b).

16. American Psychiatric Association (1994), p. 330; see also p. 329.

17. For a definition of the diagnosis of "substance-induced mood disorder," see American Psychiatric Association (1994), pp. 374–375. For specific references to antidepressants causing mania, see the same source (pp. 331, 371).

18. See Chapter 4 for the rates of drug-induced mania. A recent clinical trial of Prozac for children and adolescents with depression demonstrated a rate of 6 percent (Emslie et al., 1997).

19. Discussed with citations to the literature in Breggin (1991) and Breggin (1997a), p. 57. See also Myslobodsky (1986).

20. Anosognosia is discussed in Breggin (1989a, 1989b, 1991, 1997a); Fisher (1989); and Myslobodsky (1986). Fisher's paper is especially important in establishing that anosognosia, much like short-term memory difficulty, is a common characteristic of any form of generalized brain dysfunction.

Chapter 4

1. No single chapter can cover all the hazards of psychiatric medications. Even in this book, serious or life-threatening side effects may sometimes be omitted. For a more complete picture, the reader should consult several different medical sources regarding any particular drug. Most of the adverse drugs effects listed in this chapter are described in a variety of readily available medical sources (see Appendix A). Therefore, specific citations will be given only in those instances where further information or confirmation seems useful.

2. Bender (1998b).

3. Lazarou (1998).

4. Grady (1998) and Weis (1998). These newspaper reports contain commentaries about the *JAMA* publication.

5. Spieb-Kiefer et al. (1998).

6. *Physicians' Desk Reference* (1998), p. 860, column 3, line 10.

7. In evaluating the studies used for the approval of Prozac for depression, the FDA's medical reviewer for adverse effects, Richard Kapit, M.D. (1986, p. 18), reported that the rate of Prozac-induced psychotic mania was three times that for the comparison tricyclic antidepressant. Of the thirty-three reported cases of mania, twenty-three occurred in patients with no history of mania. See also the related discussion in Breggin (1997a), p. 86.

8. American Psychiatric Association (1994), p. 330; see also p. 329. Peter Breggin has been a medical expert in cases of drug-induced mania that resulted in homicide.

9. The clinical trials for Prozac are discussed in detail in Breggin and Breggin (1994).

10. Emslie et al. (1997). Breggin (1995) first noticed this ominous finding of a 6 percent rate of Prozac-induced mania in children when he read a pre-publication report on Emslie's research in a psychiatric newspaper. In a letter to the newspaper, Breggin warned about the high rates of mania. The newspaper noted that Emslie declined to respond.

11. R. W. Pies (1998), for example, drew his basic data from Maxmen and Ward, who in turn obtained their data from a review of the literature.

12. Maxmen and Ward do not provide rates for the "toxic psychoses." The nearest related syndromes they report are "hypomania and mania," "confusion and disorientation," and the symptoms of hallucinations and delusions. As described in Chapter 3 of the present volume, doctors sometimes specify such symptoms as memory impairments, agitation, and excitement when, in fact, the patient is suffering from a more global toxic psychosis.

13. Maxmen and Ward (1995), p. 287.

14. Specifically, after reviewing hospital charts, Davies et al. (1971) found even higher rates for "forgetfulness, agitation, illogical thoughts, disorientation, increased insomnia, and at times, delusional thoughts" among patients who were taking tricyclic antidepressants.

15. Emslie et al. (1997).

16. A detailed analysis of the hazards of these drugs—including detailed documentation of this section—can be found in Breggin's *Talking Back to Ritalin* (1998a). See also Breggin (1999a, 1999b, 1999c).

17. See ibid.

18. Ritalin-induced psychoses are discussed, with citations from the literature, in Breggin (1998a), pp. 14–20.

19. El-Zein et al. (2004) and (2006).

20. Growth inhibition is reviewed in Breggin (1998a), pp. 25–28 and Breggin (1999a, 1999b, 1999c). There are many studies confirming growth suppression (e.g., Safer et al., 1975) and disruption of growth hormone cycles (reviewed in Jacobovitz et al., 1990).

21. For the scientific community, Breggin (1998d, 1999a, 1999b, 1999c) has reviewed stimulant adverse effects including persistent and irreversible brain changes, such as cell death.

22. Dukes (1997), Medawar (1997), and Moore (1997). The most comprehensive criticisms can be found in Breggin and Breggin (1994), with an update in Breggin (1997a).

23. Emslie et al. (1997).

24. Breggin (1992a) reported a case of depression upon withdrawal from Prozac.

25. Schatzberg, Cole, and DeBattista (1997), p. 77. Cole cites Fisher et al. (1992), who demonstrated an increased rate of suicidality among patients on Prozac compared to those on trazodone.

26. Breggin and Breggin (1994) and Breggin (1997a) review the evidence for suicide and murder committed by individuals taking SSRIs. Peter Breggin has been a medical expert in some of the product liability cases brought against Eli Lilly, the manufacturer of Prozac. Among these was the Wesbecker case, the only one thus far to go to court. (For testimony, see Breggin, 1994.) Wesbecker shot twelve people, killing eight, and then shot himself to death. His psychiatrist suspected that Wesbecker had become psychotic on Prozac and stopped it shortly before the tragic violence occurred. As noted, this particular case was secretly settled by the drug company during the trial. However, news of the settlement was withheld from the judge and the jury, and the plaintiffs presented a watered-down case to the jury in order to bring about a more certain victory for Lilly. In short, the plaintiffs secretly took money in return for which, in cooperation with Lilly, they manipulated the trial. After the trial, the judge, John Potter, became outraged when he discovered these manipulations. He changed the verdict from "dismissed without prejudice by the jury" to "settled with prejudice." The Kentucky Supreme Court found that Lilly had manipulated the legal system and possibly even committed "fraud." (See Trial court's authority, 1996; Gibeaut, 1996; and Varchaver, 1995. Discussed in more detail, and with additional citations, in Breggin, 1997a.) Lilly continues to make false claims that it won a jury verdict in the Wesbecker case. In response to news in 1998 that a youngster was taking Prozac at the time he allegedly killed his parents and shot several classmates, Lilly issued a statement in defense of Prozac through the Associated Press (1998). According to this AP release, in the Wesbecker case "the victim's families sued Lilly, but a jury found Prozac wasn't responsible." In fact, Lilly paid off the families before the trial was over in return for their cooperation in presenting a weaker case to the jury. Also according to the AP release, Lilly has "successfully argued" in "scores of court cases" that Prozac was not the cause of violence. In fact, no other Prozac product-liability cases had gone to court. Since then, in April 1999, Eli Lilly finally won a jury trial in the U.S. District Court of Hawaii in the case of Forsyth v. Eli Lilly (Civil No. 95–00185ACK). Peter Breggin, who was not involved in the Forsyth case, has also been a medical expert in several cases of Prozac-related suicide or violence that were quietly settled.

27. Clayton et al. (2002); Williams et al. (2006).

28. Kennedy et al. (2000).

29. Clayton et al. (2002).

30. Bolton et al. (2006); Csoka and Susko. (2006).

31. Balhara et al. (2007).

32. Duloxetine: New indication. (2006).

33. Wolfe (2005), p. 3.

34. Lenzer (2005).

35. Russell (2007).

36. Dietary instructions can be found in Bezchlibnyk-Butler and Jeffries (2005).

37. A detailed analysis of the hazards of these drugs—including documentation of the observations in this section—can be found in Breggin (1997a, 1998b).

38. Barker et al. (2004).

39. See Breggin (1997a, 1998b) for a detailed analysis of the adverse behavioral and mental effects of benzodiazepines.

40. For documentation of the banning of Halcion in England, see Asscher (1991) and Brahams (1991).

41. Glass et al. (2005).

42. Sivertsen et al. (2006).

43. Bender (1998).

44. Perlis et al. (2006).

45. An extensive review of adverse effects of lithium is found in Breggin (1983, 1997a).

46. Adverse effects of neuroleptics on the central nervous system (CNS) are discussed extensively in Breggin (1983a, 1990, 1991, 1993, 1997a).

47. See also Breggin and Breggin (1994) and Breggin (1997a) for discussions of violence against self or others from drug-induced akathisia.

48. Pies (1998, p. 117) cites a yearly incidence of 4–5 percent per *cumulative* year for most patients and 20 percent per *cumulative* year for the elderly. These figures are consistent with the American Psychiatric Association's (1980, 1992) task force reports on tardive dyskinesia. Bezchlibnyk-Butler and Jeffries (1996) estimate that 37 percent of patients will develop TD in the first five years and 56 percent after ten years. Breggin (1991, 1997a) discusses the nature and incidence of TD in much more detail.

49. Many TD studies are conducted while the patient remains medicated, suppressing manifestations of the symptoms. Minimal or even mild cases are sometimes excluded from TD studies (as discussed in Breggin, 1991). And, as noted, studies often do not include data on tardive akathisia, which itself can occur at a high rate. Gualtieri and Sovner (1989) estimate the prevalence of tardive akathisia at 13–18 percent and call it "a significant health issue." Nonetheless, the drug companies have not included references to this disorder in the labels for neuroleptic drugs, and the FDA shows no signs of requiring such inclusion.

50. Many of these cases were carefully investigated as part of Peter Breggin's forensic work in medical malpractice and product liability suits.

51. Discussed in Breggin (1997a), pp. 49–51. See also Rosebush and Stewart (1989).

52. Addonizio et al. (1986) reviewed the charts of eighty-two male inpatients in a psychiatric unit and found a 2.4 percent rate of diagnosed NMS.

53. Ananth et al. (2004).

54. Ramaswamy et al. (2004).

55. Discussed in Breggin (1997a), p. 67. Recent research includes Inuwa et al. (1994).

56. Shirzadi and Ghaemi (2006).

57. The quote is from Julien (1997), p. 16.

58. Julien (1997), p. 21. Also see Stowe, Strader, and Nemeroff (1998), p. 981.

59. Koch et al. (1996).

60. The hazards of various psychiatric drugs to the fetus are discussed in Stowe, Strader, and Nemeroff (1998).

Chapter 5

1. Karp (2006).

2. "Impact of Direct-to-Consumer Advertising" (2003).

3. The peer-reviewed journal *PLoS Medicine* published in 2006 a collection of six articles on disease mongering, three of which discuss how pharmaceutical companies "sell" ADHD, bipolar disorder, and sexual dysfunction in males and females. Freely available at: http://collections.plos.org/plosmedicine/disease mongering–2006.php.

4. See Breggin (1983b, 1997a) for a more detailed description of this process of "iatrogenic helplessness"—the reinforcement of denial in patients by causing brain damage or dysfunction through drugs, electroshock, or psychosurgery, combined with the doctor's own denial of both the patients' problems and their iatrogenic brain dysfunction.

5. Empathy in therapy is the subject of *The Heart of Being Helpful* (Breggin, 1997b).

6. For a discussion of placebos, including the highly variable and sometimes extremely high rates of placebo effect, see Fisher and Greenberg (1989).

Chapter 6

1. Quitkin et al. (1998).

2. Bezchlibnyk-Butler and Jeffries (2005).

3. Peter Breggin has seen examples of such "recordkeeping" while examining internal documents at drug companies as an expert witness for plaintiffs in product liability cases.

4. Reported by Peter R. Breggin, who attended this seminar.

5. For examples of the kind of information discovered by a medical expert on examining sealed drug companies' documents see Breggin (1997a) concerning Eli Lilly and Prozac, and Breggin (2006b, c, and d) for GlaxoSmithKline and Paxil.

6. Breggin and Breggin (1994).

7. Similar observations were made earlier in Breggin and Breggin (1994) and Breggin (1997a).

8. Green (2003).

9. Temple (1991); discussed in Breggin (1997a), pp. 229–230.

10. This observation is discussed and documented in detail in Breggin and Breggin (1994); it is also summarized and updated in Breggin (1997a).

11. This process is discussed, with accompanying examples, in Breggin (1997a, 1998b).

12. Government Accounting Office (1990), pp. 25, 74–78.

13. Leber (1992), p. 6.

14. See, for example, Grohol (1997).

15. Cohen and Karsenty (1998).

16. Chen (2007).

17. Temple (1987); discussed in Breggin (1997a), pp. 85–86.

18. IMS Health (1999). The total drug promotion budget in the U.S. in 1998 was over $5.8 billion.

Chapter 7

1. Tucker (1997), p. 159.

2. See Fisher and Greenberg (1989, 1997) for two of the best accounts of the comparative effectiveness of drugs and psychotherapy for the full range of emotional problems. Psychotherapy comes out surprisingly well. A recent survey by *Consumer Reports* (November 1994) indicates that clients of psychotherapy were as satisfied as, and usually found the experience more rewarding than, those who were treated with drugs alone or who received drugs in addition to counseling. This finding held true regardless of the problems for which treatment was sought. Social workers, psychologists, and doctors were rated as equally effective in this survey, the largest of its kind ever undertaken.

3. Here are some of the drug-ad slogans that appeared in the July 1998 issue of the *American Journal of Psychiatry:* "Paxil means peace," "Make your first choice Prozac for both restful nights and productive days," "Gentler days ahead"

(Risperdal), "I got my mommy back" (Effexor), "Put it to the test" (Remeron), "Antipsychotic power for routine use" (Zyprexa), "Prescribe Adderall—it may make a difference," "Bringing out the best in nature" (Eskalith lithium tablets), "Out of chaos comes control" (Seroquel), and "Yes!" (Zoloft).

4. Cohen (in press).

5. Drummond (1997).

6. As documented in Sherman (1998), the proportion of visits to a psychiatrist that included an antidepressant prescription increased from 53.5 percent in 1985 to 70.9 percent in 1994. Overall, the number of visits in which a psychiatric drug was prescribed jumped from 33 million in 1985 to 46 million in 1994.

7. See, generally, Morris et al. (1997) and Schommer and Widerholt (1997).

8. Grohol (1997), p. 244.

9. Yearly editions of *Physicians' Desk Reference* are published by Medical Economics in New Jersey. They can be found in bookstores and libraries.

10. Cormack et al. (1994) report that, within a six-month monitoring period, elderly long-term users of benzodiazepines reduced their drug use on average by two-thirds (compared to a control group) after receiving a letter from their doctor describing the risks of drug use and suggesting that the use be gradually decreased and, in time, stopped. Nearly one-fifth of those who received the letter completely stopped their drug use. See also Wylie (1995).

11. Here is an example of sensitization: When given amphetamines that are then withdrawn over a period of time, many animals respond with heightened sensitivity to future administrations of the drug.

12. See Otto, Pollack, and Barlow (1995).

13. Moncrieff (2006a) suggests that a distinct and sometimes intense anxiety or fear of withdrawal may actually precipitate a relapse.

14. Breeding (1998) suggests that "[w]ithin the framework of biopsychiatry, hopelessness is a rational response"; he also emphasizes that the qualities of hope and courage are necessary to overcome the fear of withdrawing from drugs.

Chapter 8

1. Breggin (1991, 1997a, 1998a); Breggin and Breggin (1994).

2. Noyes et al. (1991), p. 1621.

3. Taylor (1999).

4. van Geffen et al. (2005).

5. Kramer et al. (1961).

6. Koopowitz and Berk (1995).

7. Glenmullen (2005).

8. Pacheco (2002).

Chapter 9

1. Warner et al. (2006).

2. Young and Currie (1997). Even with respect to tardive dyskinesia, an often irreversible movement disorder frequently produced by neuroleptic drugs and mentioned in all information sources about these drugs, surveys show that psychiatrists admit that they routinely fail even to *mention* this effect to patients before prescribing (review by Cohen, 1997).

3. Rosenbaum et al. (1998).

4. Young and Currie (1997).

5. Ibid., p. 28.

6. World Task Force, quoted in World Psychiatric Association (1993), p. 47.

7. To access this Pharmacology Glossary, go to http://bumc.bu.edu/Dept/Content.aspx?DepartmentID=65&PageID=7799#d.

8. Shader and Greenblatt (1993), p. 1402.

9. Medawar (1992); Breggin and Breggin (1994); Grinspoon (1970).

10. See Medawar (1997). Social Audit's Web site (www.socialaudit.org.uk) includes detailed correspondence between Medawar and various scientists and officials of Britain's Medicines Control Agency regarding its investigation of antidepressant withdrawal reactions. See also Moore (1997).

11. See *DSM-IV* (American Psychiatric Association, 1994).

12. Ibid., p. 184.

13. Ibid., p. 185

14. Ibid.

15. Haddad, Lejoyeux, and Young (1998), p. 1105.

16. Lader (1991), p. 56.

17. Marks (1978), p. 2.

18. APA Task Force (1990).

19. Jaffe (1980). See also *DSM-IV* (American Psychiatric Association, 1994), which draws similarities between withdrawal syndromes of all tranquilizing and sedative drugs, including antianxiety drugs and alcohol.

20. Salzman (1992), p. 146.

21. Ibid.

22. Petursson (1994).

23. Fialip et al. (1987).

24. Rickels et al. (1991).

25. Ashton (1994).

26. Ibid.; see also Swantek et al. (1991), and Denis et al. (2006).

27. Denis et al. (2006).

28. Wolfe (1997).

29. Garner, Kelly, and Thompson (1993).

30. Ghadirian (1986); Hartman (1990); Mirin et al. (1981).

31. Dilsaver, Greden, and Snider (1987).

32. Law, Petty, and Kazdin (1981).

33. Gualtieri and Staye (1979).

34. Webster (1973).

35. Dilsaver (1990); Lawrence (1985).

36. Wolfe (1997).

37. Frenkel et al. (1992), p. 111.

38. Dilsaver (1994), p. 107.

39. Schatzberg et al. (1997b), p. 5.

40. Dilsaver (1990); Lawrence (1985).

41. Liskin et al. (1985), p. 46.

42. Ibid., p. 47.

43. Schatzberg et al. (1997b), p. 5.

44. Haddad (1997), p. 21.

45. Schatzberg et al. (1997b), p. 8.

46. Therrien and Markowitz (1997); Thompson (1998).

47. Schatzberg et al. (2006), and Shelton (2006). See also Therrien and Markowiz (1997); Thompson (1998).

48. Stoukides and Stoukides (1991).

49. Szabadi (1992).

50. Reported by Peter R. Breggin, in Breggin and Breggin (1994), pp. 105–106.

51. Breggin (1992a).

52. Bloch et al. (1995).

53. Feth et al. (2006).

54. Giakas and Davis (1997).

55. Einbinder (1995).

56. Farah and Lauer (1996).

57. Wolfe (1997).

58. Medawar (1997); see also www:socialaudit.org.uk.

59. Goldstein et al. (1999).

60. Thompson (1998).

61. Perahia et al. (2005).

62. Hindmarch et al. (2000).

63. Pollock (1998), p. 535.

64. *Physicians' Desk Reference* (2007), p. 1533.

65. Lejoyeux and Adès (1997), p. 11.

66. Benazzi (1998a).

67. Benazzi (1998b).

68. Campagne (2005).

69. Montalbetti & Zis (1988); Otani et al. (1994); Peabody (1987); Theilman and Christenbury (1986).

70 Menza (1986).

71. Rocha et al. (1998).

72. Dackis and Gold (1990), p. 16.

73. Lago and Kosten (1994).

74. Schatzberg, Cole, and DeBattista (1997), p. 352.

75. *DSM-IV* (American Psychiatric Association, 1994), pp. 208–209, 225–226.

76. Whalen and Henker (1997).

77. Rappoport et al. (1978).

78. Askevold (1959); DeVeaugh-Geiss and Pandurangi (1982). See review by Walsh and Dunn (1998).

79. Klein and Bessler (1992).

80. Schwartz and Rushton (2004).

81. One study by Nolan, Gadow, and Sprafkin (1999) examined stimulant medication withdrawal during long-term treatment of children diagnosed with ADHD and with chronic multiple tic disorders. Unfortunately, although the study could have answered many questions about the withdrawal syndrome in children, it only reported on the narrow issue of whether or not tics worsened during withdrawal (they did not), and failed to report on *any* other symptoms expected to occur during stimulant withdrawal.

82. Schatzberg, Cole, and DeBattista (1997), p. 352

83. Ibid.

84. Keely and Licht (1985), p. 123.

85. Schou (1993), p. 515.

86. Lapierre et al. (1980); Christodoolou and Lykouras (1982).

87. Klein et al. (1981), p. 255.

88. Suppes et al. (1991).

89. Faedda et al. (1993).

90. Goodwin (1994), p. 149

91. Cavanaugh et al. (2004).

92. Balon et al. (1984).

93. Goodwin (1994).

94. Heh et al. (1988).

95. Darbar et al. (1996).

96. Jess et al. (2004).

97. Tran et al. (2005).

98. Tranter and Healy (1998).

99. Eppel and Mishra (1984).

100. Leipzig (1992), p. 414. The psychological and physical symptoms of a particularly severe case of neuroleptic withdrawal in a six-year-old child are described by Maisami and Golant (1991).

101. Tranter and Healy (1998), p. 308.

102. Lal and AlAnsari (1986) review eleven cases of Tourette-like syndrome that developed after neuroleptic withdrawal. This syndrome has also been observed after Clozaril withdrawal by Poyurovsky et al. (1998).

103. Gualtieri (1993); Barnes and Braude (1994).

104. Lang (1994); Sachdev (1995); Weller and McKnelly (1983).

105. Dilsaver (1994).

106. Weinberger et al. (1981); Witschy et al. (1984).

107. Reviewed in Breggin (1997a).

108. Silva et al. (1993).

109. Sovner (1995), p. 221.

110. Gualtieri (1993).

111. May et al. (1995), p. 156.

112. Amore and Zazzeri (1995); Spivak et al. (1990); Surmont et al. (1984).

113. Pies (1998), p. 176.

114. Stanilla et al. (1997).

115. Poyurovski et al. (1998).

116. Staedt et al. (1996).

117. Shiovitz et al. (1996).

118. Ahmed et al. (1998).

119. Goudie et al. (1999).

120. Kim and Staab (2005).

121. Perenyi et al. (1985), p. 430.

122. Viguera et al. (1997).

123. Pies (1998), p. 176.

124. Gilbert et al. (1995).

125. Baldessarini and Viguera (1995).

126. See Cohen (1997a).

127. Baldessarini and Viguera (1995).

128. Snowden and Roy-Birne (1998).

129. Bridges-Parlet et al. (1997).

130. Lifshitz et al. (1991).

131. When neuroleptics suppress dopamine transmission, acetylcholine activity increases, probably as a compensatory mechanism. The resulting disturbance in dopamine-acetylcholine balance causes or contributes to abnormal movements. Anticholinergic drugs are prescribed to suppress cholinergic overactivity. Of course, the brain also tries to compensate for the effects of these drugs, and the compensatory mechanisms take over when the drugs are abruptly removed.

132. Luchins et al. (1980).

133. McInnis and Petursson (1985), p. 297.

134. See Manos et al. (1981); Baker et al. (1983).

135. Tandon et al. (1989), p. 712.
136. Brown et al. (1986).
137. Toru et al. (1981).
138. Yassa (1985).
139. Baker et al. (1983), p. 585.
140. Ben Hadj et al. (1995).
141. Barr et al. (1994).
142. Rauch et al. (1996).
143. Amsden and Georgian (1996).
144. Arya (1996); Fava et al. (1997).
145. Therrien and Markovitz (1997).
146. Gilbert et al. (1995).
147. Amsden and Georgian (1996), p. 686.
148. See Kane and Lieberman (1992).
149. Levinson-Castiel et al. (2006).

Chapter 10

1. See Breggin (1998a) for suggested readings, basic principles of parenting, and information about parent training classes and types of consultations available.

2. See the consensus development conference panel report published by the National Institutes of Health (1998). In addition, Breggin (1998a) provides an analysis of reviews and studies confirming that stimulants do not improve learning or academic performance.

3. According to the National Institutes of Health (1998) consensus statement, "there are no data on the treatment of ADHD, inattentive type."

4. Breggin (1998a).

Chapter 11

1. Some of the many reasons not to trust psychiatric research, drug companies, and biological psychiatry are discussed in earlier chapters of the present book and documented in detail in Breggin (1991, 1997a, 1998a), Breggin and Breggin (1994, 1998), Moore (1997, 1998), and Ross and Pam (1995).

2. See Breggin (1997a), Breggin and Breggin (1994), and Moore (1997).

3. The failure to prove long-term positive effects and the overall flimsiness of any claims for the efficacy of psychiatric drugs have been extensively reviewed by Breggin (1991, 1997a, 1998a) and Breggin and Breggin (1994). See also Cohen (1997a), Fisher and Fisher (1996), Fisher and Greenberg (1989), Jacobs (1995), and Mosher and Burti (1994), as well as Chapter 2 of the present book.

4. See ibid.

Chapter 12

1. Perlin (1997) points out that failure to conduct psychotherapy properly is rarely a basis for a successful malpractice suit, and Simon (1997) describes the conditions under which psychiatrists are successfully sued in regard to treatment with medication and the frequency with which these lawsuits are initiated. Psychotherapists are more likely to be sued for unethical conduct, such as having sex with a patient, than for errors committed during the provision of treatment.

2. Perlin (1997).

Chapter 13

1. Many of the ideas in this chapter were first developed by Peter Breggin in *Beyond Conflict* (St. Martin's Press, 1992), *The Heart of Being Helpful* (Springer Publishing Company, 1997), and "Psychotherapy in emotional crises without resort to psychiatric medication" (*The Humanistic Psychologist*, 1998). Though presented in a new form, the material in this chapter draws on all three sources, and we wish to thank the publishers for providing earlier opportunities to develop these ideas in print.

2. Psychotherapy is a helping relationship. The experience and training of the therapist are obviously important, but what really makes therapy unique is the setting—especially given that the focus is limited to the client's problems and needs rather than those of the therapist, and all personal contact is limited to the professional relationship and the sessions. These limits make it safer for the client and the therapist to concentrate on the intimate details of the client's life. They allow for a caring relationship without extensive complications. And they make therapy very different from personal relationships, even those in which people offer or receive help. Although these limits protect the therapy relationship, they also circumscribe its goals: Therapy cannot be as healing as a mutually satisfying love relationship. On the other hand, it can certainly help a person to achieve a love relationship.

3. Breggin (1997b).

4. Breggin (1997b) describes empathy as the "heart of being helpful." In particular, he introduces the concept of empathic self-transformation to explain the therapist's or helper's task of becoming open to the person who is suffering.

5. Family therapy and family life are also discussed in Breggin (1997b).

Bibliography

Abramson, John. (2004). *Overdo$ed America: The broken promise of American medicine*. New York: HarperCollins.

Addonizio, G., Susman, V., & Roth, S. (1986). Symptoms of neuroleptic malignant syndrome in 82 consecutive inpatients. *American Journal of Psychiatry, 143*, 1587–1590.

Ahmed, S., Chengappa, K. N., Naidu, V. R., Baker, R. W., Parepally, H., & Schooler, N. R. (1998). Clozapine withdrawal-emergent dystonias and dyskinesias: A case series. *Journal of Clinical Psychiatry, 59*, 472–477.

American Psychiatric Association (1990). *American Psychiatric Association Task Force on Benzodiazepine Dependence, Toxicity, and Abuse*. Washington, D.C.: American Psychiatric Press.

———. (1992). *Tardive dyskinesia: A task force report*. Washington, D.C.: American Psychiatric Association.

———. (1994). *Diagnostic and statistical manual of mental disorders, fourth edition (DSM-IV)*. Washington, D.C.: American Psychiatric Association.

———. (2005, May 4). Mental illness stigmas are receding, but misconceptions remain. Release no. 05–24. Retrieved June 2, 2006 from: http://www.psych.org/news_room/press_releases/05–24APANewsReleaseonPoll-%20final.pdf.

Amore, M., & Zazzeri, N. (1995). Neuroleptic malignant syndrome after neuroleptic discontinuation. *Progress in Neuro-Psychopharmacology and Biological Psychiatry, 19*, 1323–1334.

Amsden, G. W., & Georgian, F. (1996). Orthostatic hypotension induced by sertraline withdrawal. *Pharmacotherapy, 16*, 684–686.

Ananth, J., Parameswaran, S., Gunatilake, S., Burgoyne, K., & Sidohm, T. (2004). Neuroleptic malignant syndrome and atypical antipsychotic drugs. *Journal of Clinical Psychiatry, 65*, 464–470.

Angell, Marcia B. (2004). *The truth about drug companies: How they deceive us and what to do about it*. New York: Random House.

Antonuccio, D. O., Danton, W. G., & DeNelsky, G. Y. (1994). Psychotherapy: No stronger medicine. *Scientist Practitioner, 4*, 2–18.

_____. (1995). Psychotherapy versus medication for depression: Challenging the conventional wisdom with data. *Professional Psychology: Research and Practice, 26,* 574–585.

Antonuccio, D. O., Danton, W. G., DeNelsky, G. Y., Greenberg, R. P., & Gordon, J. S. (1999). Raising questions about antidepressants. *Psychotherapy and Psychosomatics, 68,* 3–14.

Antonuccio, D., Ward, C., & Tearnan, B. (1989). The behavioral treatment of unipolar depression in adult outpatients. In M. Hersen, R. M. Eisler, & P. M. Miller (Eds.), *Progress in behavior modification.* Orlando, Fla.: Academic Press.

Armstrong, L. (1993). *And they call it help: The psychiatric policing of America's children.* New York: Addison-Wesley.

Armstrong, T. (1995). *The myth of the A.D.D. child.* New York: Dutton.

Arya, D. K. (1996). Withdrawal after discontinuation of paroxetine. *Australian and New Zealand Journal of Psychiatry, 30,* 702.

Ashton, H. (1991). Protracted withdrawal syndromes from benzodiazepines. *Journal of Substance Abuse Treatment, 8,* 19–28.

_____. (1994). The treatment of benzodiazepine dependence. *Addiction, 89,* 1535–1541.

Askevold, F. (1959). The occurrence of paranoid incidents and abstinence delirium in abusers of amphetamines. *Acta Psychiatrica et Neurologica Scandinavica, 34,* 145–164.

Asscher, A. W. (1991, October 1). Dear Doctor/Dentist/Pharmacist: Withdrawal of triazolam. (Letter). Committee on Safety of Medicines, London, England.

Associated Press. (1998, June 5). (Indianapolis). Maker of Prozac defends product. Original press release.

Baker, L. A., Cheng, L. Y., & Amara, I. B. (1983). The withdrawal of benztropine mesylate in chronic schizophrenic patients. *British Journal of Psychiatry, 143,* 584–590.

Baldessarini, R. J., & Viguera, A. C. (1995). Neuroleptic withdrawal in schizophrenic patients. *Archives of General Psychiatry, 52,* 189–192.

Balhara, Y., Sagar, R., & Varghese, S. T. (2007). Bleeding gums: Duloxetine may be the cause. *Journal of Postgraduate Medicine, 53,* 44–45.

Balon, R., Yeragani, V. K., Pohl, R. B., & Gershon, S. (1988). Lithium discontinuation: Withdrawal or relapse? *Comprehensive Psychiatry, 29,* 330–334.

Barker, M. J., Greenwood, K. M., Jackson, M., & Crowe, S. F. (2004). Persistence of cognitive effects after withdrawal from long-term benzodiazepine use: A meta-analysis. *Archives of Clinical Neuropsychology, 19,* 437–454.

Barnhart, W. J., Makela, E. H., & Latocha, M. J. (2004). SSRI-induced apathy syndrome: A clinical review. *Journal of Psychiatric Practice, 10,* 196–199.

Barr, L. C., Goodman, W. K., & Price, L. H. (1994). Physical symptoms associated with paroxetine discontinuation. *American Journal of Psychiatry, 151,* 289.

Beck, A. T., Rush, A. J., Shaw, B. F., & Emery, G. (1979). *Cognitive therapy of depression.* New York: Guilford Press.

Benezzi, F. (1998a). Nefazodone withdrawal symptoms. *Canadian Journal of Psychiatry, 43,* 194–195.

_____. (1998b). Mirtazapine withdrawal symptoms. *Canadian Journal of Psychiatry, 43,* 525.

Bender, K. J. (1998a, May). New warning of depression with Acutane could apply to other medications. *Psychiatric Times,* p. 1.

_____. (1998b, May). Researchers report dramatic change in psychotropic medication use. *Psychiatric Times,* p. 32.

Ben Hadj, A., Dogui, M., Ben Ammou, S., & Loo, H. (1995). Antiparkinson drugs in neuroleptic treatment: Comparative study of progressive and abrupt withdrawal. *Encèphale, 21,* 209–215.

Bezchlibnyk-Butler, K. Z., & Jeffries, J. J. (Eds.). (1996). *Clinical handbook of psychotropic drugs.* Seattle: Hogrefe & Huber.

_____. (2005). *Clinical handbook of psychotropic drugs* (15th revised edition). Ashland, OH: Hogrefe & Huber.

Blader, J. C., & Carlson, G. A. (2007, Feb. 15, in press). Increased rates of bipolar disorder diagnoses among U.S. child, adolescent, and adult inpatients, 1996–2004. *Biological Psychiatry.*

Bleuler, M. (1978). *The schizophrenic disorders.* New Haven: Yale University Press.

Bloch, M., Stager, S. V., Braun, A. R., & Rubinow, D. R. (1995). Severe psychiatric symptoms associated with paroxetine withdrawal. *The Lancet, 346,* 57.

Bola, J., Mosher, L., & Cohen, D. (2005). The Soteria project and community treatment of psychosis. In S. Kirk (Ed.), *Mental disorders in the social environment: Critical perspectives* (pp. 389–406). New York: Columbia University Press.

Bolton, J. M., Sareen, J., & Reiss, J. P. (2006). Genital anaesthesia persisting six years after sertraline discontinuation. *Journal of Sex and Marital Therapy, 32,* 327–330.

Brahams, D. (1991, October 12). Triazolam suspended. *The Lancet, 338,* 938.

Breeding, J. (1998, Winter). Drug withdrawal and emotional recovery. *The Rights Tenet,* pp. 9–12.

Breggin, P. R. (1983a). *Psychiatric drugs: Hazards to the brain.* New York: Springer.

_____. (1983b). Iatrogenic helplessness in authoritarian psychiatry. In R. F. Morgan (Ed.), *The iatrogenics handbook.* Toronto: IPI Publishing Company.

_____. (1990). Brain damage, dementia and persistent cognitive dysfunction associated with neuroleptic drugs: Evidence, etiology, implications. *Journal of Mind and Behavior, 11,* 425–464.

_____. (1991). *Toxic psychiatry: Why therapy, empathy and love must replace the drugs, electroshock and biochemical theories of the "new psychiatry."* New York: St. Martin's Press.

_____. (1992a). A case of fluoxetine-induced stimulant side effects with sui-
cidal ideation associated with a possible withdrawal syndrome ("crashing").
International Journal of Risk and Safety in Medicine, 3, 325–328.

_____. (1992b). *Beyond conflict: From self-help and psychotherapy to peace-
making.* New York: St. Martin's Press.

_____. (1993). Parallels between neuroleptic effects and lethargic encephalitis:
The production of dyskinesias and cognitive disorders. *Brain and Cognition,
23*, 8–27.

_____. (1994, October 17–19). Testimony in *Joyce Fentress et al. v. Shea Com-
munications et al. ["The Wesbecker Case"].* Jefferson Circuit Court, Division
One, Louisville, Kentucky, No. 90-CI–06033, Vol. 16.

_____. (1995, September). Prozac "hazardous" to children. *Clinical Psychiatry
News,* p. 10.

_____. (1997a). *Brain-disabling treatments in psychiatry: Drugs, electroshock,
and the role of the FDA.* New York: Springer.

_____. (1997b). *The heart of being helpful.* New York: Springer.

_____. (1998a). *Talking back to Ritalin: What doctors aren't telling you about
stimulants for children.* Monroe, Maine: Common Courage Press.

_____. (1998b). Analysis of adverse behavioral effects of benzodiazepines with
a discussion of drawing scientific conclusions from the FDA's Spontaneous
Reporting System. *Journal of Mind and Behavior, 19*, 21–50.

_____. (1998c). Psychotherapy in emotional crises without resort to psychi-
atric medication. *The Humanistic Psychologist, 25*, 2–14.

_____. (1998d). Risks and mechanism of action of stimulants. *NIH consensus
development conference program and abstracts: Diagnosis and treatment of
attention deficit hyperactivity disorder,* pp. 105–120. Rockville, Md.: National
Institutes of Health.

_____. (1999a). Psychostimulants in the treatment of children diagnosed with
ADHD: Part I—Acute risks and psychological effects. *Ethical Human Sciences and Services 1*, 13–33.

_____. (1999b). Psychostimulants in the treatment of children diagnosed with
ADHD: Part II—Adverse effects on brain and behavior. *Ethical Human Sciences and Services 1*, 213–242.

_____. (1999c). Psychostimulants in the treatment of children diagnosed with
ADHD: Risks and mechanism of action. *International Journal of Risk and Safety
in Medicine 12*, 3–35. This simultaneously published version combines 1999a
and 1999b.

_____. (2000). *Reclaiming our children: A healing plan for a nation in crisis.*
Cambridge, Mass: Perseus Books.

_____. (2001a). *Talking back to Ritalin, revised edition.* Cambridge, MA:
Perseus Books.

_____. (2001b). *The antidepressant fact book.* Cambridge, MA: Perseus Books.

_____. (2002a). *The Ritalin fact book*. Cambridge, MA: Perseus Books.

_____. (2002b). Fluvoxamine as a cause of stimulation, mania, and aggression with a critical analysis of the FDA-approved label. *International Journal of Risk and Safety in Medicine, 14,* 71–86.

_____. (2003). Suicidality, violence and mania caused by selective serotonin reuptake inhibitors (SSRIs): A review and analysis. *Ethical Human Sciences and Services, 5,* 225–246. Simultaneously published in the *International Journal of Risk and Safety in Medicine 16,* 31–49, 2003/2004.

_____. (2006a). Recent regulatory changes in antidepressant labels: Implications for activation (stimulation) in clinical practice. *Primary Psychiatry, 13,* 57–60.

_____. (2006b). Court filing makes public my previously suppressed analysis of Paxil's effects. *Ethical Human Psychology and Psychiatry, 8,* 77–84.

_____. (2006c). How GlaxoSmithKline suppressed data on Paxil-induced akathisia: Implications for suicide and violence. *Ethical Human Psychology and Psychiatry, 8,* 91–100.

_____. (2006d) Drug company suppressed data on paroxetine-induced stimulation: Implications for violence and suicide. *Ethical Human Psychology and Psychiatry, 8,* 255–263.

_____. (2006e). Intoxication anosognosia: The spellbinding effect of psychiatric drugs. *Ethical Human Psychology and Psychiatry, 8,* 201–215.

Breggin, P. R., & Breggin, G. (1994). *Talking back to Prozac: What doctors aren't telling you about today's most controversial drug.* New York: St. Martin's Press.

_____. (1998). *The war against children of color.* Monroe, Maine: Common Courage Press.

Breggin, P. R., & Stern, E. M. (Eds.). (1996). *Psychosocial approaches to deeply disturbed patients.* New York: Haworth Press. Also published as *The Psychotherapy Patient, 9*(3/4), 1996.

Bridges-Parlet, S., Knopman, D., & Steffes, S. (1997). Withdrawal of neuroleptic medications from institutionalized dementia patients: Results of a double-blind, baseline-treatment controlled pilot study. *Journal of Geriatric Psychiatry and Neurology, 10,* 119–126.

Brown, C. S., Wittkowsky, A. K., & Bryant, S. G. (1986). Neuroleptic-induced catatonia after abrupt withdrawal of amandatine during neuroleptic therapy. *Pharmacotherapy, 6,* 193–195.

Burton Goldberg Group. (1994). *Alternative medicine: The definitive guide.* Fife, Wash.: Future Medicine Publishing.

Campagne, D. M. (2005, July). Venlafaxine and serious withdrawal symptoms: Warning to drivers. *Medscape General Medicine, 7,* no. 22. http://www.medscape.com/viewarticle/506427 (accessed February 8, 2006).

Caplan, P. (1995). *They say you're crazy: How the world's most powerful psychiatrists decide who's normal.* New York: Addison-Wesley.

Carlson, P. (1998, June 9). Ailments for what cures you. *Washington Post,* p. D1.

Cavanaugh, J., Smyth, R., and Goodwin, G. (2004). Relapse into mania or depression following lithium discontinuation: A 7-year follow-up. *Acta Psychiatrica Scandinavia, 109*, 91–95.

Ceccherini-Nelli, A., Bardellini, L., Cur, A., Guazzelli, M., Maggini, C., & Dilsaver, S. C. (1993). Antidepressant withdrawal: Prospective findings. *American Journal of Psychiatry, 150*, 165.

Chen, M. (2007, Feb. 7). "Drugmakers hurry sales, delay safety studies." *The New Standard.* http://newstandardnews.net/content/index.cfm/items/4269.

Cherland, E. and Fitzpatrick, R. (1999). Psychotic side effects of psychostimulants: A 5-year review. *Canadian Journal of Psychiatry, 44*, 811–813.

Chouinard, G., & Jones, B. (1980). Neuroleptic-induced supersensitivity psychosis: Clinical and pharmacologic characteristics. *American Journal of Psychiatry, 137*, 16–21.

_____. (1982). Neuroleptic-induced supersensitivity psychosis, the "hump course," and tardive dyskinesia. *Journal of Clinical Psychopharmacology, 2*, 143–144.

Christodolou, G. N., & Lykouras, E. P. (1982). Abrupt lithium discontinuation in manic-depressive patients. *Acta Psychiatrica Scandinavica, 65*, 310–314.

Clayton, A. H., Pradko, J. F., Croft, H. A., Montano, C. B., Leadbetter, R. A., Bolden-Watson, C., Bass, K. I., Donahue, R. M., Jamerson, B. D., and Metz, A. (2002). Prevalence of sexual dysfunction among newer antidepressants. *Journal of Clinical Psychiatry, 63*, 357–366.

Cohen, D. (1997a). A critique of the use of neuroleptic drugs in psychiatry. In S. Fisher & R. P. Greenberg (Eds.), *From placebo to panacea: Putting psychotropic drugs to the test* (pp. 173–228). New York: John Wiley & Sons.

_____. (1997b). Psychiatrogenics: The introduction of chlorpromazine in psychiatry. *Review of Existential Psychology and Psychiatry, 23*, 206–233.

_____. (2001). Commentary: Electroconvulsive treatment, neurology, and psychiatry. *Ethical Human Sciences and Services, 3*(2), 127–129.

_____. (2001). How to detoxify from common illusions about psychiatric medication. *Ethical Human Sciences and Services, 3*(3), 207–211.

_____. (2001). Medication-free minors with schizophrenia. *American Journal of Psychiatry, 158*(2), 324.

_____. (2002). Research on the drug treatment of schizophrenia: A critical evaluation and implications for social work education. *Journal of Social Work Education, 38*, 217–239.

_____. (2003). Review of W. Kneeland & C. Warren's "Pushbutton Psychiatry: A History of Electroshock in America." *Journal of the History of Behavioral Sciences, 39*, 417–418.

_____. (2003). The psychiatric medication history: Context, meaning, and purpose. *Social Work in Mental Health: The Journal of Behavioral and Psychiatric Social Work, 1*, 5–28.

_____. (2003, August 11). Antidepressant debate. *New York Times*. [letter]

_____. (2004, January 20). The risks of antidepressant withdrawal. *New York Times*. [letter]

_____. (2005). Clinical psychopharmacology trials: "Gold standard" or fool's gold? In S. Kirk (Ed.), *Mental disorders in the social environment: Critical perspectives* (pp. 347–367). New York: Columbia University Press.

_____. (2006). Foreword. In Jay Joseph, *The Missing Gene: Psychiatry, Heredity, and the Fruitless Search for Genes* (pp. 1–3). San Francisco: Algora Publishing.

_____. (2006). How does the decision to medicate children arise in ADHD? Views of parents and professionals in Canada. In G. Lloyd, J. Stead, & D. Cohen (eds.), *Critical new perspectives on ADHD* (pp. 137–155). London & New York: Routledge.

_____. (2006). Critiques of the 'ADHD enterprise.' In G. Lloyd, J. Stead, & D. Cohen (eds.), *Critical new perspectives on ADHD* (pp. 12–33). London & New York: Routledge.

_____. (2007). Helping individuals withdraw from psychiatric drugs. *Journal of College Student Psychotherapy.*

Cohen, D. (Ed.). (1990). Challenging the therapeutic state: Critical perspectives on psychiatry and the mental health system [Special Issue]. *Journal of Mind and Behavior, 11*(3 & 4).

_____. (1994). Challenging the therapeutic state, Part II: Further disquisitions on the mental health system [Special Issue]. *Journal of Mind and Behavior, 15*(1 & 2).

Cohen, D., & Cohen, H. (1986). Biological theories, drug treatments, and schizophrenia: A critical assessment. *Journal of Mind and Behavior, 7*, 11–36.

Cohen, D., & Hoeller, K. (2003). Screening for depression: Medicine or telemarketing? *Ethical Human Sciences and Services, 5*, 3–6.

Cohen, D., & Jacobs, D. (1998). A model consent form for psychiatric drug treatment. *International Journal of Risk and Safety in Medicine, 11*, 161–164.

_____. (2007). Randomized controlled trials of antidepressants: Clinically and scientifically irrelevant. *Debates in Neuroscience*, DOI 10. 1007.

Cohen, D., & Karsenty, S. (1998). The social construction of the side effects of anxiolytic drugs. Unpublished manuscript.

Cohen, D., & Leo, J. (2004). ADHD and neuroimaging: An update. *Journal of Mind and Behavior, 25*, 161–166.

Cohen, D., & Leo, J. (Eds.), with commentaries by T. Stanton, D. Smith, K. McCready, D.B. Stein, P. Oas, M. Laing, B. Kean, & S. Parry. (2002). A boy who stops taking stimulants for "ADHD": Commentaries on a *Pediatrics* case study. *Ethical Human Sciences and Services, 4*, 189–209.

Cohen, D., & McCubbin, M. (1990). The political economy of tardive dyskinesia: Asymmetries in power and responsibility. *Journal of Mind and Behavior, 11*, 465–488.

Cohen, D., McCubbin, M., Collin, J., & Perodeau, G. (2001). Medications as social phenomena. *Health*, 5(4), 441–469.

Cohen, J. S. (2001). *Overdose: The case against the drug companies*. New York: Penguin Putnam.

Colbert, T. (1996). *Broken brains or wounded hearts: What causes mental illness*. Santa Ana, Calif.: Kevco.

Coles, G. (1987). *The learning mystique: A critical look at "learning disabilities."* New York: Pantheon Books.

Cooper, W. O., Arbogast, P. G., Ding, H., Hickson, G. B., Fuchs, D. C., and Ray, W. (2006). Trends in prescribing of antipsychotic medications for U.S. children. *Ambulatory Pediatrics*, 6, 79–83.

Cormack, M. A., Sweeney, K. G., Hughes-Jones, H., & Foot, G. A. (1994). Evaluation of an easy, cost-effective strategy for cutting benzodiazepine use in general practice. *British Journal of General Practice*, 44, 5–8.

Coupland, N. J., Bell, C. J., & Potokar, J. P. (1996). Serotonin reuptake inhibitor withdrawal. *Journal of Clinical Psychopharmacology*, 16, 356–362.

Critser, G. (2005). *Generation Rx: How prescription drugs are altering American lives, minds, and bodies*. Boston: Houghton Mifflin Company.

Csoka AB, Shipko S. (2006). Persistent sexual side effects after SSRI discontinuation. *Psychotherapy & Psychosomatics*, 75, 187–188.

Danton, W. C., & Antonuccio, D. O. (1997). A focused empirical analysis of treatments for panic and anxiety. In S. Fisher & R. P. Greenberg (Eds.), *From placebo to panacea: Putting psychotropic drugs to the test* (pp. 229–280). New York: John Wiley & Sons.

Darbar, D., Connachie, A. M., Jones, A. M., & Newton, R. W. (1996). Acute psychosis associated with abrupt withdrawal of carbamazepine following intoxication. *British Journal of Clinical Practice*, 50, 350–351.

Davies, R. K., Tucker, G. J., Harrow, M., & Detre, T. P. (1971). Confusional epi-sodes and antidepressant medication. *American Journal of Psychiatry*, 128, 95–99.

DEA (Drug Enforcement Administration). (1995b, October). *Methylphenidate (A background paper)*. Washington, D.C.: Drug and Chemical Evaluation Section, Office of Diversion Control, DEA. Obtained through the Freedom of Information Act.

de Girolamo, G. (1996). WHO studies of schizophrenia: An overview of the results and their implications for an understanding of the disorder. In P. Breggin & E. M. Stern (Eds.), *Psychosocial approaches to deeply disturbed patients* (pp. 213–231). New York: Haworth Press. [Also published as *The Psychotherapy Patient*, 9(3/4), 1996.]

DeVeaugh-Geiss, J., & Pandurangi, A. (1982). Confusional paranoid psychosis after withdrawal from sympathomimetic amines: Two case reports. *American Journal of Psychiatry*, 139, 1190–1191.

Dilsaver, S. C. (1994). Withdrawal phenomena associated with antidepressant and antipsychotic agents. *Drug Safety, 10,* 103–114.

Dilsaver, S. C., Greden, J. F., & Snider, R. M. (1987). Antidepressant withdrawal syndromes: Phenomenology and physiopathology. *International Clinical Psychopharmacology, 2,* 1–19.

Di Masi, J., & Lasagna, L. (1995). The economics of psychotropic drug development. In F. Bloom & D. Kupfer (Eds.), *Psychopharmacology: The fourth generation of progress* (pp. 1883–1895). New York: Raven.

Drummond, E. H. (1997). *Overcoming anxiety without tranquilizers: A groundbreaking program for treating chronic anxiety.* New York: Dutton.

Dukes, M.N.G. (1996). *Meyler's side effects of drugs.* New York: Elsevier.

_____. (1997). Editorial. *International Journal of Risk and Safety in Medicine, 10,* 67–69.

Duloxetine: New indication. Depression and diabetic neuropathy: Too many adverse effects. (2006). *Prescrire International, 15,* 168–172.

Einbinder, E. (1995). Fluoxetine withdrawal? *American Journal of Psychiatry, 152,* 1235.

El-Zein, R. A., Abdel-Rahman, S. Z., Hay, M. J., Lopez, M. S., Bondy, M. L., Morris, D. L., and Legator MS. Cytogenetic effects in children treated with methylphenidate. *Cancer Letters, 230,* 284–291.

El-Zein, R. A., Hay, M. J., Lopez, M. S., Bondy, M. L., Morris, D. L., Legator, M. S., and Abdel-Rahman, S. Z. (2006). Response to comments on 'Cytogenetic effects in children treated with methylphenidate' by El-Zein et al. *Cancer Letters, 231,* 146–148.

Emslie, G. J., Rush, A. J., Weinberg, W. A., Kowatch, R. A., Hughes, C. W., Carmody, T., & Rintelmann, J. (1997). A double-blind, randomized placebo-controlled trial of fluoxetine in children and adolescents with depression. *Archives of General Psychiatry, 54,* 1031–1037.

Eppel, A. B., & Mishra, R. (1984). The mechanism of neuroleptic withdrawal. *Canadian Journal of Psychiatry, 29,* 508–509.

Faedda, G. L., Tondo, L., Baldessarini, R. J., Suppes, T., & Tohen, M. (1993). Outcome after rapid vs. gradual discontinuation of lithium in bipolar disorders. *Archives of General Psychiatry, 50,* 448–455.

Farah, A., & Lauer, T. E. (1996). Possible venlafaxine withdrawal syndrome. *American Journal of Psychiatry, 153,* 576.

Fava, G. A., & Grandi, S. (1995). Withdrawal syndromes after paroxetine and sertraline discontinuation. *Journal of Clinical Psychopharmacology, 15,* 374–375.

Fava, M., Mulroy, R., Alpert, J., Nierenberg, A. A., & Rosenbaum, J. F. (1997). Emergence of adverse effects following discontinuation of treatment with extended-release venlafaxine. *American Journal of Psychiatry, 154,* 1760–1762.

FDAAdvisoryCommittee.com. (2004, February 2). Antidepressant Strengthened Warnings About Pediatric Suicidality Risk Needed Immediately, Cmte. Says. Downloaded from Web site.

Feth, N., Cattaan-Ludewig, K., and Sirot, E. J. (2006). Electric sensations: Neglected symptom of escitalopram discontinuation. *American Journal of Psychiatry, 163,* 160.

Fialip, J., Aumaitre, O., Eschalier, A., Dordain, G., & Lavarenne, J. (1987). Benzodiazepine withdrawal seizures: Analysis of 48 case reports. *Clinical Neuropharmacology, 10,* 538–544.

Fishbain, D. A., Rosomoff, H. L., & Rosomoff, R. S. (1992). Detoxification of nonopiate drugs in the chronic pain setting and clonidine opiate detoxification. *Clinical Journal of Pain, 8,* 191–203.

Fisher, C. M. (1989). Neurological fragments. II. Remarks on anosognosia, confabulation, memory, and other topics; and an appendix on self-observation. *Neurology, 39,* 127–132.

Fisher, R., & Fisher, S. (1996). Antidepressants for children: Is scientific support necessary? *Journal of Nervous and Mental Disease, 184,* 99–102.

Fisher, S., Bryant, S. G., & Kent, T. A. (1993). Postmarketing surveillance by patient self-monitoring: Trazodone versus fluoxetine. *Journal of Clinical Psychopharmacology, 13,* 235–242.

Fisher, S., & Greenberg, R. (Eds.). (1989). *The limits of biological treatments for psychological distress: Comparisons with psychotherapy and placebo.* Hillsdale, N.J.: Lawrence Erlbaum.

_____. (1997). *From placebo to panacea: Putting psychiatric drugs to the test.* New York: Wiley.

Food and Drug Administration (FDA). (2004a, March 22). FDA issues Public Health Advisory on cautions for use of antidepressants in adults and children. Rockville, Maryland. www.fda.gov.

Food and Drug Administration (FDA). (2004b, September 14). Transcript of Meeting of the Center for Drug Evaluation and Research. Joint meeting of the CDER Psychopharmacologic Drugs Advisory Committee and the FDA Pediatric Advisory Committee. Bethesda, Maryland. www.fda.gov.

Food and Drug Administration (FDA) (2005a, January 26). Class suicidality labeling language for antidepressants. Food and Drug Administration, Rockville, Maryland. www.fda.gov.

Food and Drug Administration (FDA). (2005b, January 26). Medication guide: About using antidepressants in children and teenagers. Food and Drug Administration, Rockville, MD. Obtained from www.fda.gov.

Food and Drug Administration (FDA) (2005c, September 28). FDA issues Public Health Advisory on Strattera (atomoxetine) for Attention Deficit Disorder. Food and Drug Administration, Rockville, MD. Obtained from www.fda.gov.

Food and Drug Administration (FDA) (2005d, June 30). FDA statement on Concerta and methylphenidate for June 30 PAC. (Pediatric Advisory Committee briefing information, June 29, 2005) www.fda.gov.

Food and Drug Administration (FDA) (2006, March 14). Summary of psychiatric and neurological adverse events from June 2005 1-year post pediatric exclusivity reviews of Concerta and other methylphenidate products. Table 2: Brief case summaries of psychiatric adverse events for Concerta, immediate-release methylphenidate, and extended release methylphenidate (N=52). www.fda.gov.

Food and Drug Administration (FDA). (2007, February 21). FDA News: FDA directs ADHD drug manufacturers to notify patients about cardiovascular adverse events and psychiatric adverse events. www.fda.gov.

Fried, S. M. (1998). *Bitter pills: Inside the hazardous world of legal drugs.* New York: Bantam Doubleday Bell.

Gaines, D. (1992). *Teenage wasteland: Suburbia's dead end kids.* New York: HarperPerennial.

GAO (Government Accounting Office). (1990, April). *FDA drug review: Postapproval risks 1976–1985.* Report to the Chairman, Subcommittee on Human Resources and Intergovernmental Relations, Committee on Government Operations, House of Representatives.

Garner, E. M., Kelly, M. W., & Thompson, D. F. (1993). Tricyclic antidepressant withdrawal syndrome. *Annals of Pharmacotherapy, 27,* 1068–1072.

Garrland, E. J., and Baerg, E. A. (2001). Amotivational syndrome associated with selective serotonin reuptake inhibitors in children and adolescents. *Journal of Child & Adolescent Psychopharmacology, 11,* 181–186.

Gelperin, K. and Phelan, K. (2006, May 3). Psychiatric adverse events associated with drug treatment of ADHD: Review of postmarketing safety data. Food and Drug Administration, Rockville, MD.

Geurian, K., & Burns, I. (1994). Detailed description of a successful outpatient taper of phenobarbital therapy. *Archives of Family Medicine, 3,* 458–460.

Ghadirian, A. M. (1986). Paradoxical mood response following antidepressant withdrawal. *Biological Psychiatry, 21,* 1298–1300.

Giakas, W. J., & Davis, J. M. (1997). Intractable withdrawal from venlafaxine treated with fluoxetine. *Psychiatric Annals, 27,* 85–92.

Gibeaut, J. (1996, August). Mood-altering verdict. *American Bar Association Journal,* p. 18

Gilbert, P. L., Harris, J., McAdams, L. A., & Jeste, D. V. (1995). Neuroleptic withdrawal in schizophrenic patients: A review of the literature. *Archives of General Psychiatry, 52,* 173–188.

Gillberg, C., Melander, H., von Knorring, A. L., Janols, L. O., Thernlund, G., Hagglof, B., Eidevall-Wallin, L., Gustafsson, P., & Kopp, S. (1997). Long-term stimulant treatment of children with attention-deficit hyperactivity disorder symptoms: A randomized, double-blind, placebo-controlled trial. *Archives of General Psychiatry, 54,* 857–864.

Glass, J., Lanctot, K. L., Herrmann, N., Sproule, B. A., Busto, U. E. (2005). Sedative hypnotics in older people with insomnia: meta-analysis of risks and benefits. *British Medical Journal, 331*(7526), 1169.

GlaxoSmithKline (2006, May). Important Prescribing Information (Dear Healthcare Provider Letter). [About clinical worsening and suicide in adults taking Paxil]. Philadelphia, Pennsylvania.

Glenmullen, J. (2000). *Prozac backlash.* New York: Simon and Schuster.

Glenmullen, J. (2005). *The antidepressant solution: A step-by-step guide to safely overcoming antidepressant withdrawal, dependence, and "addiction."* New York: Free Press.

Goldstein, T., Frye, M., Denicoff, K., Smith-Jackson, E., Leverich, G., Bryan, A., Ali, S., and Post, R. (1999). Antidepressant discontinuation-related mania: Critical prospective observation and theoretical implications in bipolar disorder. *Journal of Clinical Psychiatry, 60,* 563–567.

Goodwin, G. M. (1994). Recurrence of mania after lithium withdrawal: Implications for the use of lithium in the treatment of bipolar affective disorder. *British Journal of Psychiatry, 164,* 149–152.

Goozner, Merrill. (2004). *The $800 million pill: The truth behind the cost of new drugs.* Berkeley: University of California Press.

Gorman, J. M. (1997). *The essential guide to psychiatric drugs.* New York: St. Martin's Press.

Goudie, A. J., Smith J. A., Robertson, A., & Cavanagh, C. (1999). Clozapine as a drug of dependence. *Psychopharmacology, 142,* 369–374.

Grady, D. (1998, April 15). Reactions to prescribed drugs kill tens of thousands, study shows. *New York Times,* p. A1.

Green, A. (1989). Physical and sexual abuse of children. In H. Kaplan & B. Sadock (Eds.), *Comprehensive textbook of psychiatry* (pp. 1962–1970). Baltimore: Williams and Wilkins.

Green, A. (2003). Withdrawal symptoms are very frequent and difficult to treat. *British Medical Journal, 324.* Available at: http://www.bmj.com/cgi/eletters/324/7332/260.

Greenberg, R., Bornstein, R., Greenberg, M., & Fisher, S. (1992). A meta-analysis of antidepressant outcome under "blinder" conditions. *Journal of Consulting and Clinical Psychology, 60,* 664–669.

Grohol, J. M. (1997). *The insider's guide to mental health resources online.* New York: Guilford Press.

Gualtieri, C. T., & Sovner, R. (1989). Akathisia and tardive akathisia. *Psychiatric Aspects of Mental Retardation Reviews, 8,* 83–87.

Gualtieri, C. T., & Staye, J. (1979). Withdrawal symptoms after abrupt cessation of amitriptyline in an eight-year-old boy. *American Journal of Psychiatry, 136,* 457–458.

Haddad, P. (1997). Newer antidepressants and the discontinuation syndrome. *Journal of Clinical Psychiatry,* 58 (supplement 7), 17–22.

Haddad, P., Lejoyeux, M., & Young, A. (1998). Antidepressant discontinuation reactions are preventable and easy to treat. *British Medical Journal, 316,* 1105–1106.

Hall, S. S. (1998, February 13). Our memories, our selves. *New York Times Magazine,* pp. 26–33, 49, 56–57.

Hardman, J. G., & Limbird, L. E. (1996). *Goodman and Gilman's The Pharmacological basis of therapeutics,* 9th ed. New York: McGraw-Hill.

Hartman, P. M. (1990). Mania or hypomania after withdrawal from antidepressants. *Journal of Family Practice, 30,* 471–472.

Healy, D. (1997). *The Antidepressant era.* Cambridge, MA: Harvard University.

Healy, D. (2004). *Let them eat Prozac: The unhealthy relationship between the pharmaceutical industry and depression.* New York and London: New York University Press.

Hegarty, J. M. (1996). Antipsychotic drug withdrawal. *Current Approaches to Psychoses, 5,* 1–4.

Heh, C.W.C., Sramek, J., Herrera, J., & Costa, J. (1988). Exacerbation of psychosis after discontinuation of carbamazepine treatment. *American Journal of Psychiatry, 145,* 878–879.

Hindmarch, I., Kimber, S., & Cockle, S. M. (2000). Abrupt and brief discontinuation of antidepressant treatment: Effects on cognitive function and psychomotor performance. *International Clinical Psychopharmacology, 15,* 305–318.

Hoehn-Saric, R., Lipsey, J. R., & McLeod, D. A. (1990). Apathy and indifference in patients on fluvoxamine and fluoxetine. *Journal of Clinical Psychopharmacology, 10,* 343–345.

Horgan, J. (1999, March 21). Placebo nation. *New York Times,* p. 15.

Impact of direct-to-consumer advertising on prescription drug spending. (June 2003). The Henry Kaiser Family Foundation. Posted on: www.kff.org

IMS Health. (1999, April 21). U.S. pharmaceutical industry spent more than $5.8 billion on product promotion in 1998 [available online at http://www.imshealth.com].

INCB (International Narcotics Control Board). (1996, November). *Control of use of methylphenidate in the treatment of ADD: Expert meeting on amphetamine-type stimulants, Shanghai, 25–29 November 1996.* Vienna, Austria: INCB.

————. (1997, March 4). INCB sees continuing risk in stimulant prescribed for children. *INCB Annual Report Background Note No. 4.* Vienna, Austria: INCB.

Inuwa, I., Horobin, R., & Williams, A. (1994, July). A TEM study of white blood cells from patients under neuroleptic therapy. *ICEM 13-Paris* [International Congress of Electron Microscopy], pp. 1091–1092.

Jacobovitz, D., Sroufe, L. A., Stewart, M., & Leffert, N. (1990). Treatment of attentional and hyperactivity problems in children with sympathomimetic drugs: A comprehensive review. *Journal of the American Academy of Child and Adolescent Psychiatry, 29,* 677–688.

Jacobs, D. (1995). Psychiatric drugging: Forty years of pseudo-science, self-interest, and indifference to harm. *Journal of Mind and Behavior, 16,* 421–470.

Jacobs, D., & Cohen, D. (1999). What is really known about psychological alterations produced by psychiatric drugs? *International Journal of Risk and Safety in Medicine, 12*(1), 37–47.

_____. (1999). What is really known about psychological alterations produced by psychiatric drugs? *International Journal of Risk and Safety in Medicine, 12*(2).

_____. (2004). Hidden in plain sight: DSM-IV's rejection of the categorical approach to diagnosis. *Review of Existential Psychology & Psychiatry. 26,* 81–96.

Jaffe, J. (1980). Drug addiction and drug abuse. In L. S. Goodman & A. Gillman (Eds.), *The pharmacological basis of therapeutics,* 6th ed. (pp. 535–584). New York: Macmillan.

Jess, G., Smith, D. MacKenzie, C., & Crawford, C. (2004). Carbamazapine and rebound mania. *American Journal of Psychiatry 161,* 2132–2133.

Joint Commission on Mental Illness and Mental Health. (1961). (Final Report). *Action for Mental Health.* New York: Basic Books.

Julien, R. M. (1997). *A primer of drug action.* New York: W. H. Freeman.

Kapit, R. M. (1986, October 17). Safety update. NDA 18–936 [Prozac for depression]. Internal document of the Department of Health and Human Services, Public Health Service, Food and Drug Administration, Center for Drug Evaluation and Research. Obtained through the Freedom of Information Act.

Karp, D. A. (2006). *Is it me or my meds? Living with antidepressants.* Cambridge, MA, and London: Harvard University Press.

Kassirer, Jerome P. (2005). *On the take: How America's complicity with big business can endanger your health.* Oxford and New York: Oxford University Press.

Kean, B. (2005). The risk society and Attention Deficit Hyperactivity Disorder (ADHD): A critical social research analysis concerning the development and social impact of the ADHD diagnosis. *Ethical Human Psychology and Psychiatry, 7,* 131–142.

_____. (2006). The globalization of Attention Deficit Hyperactivity Disorder and the rights of the child. *International Journal of Risk and Safety in Medicine, 18,* 195–204.

Keely, K. A., & Licht, A. L. (1985). Gradual vs. abrupt withdrawal of methylphenidate in two older dependent males. *Journal of Substance Abuse Treatment, 2,* 123–125.

Kennedy, S. H., Eisfeld, B. S., Dickens, S. E., Bacchiochi, J. R., & Bagby, R. M. (2000). Antidepressant-induced sexual dysfunction during treatment with moclobemide, paroxetine, sertraline, and venlafaxine. *Journal of Clinical Psychiatry, 61,* 276–281.

Kim, D. R., & Staab, J. P. (2005). Quetiapine discontinuation syndrome. *American Journal of Psychiatry, 162,* 1020.

King, J. R., & Hullin, R. P. (1983). Withdrawal symptoms from lithium: Four case reports and a questionnaire study. *British Journal of Psychiatry, 143,* 30–35.

Kirk, A., & Kutchins, H. (1992). *The selling of DSM: The rhetoric of science in psychiatry.* New York: Aldine De Gruyter.

Kirsch, I. (1997). Specifying nonspecifics: Psychological mechanisms of placebo effects. In A. Harrington (Ed.), *The placebo effect: An interdisciplinary exploration* (pp. 166–186). Cambridge, Mass.: Harvard University Press.

Kirsch, I., & Sapirstein, G. (1998). Listening to Prozac but hearing placebo: A meta-analysis of antidepressant medication. *Prevention and Treatment, 1,* article 0002a. [Posted June 26, 1998: http://journals.apa.org/prevention/volume1/pre0010002a.html.]

Kirsch, I., Moore, T., Scoboria, A. & Nicholls, S. (2002). The emperor's new drugs: An analysis of antidepressant medication data submitted to the U.S. Food and Drug Administration. *Prevention & Treatment, 5,* article 23, posted July 15, 2002.

Klein, H. E., Broucek, B., & Greil, W. (1981). Lithium withdrawal triggers psychotic states. *British Journal of Psychiatry, 139,* 255–264.

Klein, R. G., & Bessler, A. W. (1992). Stimulant side effects in children. In J. W. Kane & J. A. Lieberman (Eds.), *Adverse effects of psychotropic drugs* (pp. 470–496). New York: Guilford Press.

Koch, S., Jager-Roman, E., Losche, G., Nau, H., Rating, D., & Helge, H. (1996). Antiepileptic drug treatment in pregnancy: Drug side effects in the neonate and neurological outcome. *Acta Paediatrica, 85,* 739–746.

Koopowitz, L. F., & Berk, M. (1995). Paroxetine-induced withdrawal effects. *Human Psychopharmacology, 10,* 147–148.

Kramer, J. C., Klein, D. F., & Fink, M. (1961). Withdrawal symptoms following discontinuation of imipramine therapy. *American Journal of Psychiatry, 118,* 549–550.

Lacasse, J., & Leo, J. (2005). Serotonin and depression: A disconnect between the advertisements and the scientific literature. *PLoS Medicine,* 2(12), e392. Available freely online at http://medicine.plosjournals.org.

Lader, M. (1983). Benzodiazepine withdrawal states. In M. R. Trimble (Ed.), *Benzodiazepines divided* (pp. 17–31). New York: John Wiley & Sons.

_____. (1991). History of benzodiazepine dependence. *Journal of Substance Abuse Treatment, 8,* 53–59.

_____. (1992). Abuse liability of prescribed psychotropic drugs. In J. M. Kane & J. A. Lieberman (Eds.), *Adverse effects of psychotropic drugs* (pp. 77–84). New York: Guilford Press.

Lago, J. A., & Kosten, T. R. (1994). Stimulant withdrawal. *Addiction, 89,* 1477–1481.

Lal, S., & AlAnsari, E. (1986). Tourette-like syndrome following low-dose short-term neuroleptic treatment. *Canadian Journal of Neurological Sciences, 13*, 125–128.

Lang, A. E. (1994). Withdrawal akathisia: Case reports and a proposed classification of chronic akathisia. *Movement Disorders, 9*, 188–192.

Lapierre, Y. D., Gagnon, A., & Kokkinidis, L. (1980). Rapid recurrence of mania following lithium withdrawal. *Biological Psychiatry, 15*, 859–864.

Law, W., III, Petti, T. A., & Kazdin, A. E. (1981). Withdrawal symptoms after graduated cessation of imipramine in children. *American Journal of Psychiatry, 138*, 647–650.

Lawrence, J. M. (1985). Reactions to withdrawal of antidepressants, antiparkinsonian drugs, and lithium. *Psychosomatics, 26*, 869–874, 877.

Lazarou, J., Pomeranz, B. H., & Corey, P. (1998, April 15). Incidence of adverse drug reactions in hospitalized patients. *Journal of the American Medical Association, 279*, 1200–1205.

Leipzig, R. M. (1992). Gastrointestinal and hepatic effects of psychotropic drugs. In J. M. Kane & J. A. Lieberman (Eds.), *Adverse effects of psychotropic drugs* (pp. 408–430). New York: Guilford Press.

Lejoyeux, M., & Adès, J. (1997). Antidepressant discontinuation: A review of the literature. *Journal of Clinical Psychiatry, 58* (supplement 7), 11–16.

Lenzer, J. (2005, September 27). Drug secrets: What the FDA isn't telling. *Slate*. www/slate.com/id/2126918/.

Leo, J., & Cohen, D. (2003). Broken brains or flawed studies? A critical review of ADHD brain imaging research. *Journal of Mind and Behavior, 24*, 29–56.

Levinson-Castiel, R., Merlob, P., Linder, N., Sirota, L., & Klinger, G. (2006). Neonatal abstinence syndrome after in utero exposure to selective serotonin reuptake inhibitors in term infants. *Archives of Pediatric and Adolescent Medicine 160*, 173–176.

Lewontin, R. C. (1992). *Biology as ideology*. New York: HarperPerennial.

Lewontin, R. C., Rose, S., & Kamin, L. (1984). *Not in our genes: Biology, ideology, and human nature*. New York: Pantheon Books.

Lieberman, J. A. (2006). Comparative effectiveness of antipsychotic drugs. *Archives of General Psychiatry, 63*, 1069–1072.

Lieberman, J. A., Stroup, T. S., McEvoy, J. P., Swartz, M. S., Rosenheck, R. A., Perkins, D O., Keefe, R. S., Davis, S. M., Davis, C. E., Lebowitz, B. D., Severe, J., and Hsiao, J. K. (CATIE Investigators). (2005). Effectiveness of antipsychotic drugs in patients with chonic schizophrenia. *New England Journal of Medicine, 353*, 1209–1223.

Lifshitz, K., O'Keefe, R. T., Lee, K. L., Linn, G. S., Mase, D., Avery, J., Lo, E., & Cooper, T. B. (1991). Effect of extended depot fluphenazine treatment and withdrawal on social and other behaviors of Cebus apella monkeys. *Psychopharmacology, 105*, 492–500.

Liskin, B., Roose, S. P., Walsh, B. T., & Jackson, W. K. (1985). Acute psychosis following phenelzine discontinuation. *Journal of Clinical Psychopharmacology,* 5, 46–47.

Luchins, D. J., Freed, W. J., & Wyatt, R. J. (1980). The role of cholinergic supersensitivity in the medical symptoms associated with withdrawal of antipsychotic drugs. *American Journal of Psychiatry,* 137, 1395–1398.

Maisami, M., & Golant, D. (1991). Neuroleptic withdrawal. *Journal of the Academy of Child and Adolescent Psychiatry,* 30, 336.

Mander, A. J. (1986). Is there a lithium withdrawal syndrome? *British Journal of Psychiatry,* 149, 498–501.

Mander, A. J., & Loudon, J. B. (1988, July 2). Rapid recurrence of mania following abrupt discontinuation of lithium. *The Lancet,* 2, 15–17.

Manos, N., Gkiouzepas, J., & Logothetis, J. (1981). The need for continuous use of antiparkinsonian medication with chronic schizophrenic patients receiving long-term neuroleptic therapy. *American Journal of Psychiatry,* 138, 184–188.

Mant, A., & Walsh, R. (1997). Reducing benzodiazepine use. *Drug and Alcohol Review,* 16, 77–84.

Marks, I. M., De Albuquerque, A., Cottraux, J., Gentil, V., Greist, J., Hand, I., Liberman, R. L., Relvas, J. S., Tobena, A., & Tyrer, P., et al. (1989). The "efficacy" of alprazolam in panic disorder and agoraphobia: A critique of recent reports. (1989). *Archives of General Psychiatry,* 46, 668–672.

Marks, J. (1978). *The benzodiazepines: Use, overuse, misuse, abuse.* Lancaster, England: MTP.

Maxmen, J. S., & Ward, N. G. (1995). *Psychotropic drugs fast facts,* 2nd ed. New York: W. W. Norton.

May, P., London, E. B., Zimmerman, T., Thompson, R., Mento, T., & Spreat, S. (1995). A study of the clinical outcome of patients with profound mental retardation gradually withdrawn from chronic neuroleptic medication. *Annals of Clinical Psychiatry,* 7, 155–160.

McCready, K. (1995, Summer). What heals human beings? Technology or humanity—there is a choice. Report from the Center for the Study of Psychiatry and Psychology in the *Rights Tenet: Newsletter of the National Association for Rights Protection and Advocacy* (NARPA), p. 3.

McInnis, M., & Petursson, H. (1985). Withdrawal of trihexyphenidyl. *Acta Psychiatrica Scandinavica,* 71, 297–303.

Medawar, C. (1992). *Power and dependence.* London: Social Audit.

_____. (1997). The antidepressant web: Marketing depression and making medicines work. *International Journal of Risk and Safety in Medicine,* 10, 75–126.

Medawar, C., & Hardon, A. (2004). *Medicines out of control? Antidepressants and the conspiracy of goodwill.* London: Aksant Academic Publishers/Transaction.

Medical Letter (1998, February 13). Some drugs that cause psychiatric symptoms. *Medical Letter on Drugs and Therapeutics, 40,* 21–24.

Mender, D. (1994). *The myth of neuropsychiatry: A look at paradoxes, physics, and the human brain.* New York: Plenum Press.

Menza, M. A. (1986). Withdrawal syndrome in a depressed patient treated with trazodone. *American Journal of Psychiatry, 143,* 1195.

Miller, M. M., & Potter-Efron, R. T. (1990). Aggression and violence associated with substance abuse. *Journal of Chemical Dependency Treatment, 3,* 1–36.

Mirin, S. M., Schatzberg, A. F., & Creasy, D. E. (1981). Hypomania and mania after withdrawal of tricyclic antidepressants. *American Journal of Psychiatry, 138,* 87–89.

Moncrieff, J. (2006a). Why is it so difficult to stop psychiatric drug treatment? It may be nothing to do with the original problem. *Medical Hypotheses, 67,* 517–523.

Moncrieff, D. (2006b). Does antipsychotic withdrawal provoke psychosis? Review of the literature on rapid onset psychosis (supersensitivity psychosis) and withdrawal-related relapse. *Acta Psychiatrica Scandinavica, 114,* 3–14.

Moncrieff, J., & Cohen, D. (2005). Rethinking models of psychotropic drug action. *Psychotherapy and Psychosomatics, 74,* 145–153.

Moncrieff, J., & Cohen, D. (2006). Do antidepressants cause or cure abnormal brain states? *PLoS Medicine, 3*(7), e240. Available freely online at: http://medicine.plosjournals.org

Moncrieff, J. & Kirsch, I. (2006). Efficacy of antidepressants in adults. *BMJ* 331: 155–157.

Montalbetti, D. J., & Zis, A. P. (1988). Cholinergic rebound following trazodone withdrawal? *Journal of Clinical Psychopharmacology, 8,* 73.

Moore, T. J. (1995). *Deadly medicine: Why tens of thousands of heart patients died in America's worst drug disaster.* New York: Simon & Schuster.

_____. (1997, December). Hard to swallow: Hidden dangers of antidepressants. *The Washingtonian,* pp. 68–71, 140–145.

_____. (1998). *Prescription for disaster: The hidden dangers in your medicine cabinet.* New York: Simon & Schuster.

Morris, L. A., Tabak, E. R., & Gondek, K. (1997). Counseling patients about prescribed medication: 12-year trends. *Medical Care, 35,* 996–1007.

Mosher, L. (1996). Soteria: A therapeutic community for psychotic persons. In P. Breggin & E. M. Stern (Eds.), *Psychosocial approaches to deeply disturbed patients* (pp. 43–58). New York: Haworth Press. Also published as *The Psychotherapy Patient, 9*(3/4), 1996.

Mosher, L. R., & Burti, L. (1994). *Community mental health: Principles and practice.* New York: Norton.

Mosher, L., & Cohen, D. (2003). An ethical examination of electroconvulsive therapy (ECT). *Virtual Mentor: Ethics Journal of the American Medical Association*. Available online: http://www.ama-assn.org/ama/pub/category/11123.html.

Myslobodsky, M. S. (1986). Anosognosia in tardive dyskinesia: "Tardive dysmentia" or "tardive dementia"? *Schizophrenia Bulletin, 12,* 1–6.

Nolan, E. E., Gadow, K. D., & Sprafkin, J. (1999). Stimulant medication withdrawal during long-term therapy in children with comrbid attention-deficit hyperactivity disorder and chronic multiple tic disorder. *Pediatrics, 103* (4 Pt. 1), 730–737.

Noyes, R., Jr., Garvey, M. J., Cook, B., & Suelzer, M. (1991). Benzodiazepine withdrawal: Dr. Noyes and associates reply. *American Journal of Psychiatry, 148,* 1621.

Olfson M., Marcus S. C., Tedeschi, M., & Wan, G. J. (2006). Continuity of antidepressant treatment for adults with depression in the United States. *American Journal of Psychiatry, 163,* 101–108.

Opbrock, A., Delgado, P. L., Laukes, C., McGahuey, C., Katsanis, J., Moreno, F. A., & Manber, R. (2002). Emotional blunting associated with SSRI-induced sexual dysfunction. Do SSRIs inhibit emotional responses? *International Journal of Neuropsychopharmacology, 5,* 147–151.

Otani, K., Tanaka, O., Kaneko, S., Ishida, M., Yasui, N., & Fukushima, Y. (1994). Mechanisms of the development of trazodone withdrawal symptoms. *International Clinical Psychopharmacology, 9,* 131–133.

Otto, M. W., Pollack, M. H., & Barlow, D. H. (1995). *Stopping anxiety medication. A workbook for patients wanting to discontinue benzodiazepine treatment for panic disorder.* Albany, N.Y.: Graywind Publications.

Pacheco, L. (2002). Withdrawal symptoms are very frequent and difficult to treat. *British Medical Journal, 324.* Available at: http://www.bmj.com/cgi/eletters/324/7332/260.

PDR for herbal medicines. (1998). Montvale, N J : Medical Economics.

Peabody, C. A. (1987). Trazodone withdrawal and formication. *Journal of Clinical Psychiatry, 48,* 385.

Perahia, D. G., Kajdasz, D. K., Desaiah, D., & Haddad, P. M. (2005). Symptoms following abrupt discontinuation of duloxetine treatment in patients with major depressive disorder. *Journal of Affective Disorders, 89,* 207–212.

Perenyi, A., Frecska, E., Bagdy, G., & Revai, K. (1985). Changes in mental condition, hyperkinesias and biochemical parameters after withdrawal of chronic neuroleptic treatment. *Acta Psychiatrica Scandinavica, 72,* 430–435.

Perlis, R. H., Ostacher, M. J., Patel, J. K., Marangell, L. B., Zhang, H., Wisniewski, S. R., Ketter, T. A., Miklowitz, D. J., Otto, M. W., Gyulai, L., Reilly-Harrington, N. A., Nierenberg, A. A., Sachs, G. S., & Thase, M. (2006). Predictors of recurrence in bipolar disorder: Primary outcomes from the systematic treatment enhancement program for bipolar disorder (STEP-BD). *American Journal of Psychiatry, 163*, 217–224.

Perry, P. J., Alexander, B., & Liskow, B. I. (1997). *Psychotropic drug handbook,* 7th ed. Washington, D.C.: American Psychiatric Press.

Petursson, H. (1994). The benzodiazepine withdrawal syndrome. *Addiction, 89,* 1455–1459.

Physicians' Desk Reference. (1998). Montvale, N.J.: Medical Economics. (Revised annually.)

Physicians' Desk Reference. (2007). Montvale, NJ: Thomson PDR.

Pies, R. W. (1998). *Handbook of essential psychopharmacology.* Washington, D.C.: American Psychiatric Press.

Pollock, B. G. (1998). Discontinuation symptoms and SSRIs. *Journal of Clinical Psychiatry, 59*, 535–536.

Poyurovski, M., Bergman, Y., Shoshani, D., Schneidman, M., & Weizman, A. (1998). Emergence of obsessive-compulsive symptoms and tics during clozapine withdrawal. *Clinical Neuropharmacology, 21*, 97–100.

PRNewswire via News Edge Corporation. (1998, June 4). GAMIAN PR urges aggressive treatment of children/studies show poor patient compliance.

Quitkin, F. M., Adams, D. C., Bowden, C. L., Heyer, E. J., Rifkin, A., Sellers, E. M., Tandon, R., & Taylor, B. P. (1998). *Current psychotherapeutic drugs,* 2nd ed. Washington, D.C.: American Psychiatric Press.

Ramaswamy, S., Vija, D., William, M., Sattar, S. P., Praveen, F., & Petty, F. (2004). Aripiprazole possibly worsens psychosis. *International Clinical Psychopharmacology, 19*, 45–48.

Rappoport, J. L., Buchsbaum, M., Zahn, T. P., Weingartner, H., Ludlow, C., & Mikkelsen, E. (1978). Dextroamphetamine: Cognitive and behavioral effects in normal prepubertal boys. *Science, 199*, 5650–5653.

Rauch, S. L., O'Sullivan, R. L., & Jenike, M. A. (1996). Open treatment of obsessive-compulsive disorder with venlafaxine: A series of ten cases. *Journal of Clinical Psychopharmacology, 16*, 81–84.

Rickels, K., Case, W. G., Schweizer, E., Garcia-Espana, F., & Fridman, R. (1991). Long-term benzodiazepine users three years after participation in a discontinuation program. *American Journal of Psychiatry, 148*, 757–761.

Rifkin, A., Quitkin, F., Howard, A., & Klein, D. F. (1975). A study of abrupt lithium withdrawal. *Psychopharmacologia, 44*, 157–158.

Rocha, B. A., Fumagali, F., Gaintdinov, R., Jones, S. R., Ator, R., Giros, B., Miller, G. W., & Caron, M. G. (1998). Cocaine self-administration in dopamine-transporter knockout mice. *Nature Neuroscience, 1*, 132–137.

Rogers, C. (1961). Some learnings from a study of psychotherapy with schizophrenics. In C. Rogers & B. Stevens (Eds.), *On becoming a person: A therapist's view of psychotherapy* (pp. 183–196). New York: Houghton Mifflin.

_____. (1995). *A way of being.* New York: Houghton Mifflin.

Rosebush, P., & Stewart, T. (1989). A prospective analysis of 24 episodes of neuroleptic malignant syndrome. *American Journal of Psychiatry, 146,* 717–725.

Rosenbaum, J. F., Fava, M., Hoog, S. L., Ascroft, R. C., & Krebs, W. B. (1998). Selective serotonin reuptake inhibitor discontinuation syndrome: A randomized clinical trial. *Biological Psychiatry, 44,* 77–87.

Rosenbaum, J. F., & Zejecka, J. (1997). Clinical management of antidepressant discontinuation. *Journal of Clinical Psychiatry, 58* (supplement 7), 37–40.

Ross, C. A., & Pam, A. (1994). *Pseudoscience in biological psychiatry: Blaming the body.* New York: John Wiley & Sons.

Rush, A. J., Trivedi, M.H., Wisniewski, S. R., Stewart, J. W., Nierenberg, A. A., Thase, M. E., Ritz, L., Biggs, M. M., Warden, D., Luther, J. F., Shores-Wilson, K., Niederehe, G., & Fava, M. for the STAR*D study team. (2006). Bupropion, sertraline, or venlafaxine-XR after failure of SSRIs for depression. *New England Journal of Medicine, 354,* 1231–1242.

Russell, J. (2007, February 1). Cymbalta leads the way for Lilly. *The Indianapolis Star.* Retrieved February 3, 2007 from: http://www.indystar.com/apps/pbcs.dll/article?AID=/20070201/BUSINESS/702010485/–1/ZONES04.

Rybacki, J., & Long, J. W. (1998). *The essential guide to prescription drugs.* New York: HarperPerennial.

Sachdev, P. (1995). The epidemiology of drug-induced akathisia: Part II. Chronic, tardive, and withdrawal akathisias. *Schizophrenia Bulletin, 21,* 451–461.

Safer, D. J., Allen, R. P., & Barr, E. (1975). Growth rebound after termination of stimulation drugs. *Journal of Pediatrics, 86,* 113–116.

Schatzberg, A. F. (1997). Antidepressant discontinuation syndrome: An update of serotonin reuptake inhibitors. *Journal of Clinical Psychiatry, 58* (supplement 7), 3–4.

Schatzberg, A. F., Blier, P., Delgado, P. L., Fava, M., Haddad, P. M., & Shelton, R. C. (2006). Antidepressant discontinuation syndrome: Consensus panel recommendations for clinical management and additional research. *Journal of Clinical Psychiatry, 67* (suppl. 4), 27–30.

Schatzberg, A. F., Cole, J. O., & DeBattista, C. (1997). *Manual of clinical psychopharmacology,* 3rd ed. Washington, D.C./London, England: American Psychiatric Press.

Schatzberg, A. F., Haddad, P., Kaplan, E., Lejoyeux, M., Rosenbaum, J. F., Young, A. H., & Zajecka, J. (1997). Serotonin reuptake inhibitor discontinuation syndrome: A hypothetical definition. *Journal of Clinical Psychiatry, 58* (supplement 7), 5–10.

Schommer, J. C., & Wiederholt, J. B. (1997). The association of prescription status, patient age, patient gender, and patient question-asking behavior with the content of pharmacist-patient communication. *Pharmaceutical Research, 14,* 145–151.

Schou, M. (1993). Is there a lithium withdrawal syndrome? An examination of the evidence. *British Journal of Psychiatry, 163,* 514–518.

Schwartz, R. H., & Rushton, H. G. (2004). Stuttering priapism associated with withdrawal from sustained-release methylphenidate. *Journal of Pediatrics, 144,* 675–676.

Selemon, L. D., Lidow, M. S., & Goldman-Rakic, P. S. (1999). Increased volume and glial density in primate prefontal cortex associated with chronic antipsychotic drug exposure. *Biological Psychiatry, 46,* 161–172.

Shader, R. I., & Greenblatt, D. J. (1993). Use of benzodiazepines in anxiety disorders. *New England Journal of Medicine, 328,* 1398–1405.

Sharkey, J. (1994). *Bedlam: Greed, profiteering, and fraud in a mental health system gone crazy.* New York: St. Martin's Press.

Shelton, R. C. (2006). The nature of the discontinuation syndrome associated with antidepressant drugs. *Journal of Clinical Psychiatry, 67*(suppl. 4), 3–7.

Sherman, C. (1998). Shift seen in psychotropic prescribing patterns. *Clinical Psychiatry News, 26*(4). [Available on-line at http://www.medscape.com.]

Shiovitz, T. M., Welke, T. L., Tigel, P. D., Anand, R., Hartman, R. D., Sramek, J. J., Kurtz, N. M., & Cutler, N. R. (1996). Clozapine rebound and rapid onset psychosis following abrupt clozapine withdrawal. *Schizophrenia Bulletin, 22,* 591–595.

Shirzadi, A. A., & Ghaemi, N. (2006). Side effects of atypical antipsychotics: Extrapyramidal symptoms and the metabolic syndrome. *Harvard Review of Psychiatry, 14,* 152–164.

Silva, R. R., Friedhoff, A. J., & Alpert, M. (1993). Neuroleptic withdrawal psychosis in Tourette's disorder. *Biological Psychiatry, 34,* 341–342.

Sivertsen, B., Omvik, S., Pallesen, S., Bjorvatn, B., Havik, O. E., Kvale, G., Nielsen, G.H., & Nordhus, I. H. (2006). Cognitive behavioral therapy vs. zopiclone for treatment of chronic primary insomnia in older adults: A randomized controlled trial. *Journal of the American Medical Association, 295,* 2851–2858.

Snowden, M., & Roy-Birne, P. (1998). Mental illness and nursing home reform: OBRA–1987 ten years later. *Psychiatric Services, 49,* 229–233.

Sovner, R. (1995). Thioridazine withdrawal-induced behavioral deterioration treated with clonidine: Two case reports. *Mental Retardation, 33,* 221–225.

Spieb-Kiefer, C., Grohmann, R. Schmidt, L. G., & Ruther, E. (1988). Severe and life-threatening adverse reactions to psychotropic drugs. *Pharmacopsychiatry, 21,* 290–292.

Spivak, B., Weizman, A., Wolovick, L., Hermesh, H., Tyano, S., & Munitz, H. (1990). Neuroleptic malignant syndrome during abrupt reduction of neuroleptic treatment. *Acta Psychiatrica Scandinavica, 81,* 168–169.

Staedt, J., Stoppe, G., Hajak, G., & Ruther, E. (1996). Rebound insomnia after abrupt clozapine withdrawal. *European Archives of Psychiatry and Clinical Neurosciences, 246,* 79–82.

Stanilla, J. K., de Leon, J., & Simpson, G. M. (1997). Clozapine withdrawal resulting in delirium with psychosis: A report of three cases. *Journal of Clinical Psychiatry, 58,* 252–255.

Stead, J., Lloyd, G., & Cohen, D. (Eds.). (2006). *Critical new perspectives on ADHD.* London & New York: Routledge.

Stoukides, J. A., & Stoukides, C. A. (1991). Extrapyramidal symptoms upon discontinuation of fluoxetine. *American Journal of Psychiatry, 148,* 1263.

Stowe, Z. N., Strader, Jr., J. R., & Nemeroff, C. B. (1998). Psychopharmacology during pregnancy and lactation. In A. F. Schatzberg & C. B. Nemeroff (Eds.), *Textbook of psychopharmacology,* 2nd ed. (pp. 979–996). Washington, D.C.: American Psychiatric Press.

Surmont, D.W.A., Colardyn, F., & De Reuck, J. (1984). Fatal complications of neuroleptic drugs: A clinico-pathological study of three cases. *Acta Neurologica Belgica, 84,* 75–83.

Swanson, J. M. (1993, January 27–29). Medical intervention for children with attention deficit disorder. *Proceedings of the Forum on the Education of Children with Attention Deficit Disorder,* pp. 27–34. Washington, D.C.: U.S. Department of Education, Office of Special Education and Rehabilitation Services and Office of Special Education Programs, Division of Innovation and Development.

Swantek, S. S., Grossberg, G. T., Neppe, V. M., Doubek, W. G., Martin, T., & Bender, J. E. (1991). The use of carbamazepine to treat benzodiazepine withdrawal in a geriatric population. *Journal of Geriatric Psychiatry and Neurology, 4,* 106–109.

Szabadi, E. (1992). Fluvoxamine withdrawal syndrome. *British Journal of Psychiatry, 160,* 283–284.

Tandon, R., Dutchak, D., & Greden, J. F. (1989). Cholinergic syndrome following anticholinergic withdrawal in a schizophrenic patient abusing marijuana. *British Journal of Psychiatry, 154,* 712–714.

Taylor, D. (1999, September/October). Truth withdrawal: David Taylor experienced SSRI withdrawal—It's not quite like the standard texts say. *Open Mind* (National Association for Mental Health, London), p. 16.

Taylor, D., Stewart, S., & Connolly, A. (2006). Antidepressant withdrawal symptoms: Telephone calls to a national medication helpline. *Journal of Affective Disorders. 95,* 129–133.

Temple, R. (1987, December 28). *Memorandum: Fluoxetine label.* Memorandum from the director, Office of Drug Research and Review, to the director, Division of Neuropharmacology Drug Products. Internal Document of the Department of Health and Human Services, Public Health Service, Food and Drug Administration, Center for Drug Evaluation and Research. Obtained through the Freedom of Information Act.

_____. (1987, December 28). *Approval of Sertraline.* Memorandum from the director, Office of Drug Research and Review, to the director, Division of

Neuropharmacology Drug Products. Internal Document of the Department of Health and Human Services, Public Health Service, Food and Drug Administration, Center for Drug Evaluation and Research. Obtained through the Freedom of Information Act.

Theilman, S. B., & Chistenbury, M. M. (1986). Hypomania following withdrawal of trazodone. *American Journal of Psychiatry, 143,* 1482–1483.

Therrien, F., & Markowitz, J. S. (1997). Selective serotonin reuptake inhibitors and withdrawal symptoms: A review of the literature. *Human Psychopharmacology, 12,* 309–323.

Thompson, C. (1998). Discontinuation of antidepressant therapy: Emerging complications and their relevance. *Journal of Clinical Psychiatry, 59,* 541–548.

Toru, M., Matsuda, O., Makiguchi, K., & Sugano, K. (1981). Neuroleptic malignant syndrome–like state following a withdrawal of antiparkinsonian drugs. *Journal of Nervous and Mental Disease, 169,* 324–327.

Tran, K. T., Hranicky, D., Lark, T., & Jacob, N. (2005). Gabapentin withdrawal syndrome in the presence of a taper. *Bipolar Disorders, 7,* 302–304.

Tranter, R., & Healy, D. (1998). Neuroleptic discontinuation syndromes. *Journal of Psychopharmacology, 12,* 306–311.

Trial court's authority to investigate and determine the correctness and veracity of judgments. (1996, May 30). *Hon. John W. Potter, Judge, v. Eli Lilly and Company* (95-SC–580-MR). Appeal from Court of Appeals; Opinion by Justice Wintersheimer, reversing, rendered May 23, 1996. *43 K.L.S.5,* pp. 33–35.

Trifiro, G., Verhamme, K. M., Ziere, G., Caputi, A. P., Stricker, B. H., & Sturkenboom, M. C. (2006). All-cause mortality associated with atypical and typical antipsychotics in demented outpatients. *Pharmacoepidemiology & Drug Safety,*

Trivedi, M. H., Rush, A. J., Wisniewski, S. R., Nierenerg, A. A., Warden, D., Ritz, L., Norquist, G., Howland, R. H., Lebowitz, B., McGrath, P. J., Shores-Wilson, K., Biggs, M. M., Balasubramani, G. K., & Fava, M. (STAR*D Study Team). (2006). Outcomes with citalopram for depression using measurement-based care in STAR*D: Implications for clinical practice. *American Journal of Psychiatry, 163,* 28–40.

Tucker, G. J. (1997). Editorial: Putting DSM-IV in perspective. *American Journal of Psychiatry, 155,* 159–161.

Umbarger, C., Dalsimer, J., Morrison, A., & Breggin, P. (1962). *College students in a mental hospital.* New York: Grune & Stratton.

USPDI. (1998). *Drug information for the health care professional,* 18th ed. USPDI: Rockville, MD. (Revised annually.)

van Geffen, E. C., Hugtenburg, J. G., Heerdink, E. R., van Hulten, R. P., & Egberts, A. C. (2005). Discontinuation symptoms in users of selective serotonin reuptake inhibitors in clinical practice: Tapering versus abrupt discontinuation. *European Journal of Clinical Pharmacology, 61,* 303–307.

van Putten, T., & Marder, S. (1987). Behavioral toxicity of antipsychotic drugs. *Journal of Clinical Psychiatry, 48*(supp.), 13–19.

Varchaver, M. [American Lawyer News Service] (1995, September 25). Prozac verdict was a sure thing. *Fulton County Daily Report* (Atlanta).

Viguera, A. C., Baldessarini, R. J., Hegarty, J. D., van Kammen, D. P., & Tohen, M. (1997). Clinical risk following abrupt and gradual withdrawal of maintenance neuroleptic treatment. *Archives of General Psychiatry, 54,* 49–55.

Walsh, K. H., & Dunn, D. W. (1998). Complications of psychostimulants. In J. Biller (Ed.), *Iatrogenic neurology* (pp. 415–431). Boston: Butterworth-Heinemann.

Warner, C. H., Bobo, W., Warner, C., Reid, S., & Rachal, J. (2006). Antidepressant discontinuation syndrome. *American Family Physician, 74,* 449–456.

Webster, P. A. (1973). Withdrawal symptoms in neonates associated with maternal antidepressant therapy. *The Lancet, 2,* 318–319.

Weinberger, D. R., Bigelow, L. L., Klein, S. T., & Wyatt, R. J. (1981). Drug withdrawal in chronic schizophrenic patients: In search of neuroleptic-induced supersensitivity psychosis. *Journal of Clinical Psychopharmacology, 1,* 120–123.

Weis, R. (1998, April 15). Correctly prescribed drugs take heavy toll. *Washington Post,* p. A1.

Weller, R. A., & McKnelly, W. V. (1983). Case report of withdrawal dyskinesia associated with amoxapine. *American Journal of Psychiatry, 140,* 1515–1516.

West, R., & Gossop, M. (1994). Overview: A comparison of withdrawal symptoms from different drug classes. *Addiction, 89,* 1483–1489.

Wexler, B., & Cicchetti, D. (1992). The outpatient treatment of depression. *Journal of Nervous and Mental Disease, 180,* 277–286.

Whitaker, R. (2005). Anatomy of an epidemic: Psychiatric drugs and the astonishing rise of mental illness in America. *Ethical Human Psychology and Psychiatry, 7,* 19–32.

Williams, V. S., Baldwin, D. S., Hogue, S. L., Fehnelm, S. E., Hollis, K. A., Edin, H. M. (2006). Estimating the prevalence and impact of antidepressant-induced sexual dysfunction in 2 European countries: A cross-sectional patient survey. *Journal of Clinical Psychiatry, 67,* 204–210.

Witschy, J. K., Malone, G. L., & Holden, L. D. (1984). Psychosis after neuroleptic withdrawal in a manic-depressive patient. *American Journal of Psychiatry, 141,* 105–106.

Wolfe, R. M. (1997). Antidepressant withdrawal reactions. *American Family Physician, 56,* 455–462.

Wolfe, S. M. (Ed.). (2005, January). DO NOT USE: Duloxetine (Cymbalta) for major depressive disorder—Nothing special and possible liver toxicity. *Worst Pills Best Pills, 11*(1), 1–3.

World Psychiatric Association. (1993). Task force on sedative hypnotics. *European Psychiatry, 8,* 45–49.

Wylie, R. M. (1995). Reducing benzodiazepine usage. *British Journal of General Practice, 45,* 327.

Yassa, R. (1985). Antiparkinsonian medication withdrawal in the treatment of tardive dyskinesia: A report of three cases. *Canadian Journal of Psychiatry, 30,* 440–442.

Young, A. H., & Currie, A. (1997). Physicians' knowledge of antidepressant withdrawal effects: A survey. *Journal of Clinical Psychiatry, 58* (supplement 7), 28–30.

Zalsman, G., Hermesh, H., & Munitz, H. (1998). Alprazolam withdrawal delirium: A case report. *Clinical Neuropharmacology, 21,* 201–202.

Zimmerman, M., Posternak, M., Friedman, M., Attiullah, N., Baymiller, S., Boland, R., Berlowitz, S., Rahman, S., Uy, K., & Singer, S. (2004). Which factors influence psychiatrists' selection of antidepressants? *American Journal of Psychiatry, 161,* 1285–1289.

Zolpidem: Now classified as a psychotropic at risk of abuse. (2003). *Prescrire International, 2003, 12,* 60.

Index

Books by Peter R. Breggin, M.D.

*College students in a mental hospital: Contribution to the
social rehabilitation of the mentally ill* (jointly authored) (1962)

Electroshock: Its brain-disabling effects (1979)

The psychology of freedom: Liberty and love as a way of life (1980)

Psychiatric drugs: Hazards to the brain (1983)

*Toxic psychiatry: Why therapy, empathy and love
must replace the drugs, electroshock and biochemical
theories of the "new psychiatry"* (1991)

Beyond conflict: From self-help and psychotherapy to peacemaking (1992)

Talking back to prozac (coauthor Ginger Breggin) (1994)

The war against children (coauthor Ginger Breggin) (1994)

Psychosocial approaches to deeply disturbed persons
(coeditor E. Mark Stern) (1996)

*Brain-disabling treatments in psychiatry:
Drugs, electroshock and the role of the FDA* (1997)

*The heart of being helpful: Empathy and
the creation of a healing presence* (1997)

*The war against children of color: Psychiatry targets
inner city children* (coauthor Ginger Breggin) (1998)
Revision of *The war against children* (1994)

Reclaiming our children: A healing solution to a nation in crisis (2000)

Talking back to Ritalin, revised edition (2001)

The antidepressant fact book (2001)

Dimensions of empathic therapy
(coeditors Ginger Breggin and Fred Bemak) (2002)

The Ritalin fact book (2002)

Books by David Cohen, Ph.D.

Critical new perspectives on ADHD
(coeditors Gwynedd Lloyd and Joan Stead) (2006)

*Drug abuse and dependence on psychotropic medications among women,
older persons, and children* (coauthor Johanne Collin) (1998)*

Critical handbook of psychiatric drugs
(coauthors Suzanne Cailloux-Cohen and AGIDD, 1995)*

Psychotropic drugs: Psychosocial aspects
(coeditor Guilhème Pérodeau) (1997)*

Medicalization and social control
(coeditor Louise Bouchard) (1994)*

*Challenging the therapeutic state:
Further disquisitions on the mental health system* (1994)

Tardive dyskinesia and cognitive dysfunction
(coeditor Henri Cohen) (1993)

*Challenging the therapeutic state:
Critical perspectives on psychiatry and the mental health system* (1990)

*published in French